Two week loan

Please return on or before the last
date stamped below.
Charges are made for late return.

Pharmaceutical Medicine, Biotechnology and European Law

European law has been faced with increasingly complex issues emerging from rapid developments in pharmaceutical medicine and biotechnology. A team of distinguished European legal practitioners and academics reassesses the impact of European law on health care and pharmaceutical law. The essays are grouped under four themes: free movement of goods and persons, competition and intellectual property; European drug regulation; biotechnology; and product liability and transnational health care litigation. The book reviews the impact of European law on movement of health care professionals and pharmaceuticals, patent and trade mark rights, the Product Liability Directive, laws on product liability and intellectual property claims. It examines recent developments in drug regulation, particularly data protection, abridged applications for marketing authorisations and the European Medicines Evaluation Agency. A compelling analysis is made of the Biotechnology Directive morality clauses. This important study offers a valuable resource for the pharmaceutical and biotechnology industries, legal academics and practitioners alike.

DR RICHARD GOLDBERG is a Solicitor and Lecturer in Law at the University of Birmingham. He is the author of *Causation and Risk in the Law of Torts: Scientific Evidence and Medicinal Product Liability* (1999), nominated for the SPTL Book Prize in 1999.

DR JULIAN LONBAY is Senior Lecturer in Law at the University of Birmingham. His publications include *Training Lawyers in the European Community* (1990, ed.), *International Professional Practice* (1992, ed. with L. Spedding and H. Levinson), *Frontiers of Competition Law* (1994), *Enhancing the Legal Position of the European Consumer* (1996) and *Remedies for Breach of EC Law* (1997, ed. with A. Biondi).

Pharmaceutical Medicine, Biotechnology and European Law

Edited by

Richard Goldberg
and
Julian Lonbay

Institute of European Law
Faculty of Law
University of Birmingham

CAMBRIDGE
UNIVERSITY PRESS

PUBLISHED BY THE PRESS SYNDICATE OF THE UNIVERSITY OF CAMBRIDGE
The Pitt Building, Trumpington Street, Cambridge, United Kingdom

CAMBRIDGE UNIVERSITY PRESS
The Edinburgh Building, Cambridge CB2 2RU, UK
40 West 20th Street, New York NY 10011–4211, USA
10 Stamford Road, Oakleigh, VIC 3166, Australia
Ruiz de Alarcón 13, 28014 Madrid, Spain
Dock House, The Waterfront, Cape Town 8001, South Africa

http://www.cambridge.org

First published 2000

Printed in the United Kingdom at the University Press, Cambridge

Typeface Plantin 10/12 pt   *System* 3b2   [CE]

A catalogue record for this book is available from the British Library

Library of Congress Cataloguing in Publication data

Pharmaceutical medicine, biotechnology, and European law / edited
by Richard Goldberg Julian Lonbay.
     p.   cm.
ISBN 0 521 79249 5 (hb)
1. Pharmacy – Law and legislation – Europe.
2. Drugs – Law and legislation – Europe.
3. Biotechnology industries – Law and legislation – Europe.
4. Medical laws and legislation – Europe.
I. Goldberg, Richard.   II. Lonbay, Julian.
KJC6191.P48   2001
344′.04233′094–dc21   00–063011

ISBN 0 521 79249 5 hardback

Contents

Notes on the contributors

DERYCK BEYLEVELD is Professor of Jurisprudence at the University of Sheffield and Founding Director of the Sheffield Institute of Biotechnological Law and Ethics (SIBLE). His research and publications span criminology, legal and moral philosophy, contract law, product liability law, international human rights law, patents in biotechnology, and many topics in bioethics and biolaw (in both medical and non-medical fields), as well as public perception of biotechnology. His publications include *A Bibliography on General Deterrence Research* (1980); *The Dialectical Necessity of Morality* (1991); *Mice, Morality and Patents* (1993); and *Law as a Moral Judgment* (2nd edn, 1994) (the latter two with Roger Brownsword – with whom he is currently writing a book on *Human Dignity in Bioethics and Biolaw* for Oxford University Press). He is currently working on confidentiality and data protection in the context of research ethics committees, and the relationship between law and ethics in the context of the working of research ethics committees. He is a member of the co-ordinating team for a Biotechnology Fourth Framework Shared Cost Project on Plant Intellectual Property, and a participant in a Biomedicine and Health Concerted Action on the Ethical Function of Hospital Ethics Committees. He is currently Vice-Chair of Trent Multi-Centre Research Ethics Committee and is an adviser on confidentiality and data protection to the Royal College of General Practitioners, the Royal College of Paediatrics and Child Health Care and the Association of Community Health Councils of England and Wales.

ROGER BROWNSWORD LLB (London) is Professor of Law and Head of Department at the University of Sheffield. He has published two books with Deryck Beyleveld, *Mice, Morality and Patents* (1993) and *Law as a Moral Judgment* (2nd edn, 1994); and, with John Adams, *Understanding Law* (2nd edn, 1996). He is currently working on another book with Deryck Beyleveld on *Human Dignity in Bioethics and Biolaw* (Oxford University Press). He edited, with Bill Cornish and Margaret Llewelyn, *Human Genetics and the Law: Regulating a Revolution* (1998). In addition he has published several books on Contract Law and over 100 chapters in books and articles on a wide variety of topics.

WILLIAM CORNISH QC FBA, LLD is Herchel Smith Professor of Intellectual Property Law at Cambridge and President of Magdalene College. He is the author of many works on intellectual property, including *Encyclopedia of United Kingdom and European Patent Law* (1978–, with Fiona Clark, Sir Robin Jacob and others); *Piracy and Counterfeiting of Copyright Products* (1984, ed.); *Copyright in Free and Competitive Markets* (1986, ed.); and *Intellectual Property: Patents, Copyright, Trade Marks and Allied Rights* (4th edn, 1999). He edits the *International Review of Industrial Property and Copyright* and is on the editorial board of the *European Intellectual Property Review*. He is an External Academic Member, Max-Planck-Institute for Intellectual Property, Munich. Other posts include: Chairman, British Literary and Artistic Copyright Association (1981–5); Specialist Adviser on Intellectual Property to House of Lords Committee on the European Union (1981–9); President, International Association for Teaching and Research in Intellectual Property (1986–8); Vice-President, Association Littéraire et Artistique Internationale (1989–); Chairman, Working Group on Intellectual Property Rights in Universities, National Academies Policy Action Group (1993–5); and Founding Council Member of the Intellectual Property Institute.

ANTOINE CUVILLIER graduated in commercial law from the University of Paris-Nanterre and in international law from the University of Paris-Pantheon Sorbonne. He holds an LLM in international legal studies from the Washington College of Law, the American University. After experience in private practice both in the United States and France, and consultancy work for the pharmaceutical industry, he joined the European Medicines Evaluation Agency (EMEA) at its creation in 1994 as Administrator (legal affairs).

IAN DODDS-SMITH graduated from Downing College, Cambridge and is a partner and Head of the Health Care Group at CMS Cameron McKenna – a sub-group specialising in regulatory, research and product liability issues concerning the pharmaceutical and chemical sectors. His appointments include Consultant Editor to the *Personal and Medical Injuries Law Letter*, Member of the editorial board of the *Regulatory Affairs Journal* and various Royal College and Medical Research Council working parties on research issues. He is a Fellow of the Royal Society of Medicine and Member of the Drug Information Association and Federation of Insurance and Corporate Counsel. He has written widely on regulatory and product liability issues. His publications include *Pharmaceutical Medicine and the Law* (1991, ed. with Sir Abraham Goldberg); and 'Product Liability for Medicinal Products', in M. J. Powers and N. H. Harris, *Clinical Negligence* (3rd edn, 2000, with M. Spencer).

RICHARD GOLDBERG LLB (Strathclyde), LLM PhD (London) is a Solicitor and Lecturer in Law at the University of Birmingham. He is the author of *Causation and Risk in the Law of Torts: Scientific Evidence and Medicinal Product Liability* (1999), which was nominated for the SPTL Book Prize in 1999. In addition he is the author of many articles in his area of special interest – product liability, particularly in respect of pharmaceuticals. He is currently working with Professor C. J. Miller on the second edition of *Product Liability* (Oxford University Press) and a chapter on Causation in the Butterworths Common Law Series text on *Product Liability* (ed. G. Howells).

LEIGH HANCHER LLB (Glasgow), MA (Sheffield), doctorate (*cum laude*, Leiden) is Professor of European Law at the Catholic University of Brabant, Tilburg. She held the chair of Public Economic Law at the Erasmus University Rotterdam from 1991 to 1997 and in the first half of 1996 she held the visiting chair of Natural Resources Law at the University of Calgary, Alberta. She is the author of numerous works in European law, including *EC Electricity Law* (1991); *Regulating for Competition, Government, Industry and the Pharmaceutical Sector in Britain and France* (1992); and *EC State Aids Law* (2nd edn, 1999). She is a regular contributor to leading EC law journals and a member of the editorial boards of various law journals and European law associations.

JONATHAN HARRIS (BA 1994, BCL 1995, MA Oxon. 1998) is a Reader in Law at the University of Nottingham and former Lecturer in Law at the University of Birmingham. He specialises in Private International Law. He has written articles on all aspects of the subject in journals such as the *Modern Law Review, Law Quarterly Review, Oxford Journal of Legal Studies, Lloyd's Maritime and Commercial Law Quarterly* and *European Law Review.* He has also written chapters in a number of edited volumes. He is on the editorial board of *Civil Justice Quarterly* and a contributing editor to the *Journal of International Trust and Corporate Planning.*

BELINDA ISAAC (née Mills) LLB (Northumberland), PhD (London) is a Solicitor and partner at Arnander Irvine and Zietman (formerly Llewelyn Zeitman) and specialises in intellectual property matters. She has published numerous articles on trade mark issues and is author of *Brand Protection Matters* (2000). She is a board member of the *European Trade Mark Reports* and is a correspondent for the *Entertainment Law Review.*

MARGARET LLEWELYN LLB PhD (Wales) is a Senior Lecturer in Law at the University of Sheffield and Deputy Director of the Sheffield Institute for Biotechnology Law and Ethics (SIBLE). She was a Research Fellow at the Max- Planck Institute for Intellectual Property Law in Munich, a Researcher at Queen Mary College, University of London and, more recently, Senior Lecturer at the University of Central Lancashire. Her primary area of research is the legal protection of genetic material. She has published extensively in journals such as the *European Intellectual Property Review, BioScience Law Review* and *Intellectual Property Quarterly* as well as contributing to a number of collected works. In addition to her published work she has given national and international conference papers and advises organisations such as the United Nations, the European Parliament, the Royal Society and various National Academies of Science. Her current work focuses on the review of Article 27(3)(b) of the Agreement on Trade Related Aspects of Intellectual Property within the WTO. She is also co-ordinating an EU-funded project into attitudes towards plant intellectual property within the European plant breeding industry. She writes extensively on the subject of second tier/utility model protection and the problems of providing appropriate and effective protection for small to medium-sized enterprises. She is co-editor, with Roger Brownsword and Professor W. R. Cornish, of *Human Genetics and the Law: Regulating a Revolution* (1998).

JULIAN LONBAY LLB (Dundee), LLD (European University Institute, Florence) is Senior Lecturer in Law at the University of Birmingham. He is a visiting professor at the University of Limoges. He is the author of *Training Lawyers in the European Community* (1990, ed. with Brown, Tridimas and Platt) and *International Professional Practice* (1992, ed. with Spedding and Levinson) and many works on European law. He has undertaken research on professional mobility in Europe for the European Commission, the Law Societies of the British Isles and the Lord Chancellor's Advisory Committee on Legal Education, amongst others. He is a member of the Scientific Committee of Cicero (a pan-European Research Group in relation to legal education) and is second Vice-President of the European Law Faculty Association. He is a regular contributor to the *International and Comparative Law Quarterly* on the free movement of persons.

Preface

Both pharmaceutical medicine and biotechnology are rapidly developing scientific disciplines. European law has had to grapple with the complex issues that have emerged from these areas over the last few years. In view of this, the Institute of European Law at the University of Birmingham, in association with the Faculty of Pharmaceutical Medicine of the Royal Colleges of Physicians of the UK, convened a conference at the University of Birmingham entitled 'Aspects of European Health Care Law'. In the light of the Institute of European Law's function to provide a centre for supporting research and publication, we considered that the publication of a book on these topics would be a valuable contribution to a developing field. With the support of Cambridge University Press, we have been able to produce this collection, which will hopefully provoke a greater understanding of these issues.

We would like to thank, in particular, the President of the Faculty of Pharmaceutical Medicine, Professor Peter Stonier, for his assistance and encouragement in organising the conference. In addition, the conference itself was generously sponsored by Abbott Laboratories, Fournier Pharmaceuticals Ltd, Hoechst Marion Roussel Ltd and SmithKline Beecham. We would also like to thank Mrs Nadene Bryan for her secretarial and administrative assistance in respect of both the conference and the book.

The collection intends to reflect the legal position at 1 January 2000.

RICHARD GOLDBERG
JULIAN LONBAY

Foreword

This book strikingly demonstrates the reach and impact of European law in the sector of public health, and in particular medicine, the pharmaceutical industry and the medical professions.

Professionals and specialists in many different aspects of pharmaceutical medicine – on the technical side, on the clinical side, on the commercial front – are now confronted daily with the requirements of European law to an extent which, only a few years ago, was almost unimaginable.

Lawyers, for their part, have seen new fields of practice emerge, as it has proved necessary to apply the principles of European law to an increasingly Europeanised market in medical products and medical services. From a starting point forty years ago in the embryonic provisions of the EEC Treaty, a very substantial body of Community legislation and case law of the European Court of Justice has emerged in recent years. Community-wide rules on free movement, competition, patents and trade marks overlie national markets and prevail over national law. Europe-wide bodies have developed – in competition policy, in trade marks and patents, and in the testing and evaluation of medicines, to name only a few.

Within this rapidly growing field, the essays published in this book tackle a wide variety of topics: the impact of European rules in all the above areas on pharmaceuticals; the free movement of health care professionals; European drug regulation; biotechnology and the moral limits on the legal protection of inventions; product liability; and transnational health care litigation.

Among the book's qualities is the way in which the selection of topics illustrates, from different perspectives, some common themes. In the creation of the single European market, a balance has to be struck among a variety of competing interests: to mention only some, balancing the interests of free trade and fair competition with the interests of the pharmaceutical industry and the need to promote research and investment; at the same time seeking to ensure the provision of effective health services, to guarantee the rights of the health care professional, and not least to protect the concerns of the patient as well as of the public generally.

For all of these constituencies, this book will provide much of interest.

FRANCIS G. JACOBS
Advocate-General
Court of Justice of the European Communities

Editors' note

For the purposes of citation of the European treaties, the Editors have decided that with each initial reference to a Treaty Article, the new Article number should be given, followed by the old Article number in brackets and then the abbreviation for the relevant Treaty: for example, Article 47 (ex 57) EC. It is sometimes more appropriate to refer to the old Article number initially: for example, when dealing with older cases before the Court of Justice of the European Communities. Here the Article will be referred to by its original number, with the new Article number in brackets, followed by the abbreviation for the relevant Treaty: for example, Article 57 (now 47) EC.

Table of cases

CASES FROM OTHER JURISDICTIONS

AUSTRALIA

EFTA COURT

ENGLAND AND WALES

Table of treaties, European legislative instruments and national legislation

Introduction

Richard Goldberg and Julian Lonbay

This collection of essays seeks to examine several developing areas of the law relating to pharmaceutical medicine and biotechnology in the European Community. The essays address four such topics which have emerged in recent years, namely: (1) free movement of goods and persons, competition and intellectual property; (2) European drug regulation; (3) biotechnology; and (4) product liability, which is addressed along with transnational health care litigation.

The Treaty of Rome established rules on free movement of goods (Articles 28 to 30 (ex 30 to 36) EC) and competition (Articles 81 and 82 (ex 85 and 86) EC), which have had a profound effect on the use of intellectual property rights to prevent the importation of patented and trade-marked pharmaceuticals from one European State to another. Professor William Cornish's essay explains the doctrine of exhaustion of patent rights in the internal European Community (EC) and European Economic Area (EEA) market. Here, patent rights are exhausted to the extent that they cannot be used to prevent the importing of patented pharmaceuticals from one EEA State to another, when first marketing of the goods is by or with the consent of the owner of the patent for them in any of the EC/EEA countries. Although acknowledging the doctrine of exhaustion for parallel importation from one EEA State to another, Cornish convincingly argues against a rule of international exhaustion of patent rights for parallel importation of products into the EEA from countries outside it, since patent systems are incentive systems and thus patentees should be able to engage in international price discrimination. Nevertheless, he appears to take issue with Belinda Isaac's criticism of the international exhaustion principle in respect of trade mark rights. She concludes that this principle may lead to confusion amongst consumers and damage the reputation attaching to a trade mark. Cornish considers that trade mark rights are in an entirely different situation from patents, since a rule against international trade mark exhaustion would place in the hands of international producers the private equivalent of a State ban on imports. Having examined the

1

situations in which the doctrine of exhaustion of trade mark rights operates in the internal EC/EEA market, Isaac carefully considers the implications of the Court of Justice of the European Communities (ECJ) decision in *Silhouette* v. *Hartlauer*,[1] concluding that trade mark owners within the EEA may take action to prevent goods entering the EEA without their consent. In Cornish's view, the ECJ's decision does not go as far as this. Sooner rather than later, it would seem that international agreement must be reached on whether or not a doctrine of international trade mark exhaustion should be applied. Whatever the decisions in this area, the case for no rule of international exhaustion of patent rights seems strong.

Closely linked to free movement of goods is the issue of free movement of individuals involved in the health care sector. The third chapter addresses the role of health care professionals who prescribe and administer medicinal products at the marketing of medicines stage. Freedom of movement of health care professionals is important in the provision of pharmaceutical medicine across all the Member States. In addition, health care professionals, who prescribe and administer drugs to patients, must be qualified to do so. Julian Lonbay's essay examines some of the issues arising from free movement of health care professionals and patients, explaining the various phases of development of Community law and policy as it attempts to tackle difficulties raised by national differences in structures of various professions, differences in qualifications and differences in modes of provision of health care. As Lonbay shows, the EC legislation which has emerged covers health care professions in a variety of ways but leaves exposed some gaps. Questions relating to control of content of education, training and professional practice are not fully resolved. He concludes that the rights of European Union (EU) health care professionals to settle and work in other Member States are not always smoothly dealt with by Community law, the ECJ or competent national authorities, though much has been achieved.

Professor Leigh Hancher continues with an examination of parallel imports and pharmaceuticals by providing an overview, from a competition law perspective, of recent developments by the ECJ. She explains that these recent decisions by the Court were based upon the fundamental principles of free movement and competition in the Treaty of Rome, i.e. the need to secure market access for the importing of medicinal products into markets which are still subject to a considerable degree of national divergence in price regulation, with a strong emphasis on the interests of legal certainty. The need for legal certainty is strong,

---

[1] Case C-355/96 *Silhouette International Schmied* v. *Hartlauer Handelsgesellschaft* [1998] ECR I-4799.

particularly where minimal harmonisation has taken place, namely in the areas of trade mark law and certain aspects of the licensing procedure. Indeed, this need for legal certainty has been demonstrated by the Court's reformulation of the requirement of the trade mark owner's intention to partition markets by an objective test, and the rejection of a subjective approach in the *Paranova*[2] case, and the interpretation of the concept of 'essential similarity' in Article 4 of Directive 87/21 on the abridged licensing procedures in the *Generics (UK)*[3] case. Both lines of cases encourage parallel importing and intra-brand competition. Hancher concludes that the solution to parallel importation, often reiterated by the ECJ, must emanate from the Commission and the Council.

As will be seen in the first three chapters, much of health care law is affected by the trade in pharmaceuticals, both within and outside the EEA. However, all medicinal products require to be regulated and to have marketing authorisations before they are allowed to be distributed to consumers within the internal market. European law has had a considerable impact on these regulatory aspects. Ian Dodds-Smith's essay provides a critique of some of the most significant European developments in drug regulation in recent years, in focusing on data protection (the protection of know-how of research-based pharmaceutical companies) and its relationship with the European rules on abridged applications for marketing authorisations. Such rules appear to favour the generic drug industry and have created uncertainty for the regulatory authorities and both competing sides of the pharmaceutical industry. Here, it is important to appreciate the rationale behind drug regulation, namely the balance between encouraging innovation and protecting health, as well as facilitating free movement by uniform standards. His view is that, other than the limited attempt to encourage innovation with orphan drugs, the current trend in drug regulation is the encouragement of generics, which is discouraging innovation. He considers that the most recent regulatory systems are developing in a manner that erodes commercial freedoms without proper justification. The abridged procedure for the marketing authorisation of generic products in Council Directive 87/21/EEC, which revised Article 4.8 of Directive 65/65/EEC, exempts generic companies from providing the results of pharmacological and toxicological tests or clinical trials. He describes the important impact of the ECJ decision of *Scotia Pharmaceu-*

---

[2] Joined Cases C-427/93, C-429/93 and C-436/93 *Bristol-Myers Squibb and Others* v. *Paranova* [1996] ECR I-3457.

[3] Case C-368/96 *R* v. *The Licensing Authority established by the Medicines Act 1968 (acting by the Medicines Control Agency)*, *ex parte Generics (UK) Ltd*; *R* v. *Same, ex parte Wellcome Foundation Ltd*; *R* v. *Same, ex parte Glaxo Operations UK Ltd and Others (E. R. Squibb & Sons Ltd, Generics (UK) Ltd, intervening)* [1999] ECR I-7967; [1999] 2 CMLR 181.

ticals[4] which strictly interpreted the use of the published literature exemption by generic companies and stressed the protection of innovation. It has also led to an amendment to the legislative provisions controlling the published literature exemption. By contrast, the recent ECJ decision of *Generics (UK)* established that as long as 'essential similarity' can be shown between the generic product and one authorised within the Community for not less than six or ten years, a generic applicant can receive a marketing authorisation for all therapeutic indications. Dodds-Smith's view is that this decision will result in reduced innovation for the pharmaceutical industry.

Antoine Cuvillier explains how the European medicines evaluation system has evolved and how it operates. He draws attention to the important fact that the European Medicines Evaluation Agency (EMEA) was the EU's response to the challenge of an EU policy protecting public health.[5] In particular, the EMEA's role in its two new market authorisation procedures, namely the centralised procedure (under Regulation (EC) No. 2309/93) and the mutual recognition procedure, is examined. Cuvillier addresses the EMEA's position as a networking agency, bringing together the necessary European expertise that the system requires, as well as its existing guarantees of resource efficiency, independent scientific opinions and transparency. He then explores the EMEA's wider role in the legal framework of European medicines regulation, through international co-operation and harmonisation activities. Despite the fact that the EMEA has only been in full operation since February 1995, Cuvillier's view is that it has already made a significant impact on the pharmaceutical regulatory environment.

Over the past few years, one of the most controversial of the emerging areas in health care law has been the development of legal protection for biotechnological inventions, the patenting of which is important for the production of innovating pharmaceutical products. There are, however, significant moral and ethical issues which must constrain the patenting of certain types of biotechnological inventions. Deryck Beyleveld, Professor Roger Brownsword and Margaret Llewelyn provide a compelling critical analysis of the morality clauses of the Directive on the Legal Protection of Biotechnological Inventions.[6] It is their view that the

---

[4] [1995] ECR I-2851.

[5] Public health law is an increasingly important area that is reflected in the adoption of Article 152 (ex 129) EC, which confirms the public health remit of the EC. See Lonbay, below, chapter 3, for an overview of EC competence in this field. A detailed analysis of this area is beyond the scope of this volume.

[6] Directive 98/44/EC on the legal protection of biotechnological inventions [1998] OJ L213/13.

Directive has left room for interpretations which could result in a marginalisation of the morality exclusions. They doubt that the present wording of the Directive will ensure that all biotechnological inventions are subjected to a rigorous moral scrutiny by European national patent systems.

The problems associated with the liability for defective medicinal products are considerable. The thalidomide case, though establishing no liability in negligence,[7] brought home the inadequate regulatory machinery in place both in the UK and in Europe, in 1962, which in turn led to the enactment of the Medicines Act 1968, in the UK, and Directive 65/65/EEC[8] in Europe. In his essay, Richard Goldberg identifies a potential interrelationship between product liability and intellectual property in the context of medicinal products. First, he examines the nature of the development risk defence of the UK Consumer Protection Act 1987, Part I, which implemented the EC Product Liability Directive.[9] He focuses on *Commission of the European Communities* v. *United Kingdom*,[10] concerning the UK's alleged failure to implement the Directive with its version of the defence. His view is that, despite the conclusions of the Court, the Section 4(1)(e) version of the defence has been constructed in a way which, by placing its emphasis upon the conduct of producers, reflects the requirements of negligence. The essay then examines the potential role of intellectual property rights in addressing the difficulty of increased injury costs as a result of the Product Liability Directive. In reviewing the Regulation establishing the Supplementary Protection Certificate (SPC),[11] which was designed to deal with the problem of patent life erosion caused by the increased testing and authorisation requirements of new medicinal products, he submits that there is a real link between drug disasters, product liability and patent law, and that the emergence of an increase in testing time for drugs could be linked not only to the result of increased pharmacovigilance, but also to the result of product liability litigation associated with Adverse Drug Reactions (ADRs). In his view, it is feasible that increasing patent restoration, or marketing exclusivity, could be justified

---

[7] *S* v. *Distillers Co. (Biochemicals) Ltd* [1970] 1 WLR 114.

[8] Council Directive 65/65/EEC of 26 January 1965 on the approximation of provisions laid down by law, regulation or administrative action relating to proprietary medicinal products [1965] OJ L369/65; OJ spec. edn 1965–6, 20.

[9] Directive 85/374/EEC on the approximation of the laws, regulations and administrative provisions of the Member States concerning liability for defective products [1985] OJ L210/29.

[10] [1997] ECR I-2649.

[11] Regulation 1768/92 concerning the creation of a supplementary protection certificate for medicinal products [1992] OJ L182/1.

by several factors other than the erosion of patent life, which might affect the injury costs sustained by pharmaceutical companies.

The final essay is a timely reminder of the increased importance of the international element to product liability and intellectual property claims concerning pharmaceuticals. Jonathan Harris stresses the impact of Conflict of Laws on transnational health care litigation. Focusing primarily on choice of law problems, he examines the effect of the abolition of the double actionability rule by the Private International Law (Miscellaneous Provisions) Act 1995, Part III on both product liability and intellectual property claims. Harris makes some pertinent criticisms of the choice of law rules under the Act, which he considers to have created uncertainty and which are difficult to justify on policy grounds. His view is that claims involving defective medicinal products should be treated as falling within the 1995 Act but that it is unclear when a manufacturer of medicinal products will be exposed to liability in contract and/or tort. It will also be difficult to say what the applicable law will be: the same uncertainties are present in intellectual property claims.

Harris also points to the failure of the 1995 Act to address the interaction between the creation of a *lex loci delicti* choice of law rule under the Act and the jurisdictional rules in respect of torts committed abroad. It would seem that under the Brussels Convention on Jurisdiction and Judgments,[12] by virtue of the difference between the definition of 'tort' for the purposes of the Convention and the 1995 Act, defective health care product litigation between a consumer and a manufacturer could be treated as contractual, although the merits of the claim may sound in tort. An additional jurisdictional problem arises as to when a claim for infringement of a foreign intellectual property right may be brought before an English court. In this light, Harris provides an important examination of the recent pre-1995 Act claim in the Court of Appeal, *Pearce* v. *Ove Arup Partnership Ltd.*[13] Harris considers that the removal of double actionability under the 1995 Act should allow the English courts to hear cases in respect of foreign intellectual property right infringements both under the Brussels Convention on Jurisdiction and at common law. He identifies an important consequence of the 1995 Act, although one not spelled out clearly in the Act, namely that there is no longer a rule of non-justiciability in respect of the bringing of cases in English courts concerning the infringement of foreign intellectual property rights.

The issues which will be discussed are a representative selection of

[12] [1990] OJ C189/2.
[13] [1999] 1 All ER 769.

some of the current problems which are faced in pharmaceutical medicine, biotechnology and EC law. It is hoped that they will provoke readers into appreciating the significance of these problems within a wider European context.

Part I

Free movement of goods and persons, competition and intellectual property

1   The free movement of goods I: pharmaceuticals, patents and parallel trade

W. R. Cornish

Parallel importation and intellectual property

This essay is not intended for specialists in intellectual property or European Community law. It is addressed to those who, from time to time, have to wrestle with the baffling issue of when it is legal to employ patents for inventions as a means of resisting 'parallel importation', and when as a matter of policy it is desirable to do so. My underlying aim is to set out arguments so that readers can judge for themselves. The arguments vary in relation to the different types of intellectual property – a factor which is often ignored in public debates. The distinctions involved are accordingly my starting point.

Intellectual property rights (IPRs) – patents, copyright, trade marks and so on – exist to prevent those who do not have the rightholder's licence from producing and trading in certain goods or services where otherwise they would be entitled to do so. IPRs indirectly provide their owners with a freedom to trade in a market without direct competition from those with whom they have no connection. Thus composers and record producers have copyrights which they can use to attack pirates who have made illegitimate copies of their music and records; patentees of inventions can prevent their rivals from incorporating the inventive idea into their products, machines and processes.

In essence, IPRs exist on a State-by-State basis and give rights against trading activities within national (or occasionally regional) boundaries. This strict concept of territoriality means that, for instance, patents for a given invention must be obtained for each country. In consequence, a patent may be granted for the invention in one State but not in another;[1]

---

[1] This could occur because applications are not made in every country, or because the applicant fails to satisfy the legal tests for grant in some countries. The system of priority of rights, which operates internationally between different patent systems, ensures that it is extremely unusual for unconnected rivals to obtain the patent for the same invention in different countries.

or the equivalent patents may come to be owned by different persons in separate countries.[2]

The practice of parallel importation does not relate to unauthorised invasions of an exclusive right by pirates, counterfeiters and other exploiters of the protected subject-matter. It concerns trade in 'legitimate products' – goods which are initially produced and marketed by an IP rightholder, or by some associated company or licensee. Is the relevant intellectual property (be it patent, copyright, trade mark or whatever) available to stop the importation of such goods by an independent operator who quite properly buys them in one country and then tranships them to another?

This form of arbitrage sets in when the goods, though genuine rather than pirated, are differently priced in the two countries. The 'parallel importer' buys them from a proper source in the cheaper country and exports them to the more expensive place without seeking a licence, thus threatening the higher price (and generally, the higher profit) there obtaining. Does the scope of the IPR in this second country, the country of importation, require him to secure that licence, or is the right in that country subject to a rule of 'international exhaustion'? Will the answer to the question vary with the type of intellectual property in question? Will it depend on whether the product has been protected by intellectual property rights in the country where it is first marketed, so that the right-owner has already had one chance to sell free of competition from pirates and other product imitators?

In the years of IPR resurgence – the late eighties and early nineties – the United States sought to persuade negotiators of the TRIPs Agreement[3] that there should be a blanket rule of non-exhaustion of all IPRs which would operate at the international level. This was proposed as a founding principle of fair (as distinct from free) trade for the brave new World Trade Organisation. The idea met a wave of hostility and no functioning rule on the subject was imposed on the States which are

---

[2] The degree to which one IP owner is likely to have coverage in most countries varies with the type of IPR. In the case of trade marks, the possibility of rival ownership of the same or very similar marks is not uncommon. By contrast, copyright in a work of authorship is likely to exist in all significant States. There will be greater variation in respect of the so-called 'neighbouring rights' to copyright, though the TRIPs Agreement takes some major steps towards ironing out the differences.

[3] The GATT Uruguay Round, completed at Marrakesh in April 1994, created the World Trade Organisation (WTO) and included among the deals which that organisation now administers the Agreement on Trade-Related Aspects of Intellectual Property Rights (TRIPs). TRIPs represents a very considerable advance in the cause of IP internationally, not least because States which do not fulfil their TRIPs obligations may be subjected by other States (doubtless at the instance of their industries) to GATT dispute settlement procedures, backed if necessary by counter-retaliatory measures, i.e. barriers to entry of any type of GATT goods or services into the objecting country.

now ratifying the TRIPs.[4] The great majority of States consider that they are net losers from conceding IPRs, since, for the present, the really valuable rights will be owned by multinational enterprises; at best they hope to be buying some key to enhanced industrial development, which will bring its return through a gradual shift towards more domestic invention, creativity and production of goods and services. In the meantime, there is no reason to furnish a legal device which would prevent the importation of legitimate goods from cheaper markets abroad: hence, for instance, the recent introduction in New Zealand of a blanket rule in favour of international exhaustion for all intellectual property.[5]

IP policies: the divergences

Most of the world remains uninformed about IPRs. Yet if the problem over parallel imports is to be resolved in a way which makes reasonable sense, it is vital to have some grasp of the different types of protection, their particular subject-matter and the policy objectives at which the State is aiming in granting the right.

Patents are granted over technical and scientific conceptions which constitute inventions. They are therefore directed at ideas which, in a few outstanding cases, can have profound effects on the structure of industries and on the opportunities and benefits available to society as a whole. Such an effect emerges from time to time in the pharmaceutical industry, where patents can be granted both for substances which are shown for the first time to have therapeutic value and for the discovery of new uses for known substances. A new antihistamine or tranquilliser or whatever may effectively replace the drugs in previous use and the firm with the patent may increase in size and importance to a striking degree, at least for the duration of the patent.

The market power which the patent confers in these lucky cases

---

[4] The outcome is the curious declaration in Article 6 (Exhaustion) that 'For the purposes of dispute settlement under this Agreement, subject to the provisions Articles 3 and 4 above [which guarantee national treatment and most-favoured-nation treatment], nothing in this Agreement shall be used to address the issue of the exhaustion of intellectual property rights.'

Article 28 requires that national patent rights operate against the importation of the protected invention for use or sale. The argument has been made that this covers all importation including that of parallel goods, it being prohibited to argue that there is a right of exhaustion applying to them. Such a partisan proposition flies in the face of the negotiating history and the obvious intent that Member States should be left to decide for themselves whether or not to introduce international exhaustion for each type of IPR.

[5] Much to the fury of sectors of US industry. In consequence, their Government's Trade Representatives threatened New Zealand with the special trade sanctions which still operate in the US alongside the rules of the revised GATT.

allows the patentee to behave as a monopolist in an economic, rather than a merely legal, sense. Because of this potential within the system the period of grant for patents around the world is twenty years from the application for protection (or some broadly equivalent period). In the case of pharmaceuticals and agrochemicals this period can be extended – in Europe, the US and certain other countries – to take account of delays in marketing imposed by the need to satisfy food and drug safety procedures.[6]

The invention for which a patent may be granted is based on technical knowledge which is there to be discovered, and often there is a race within an industry to uncover what is widely hoped to be the next step. In most countries the patent goes to the first to apply for protection, not the first to invent. That person will acquire an exclusive right which can be asserted even against those who reach the same results by independent research. This first-past-the-post element in the patent system is a distinctive characteristic and underscores the essential objectives in adopting such a system. Patents offer the incentive to undertake the investigations which lead first to invention and subsequently to a developed and marketable product. Their opportunities are entirely dependent on market responses.

The basic assumption is that the process of invention and industrial development is so economically and socially desirable that it must be induced by a special market opportunity for a limited period. At the same time, legal protection is given only if the invention is published to the rest of an industry in the patent specification. The system aims thereby to publicise information earlier than it might otherwise become available, and so prevent repetitious research and provide a block upon which others may build.

It is very difficult to show with any exactness how far the patent system produces the effects for which it is designed. Clearly it has greater impact in some industries than others, and by common consent it is most effective in the pharmaceutical and related fields. One indication of its value lies in the fact that, for all the doubting and criticism, the degree of its use around the world continues to grow. One thing, however, is clear: if there are to be incentives that lead to research and development, and to the publishing of successful results, they have to be sufficient. As with any lottery, the greater the potential prize, even against long odds, the more attractive the risk. If therefore a patent not only gives a right against competitors who adopt the invention but also shores up international price differentials for legitimate products, its

---

[6] For further details on increasing patent protection, see below, chapter 8.

potential as a reward increases and the whole system grows in attractive power. In relation to patents, therefore, we can say that there is a real case for a rule of non-exhaustion: whether there are countervailing considerations which override it is something to which we shall come in a moment.

First, we must complete the distinctions which are needed from other forms of intellectual property. Copyright gives exclusive rights against the unauthorised copying and performing of literary and artistic works (in a broad sense), and also against misappropriations of subject-matter such as films, sound recordings and performances, which are costly to produce and much cheaper to imitate. Since protection is given only against a taking of the protected material, and therefore only to the particular expression embodied in the work or other material, and not to all embodiments of a general idea, it is plain that the prevention of unfair free-riding by others is a primary motivation behind the law's intervention (which, by way of balance, can be for much longer periods than under the patent system). But some measure of encouragement for what is culturally beneficial is also present here, and therefore raises some case in favour of a non-exhaustion rule, as with patents, though it is probably less pressing.

When we reach the law of trade marks and associated rules protecting the indicators which one competitor uses to distinguish his goods from those of others, the very purpose of the law's intervention is different. Exclusive rights are granted for marks and names in order, in some general sense, to protect their ability to indicate origin. So much is common ground. There are those today who argue that every aspect of the investment in marketing which can be associated with a mark should fall within the ambit of the property right in it; but that remains a highly controversial position, which has recently suffered some reverses at the hand of the ECJ.[7]

One aspect of this drive has been the claim that registered trade mark rights should not be subject to any concept of external exhaustion of rights. If such a rule is enacted without distinction, it must mean that even where a trade mark proprietor in two countries markets the same goods under the same mark in each country, those first sold in the cheaper market cannot be taken by a purchaser for resale in the dearer market. Since trade marks are applied to virtually all finished goods, such a rule places in the hands of international producers the private equivalent of a State ban on particular imports, in which the State will be implicated through use of its judicial and associated systems to

---

[7] See below, chapter 2.

enforce the rights. The immediate losers under such a ban are consumers inside the more expensive market, and they, their politicians and their low-price retailers are often vociferous objectors, where parallel importation is not allowed. Accordingly there is a powerful case in favour of international exhaustion when it comes to trade marks. Its detailed examination is taken up in Isaac's chapter in this volume. The one point to be stressed here is that the trade mark situation is very different from that relating to patents.

A non-exhaustion of right rule for patents?

Parallel importation sets in only where there are price differentials between markets, and the reasons why these may occur are varied. Leaving aside for the moment the special conditions affecting pharmaceuticals, we may identify some recurrent circumstances affecting patented products in general:

1. Probably the commonest cause of differing price levels between countries is the shifting of exchange rates. Goods may start their sales life at equivalent prices and veer apart over time. There are always inhibitions on too readily altering prices within a given country. To this extent the differential is fortuitous and a non-exhaustion rule may be thought not to contribute greatly to the incentives underlying the patent grant. Nonetheless, if most patent systems have a non-exhaustion rule, patentees with protection across those systems can rely on protection of their prices in whichever markets for the moment have gained in value. To that extent, non-exhaustion may after all be considered a truly significant contributor to the incentive effect.

2. Marketing needs and practices may have various effects on comparative price levels. In a higher-priced country, the distribution system may be less competitive. That is not something which it is desirable to support. On the other hand, it may require greater advertising expenditure in order to get the inventive product known and sought after. Societies differ in many ways in their appreciation of products, particularly when they are novelties. Of course the over-selling of junk is not a desirable activity, but a market system has some inherent capacity to bypass the meretricious. In worthier cases, advertising expenditure will be justified and parallel importation from cheaper countries will take on the colour of undesirable free-riding. The profits of the practice go to the parallel importer who contributes nothing to the introduction or popularising of the product.

3. Economic and social conditions differ radically between the richest

and poorest nations, making it scarcely feasible for a novel product to be offered at equivalent prices in them all. There may well be good commercial and social reasons for getting the product to less developed countries at a price that at least some substantial sector of the populace can pay – obviously so in the case of new pharmaceuticals and medical aids, improvements in food production, ideas which can form the basis of local industry, materials and machines for use in education, and so on. Yet if these low-priced products can be exported to higher-priced markets so as to undermine the commercial prospects there, the products will either be marketed at industrial country prices (i.e., for the very few) or they will not be allowed on the developing market at all. This is surely a powerful argument against international exhaustion in relation to inventive products which have patents only for a strictly limited term, yet which are the subject of the strongest incentive policy in the whole IPR field.

4. Variations in quality may exist between the products put on different markets, which may explain price differences. Many factors may dictate these differences: climate, geographical conditions, consumer preferences, cost of materials, national standards, marketing and safety controls, and so on. To take an obvious, if rather unusual, case: a television set must comply with a country's technical standards for broadcasting if it is to be usable there. Whatever the cause, in such situations parallel imports bear a potential for misleading purchasers and other users, which may not be adequately met by clear advertising or labelling.

Exhaustion in the internal EC/EEA market

For a quarter of a century, it has been settled in principle that within the European Community (and latterly within the slightly wider range of the European Economic Area), patent rights are to be considered exhausted to the extent that they may not be used to prevent the importing of patented goods from one EEA State to another. This exhaustion comes about whenever the first marketing of the goods is by or with the consent of the owner of a patent for them in any of the countries, whether or not the invention is protected by a patent in that particular country.[8] The same rule applies in relation to authors' rights, neighbouring rights to copyright, trade marks, names and similar symbols, and other intellectual property.[9]

---

[8] For the case law, see below, pp. 18–19.
[9] For the subject in detail see, e.g., W. R. Cornish, *Intellectual Property: Patents, Copyright, Trade Marks and Allied Rights* (4th edn, London: Sweet & Maxwell, 1999) ch. 18;

The rule arises from the Treaty of Rome itself, rather than from any specific rule of patent law. It is an interpretation of the Treaty's principle of free movement of goods between Member States (Article 28 (ex 30) EC),[10] as it falls to be read in the light of the limited exception to that principle, allowing for the protection of 'industrial and commercial property' (Article 30 (ex 36) EC).[11] The ECJ concluded that while these provisions left Member States free to enforce the exclusive rights in patents against commercial activities of unconnected third parties (a power which was characterised as embracing the 'essence' of the right), the rights could not also relate to goods legitimately placed elsewhere on the internal market (this being a mere 'exercise' of the right).[12]

The incantations of 'essence' and 'exercise' made a poor substitute for plain reasoning,[13] but the outcome was clear enough. The central EC policy of a unified market demanded that national patent and other IP laws should (if necessary) adopt a Community-wide doctrine of exhaustion once there had been consensual sale of the goods somewhere within the EC (or now the EEA).

'Consent' for these purposes arises wherever there is any connection – legal, economic, financial or technical – between enterprises.[14] Thus if the marketing in France is by one subsidiary of a group, or by a manufacturing licensee, and the patentee in Britain is the parent company, or another subsidiary, or the licensor, none of the latter can object to parallel importation of the French product into England. Only if the patent has been assigned so as to belong to different owners in separate countries will there be no exhaustion.[15] Even then, if this is a mere pretext within a continuing arrangement for splitting up the single

---

C. Bellamy and G. Child, *Common Market Law of Competition* (4th edn, London: Sweet & Maxwell, 1993) ch. 8.2; P. Oliver, *Free Movement of Goods in the European Community: Under Articles 30 to 36 to the Rome Treaty* (3rd edn, London: Sweet & Maxwell, 1996) ch. 8.2.

[10] The prohibition in Article 28 EC, as between Member States, is of quantitative restrictions on imports or measures having equivalent effect. An example of the latter is an injunction enforcing an IPR.

[11] After allowing exceptions to Article 28 EC, Article 30 (ex 36) EC adds a proviso: 'such prohibitions or restrictions shall not, however, amount to a means of arbitrary discrimination nor to a disguised restriction on trade between Member States'. A law which gives preference to local over other EC nationals will involve arbitrary discrimination. What characterises a *disguised* restriction on trade is much less easy to identify.

[12] *Centrafarm* v. *Sterling Drug* [1974] ECR 1147; and the cases mentioned in the subsequent footnotes.

[13] Later attempts to define the 'specific subject-matter' of the IPR went little further, since they were largely tautologous.

[14] *Centrafarm* v. *Sterling Drug*, [1974] ECR 1147.

[15] So held in relation to trade marks in *IHT* v. *Ideal Standard* [1994] ECR I-2789.

market, the arrangement may well be an infraction of the EC Rules of Competition (Article 81 (ex 85) EC).[16]

Most of the patent cases which have settled this basic principle have concerned pharmaceuticals, because in the variously regulated national markets for health products there tend to be considerable variations in prices. The products can generally be procured by determined parallel exporters and they are cheap to transport. Two types of issue have raised complications in pharmaceutical cases.

The reasons for price differentials

In the first determinative decision of the ECJ, *Centrafarm* v. *Sterling Drug*,[17] the urinary infection drug in question had been bought in the UK by the parallel importer for half the Dutch price, and then exported to the Netherlands. The patentee, seeking to protect itself under Article 30 EC, emphasised a variety of explanations for that price differential, and also claimed that the public might receive defective products if distribution could not be controlled on a national basis. The Court would not accept that any of these grounds were sufficient to displace the free movement policy. In the particular case, the price differential followed very largely from currency fluctuations between the two countries. But, over and above that, the Court was strongly in favour of a clear, undifferentiated rule which fostered a basic objective of the single market, however much it might distort patenting policy.

The absence of patent protection in the country of export

Patent protection may not have been secured in all countries of the EEA. It may not have been applied for everywhere, or the application may have been rejected (or a granted patent annulled) for failing the tests of patent validity (patentable subject-matter, adequate disclosure, etc.). In previous decades, the issue has been exacerbated in the field of pharmaceuticals because of real or supposed legal inhibitions on the securing of patents, and in particular patents for substances with a therapeutic effect. Where the drug in question was not patented in one country, its price was often lower, since (subject to medical safety regulations) competitors could put it on the market there without any patent licence. Even under EU law there could not thereafter be any parallel importing of that competitor's goods into EU States where there was patent coverage. But if the patentee (or a licensee) went on to the

[16] See, e.g., the root decision, *Consten and Grundig* v. *EC Commission* [1966] ECR 299.
[17] [1974] ECR 1147.

free country's market, that was held by the ECJ to result in sales with the patentee's consent. The goods were therefore subject to the Community-wide exhaustion of the patent.[18]

Joliet (later an ECJ judge) led those who argued that this was inconsistent and unfair.[19] Parallel imports subject to a patent could be resisted if they originated from any involuntary source. Indeed the Court applied this solution to the case where there were patents in both countries, but in the cheaper country a competitor was able to procure a compulsory licence from the State and so to enter the market without paying a full royalty, such as might have been negotiated voluntarily.[20] Yet where there was no IPR to protect the first marketing at all, the mere fact that a proprietor of rights elsewhere in the EC was connected with the goods when initially marketed made all the difference: the connection supplied 'consent' and no objection could be taken if they were afterwards exported to a Member State where there was a relevant patent. Yet the absence of a chance to make the first sale at a price derived from intellectual property protection could well explain the price differential at the root of the issue.

When Spain and Portugal joined the Union, the severe limitations on pharmaceutical patenting in their previous laws, combined with vigorous governmental price controls, meant that there had to be an interregnum against parallel exporting from those countries in this field as part of the terms of accession. When this intercession expired, the differentials remained serious enough for the issue to be brought back to the ECJ.[21] Advocate-General Fennelly proposed a revision of the earlier approach, but the Court would not accept his advice. It considered that the demands of the free movement desideratum remained determinative.

The ECJ has been left to devise a policy for exhaustion of patent rights within the EEA because the issue is too controversial for political bodies with legislative powers. So far as the issue is a general one for patents as a whole, the results of the Court's decisions are likely to remain in their present uncomfortable state until it proves possible to introduce a Community patent. This project is currently stranded amid

---

[18] *Merck* v. *Stephar* [1981] ECR 2063 (ECJ).

[19] R. Joliet 'Patented Articles and the Free Movement of Goods within the EEC' [1975] 28 *Current Legal Problems* 15; P. Demaret, *Patents, Territorial Restrictions and EEC Law: A Legal and Economic Analysis* (Verlag Chemie, 1978); W. A. Rothnie, *Parallel Imports* (London: Sweet & Maxwell, 1993), ch. 6.

[20] *Pharmon* v. *Hoechst* [1985] ECR 2281. The case was only rather arbitrarily different from *Musikvertrieb Membran* v. *GEMA* [1981] ECR 147, which concerned a statutory licence of music copyright; in that case, the Court insisted upon Community-wide exhaustion.

[21] *Merck* v. *Primecrown* [1997] 1 CMLR 83.

arguments about translation costs, which pit national emotions against the demands of efficiency. A Union-wide patent would settle whether or not there is to be protection of a claimed invention for the whole unified market; a concept of exhaustion of rights for that area would then follow the traditional concept of most patent systems. So far as concerns pharmaceutical patents in particular, it is not easy to discover just how damaging the free flow of the internal market is to patentees' profitability.[22] There is nonetheless a case for a special rule disallowing parallel imports between one country and another, even where there is consent to the initial marketing, if in the country of first marketing there is a causal relationship between the low price there and governmental policies towards selling prices of the drugs concerned. Since progress towards establishing a true common market in pharmaceuticals is so beset with difficulties, the argument for such protection is the stronger. But there can be little realistic chance of it succeeding.

Patented products entering the EEA from outside

A different policy attitude appears to predominate in the EEA, when the question is whether patent rights may be used to prevent the entry into that area from countries outside it. The national laws of most Member States traditionally allowed the patent right to be asserted against the importation of patented goods even though they were initially marketed by the patentee or an associate elsewhere. There were differences in the principles to be applied, but these went to the issue of notice: must sufficient indication be given that no licence for international movement of the products was being granted? Or was there no exhaustion of right unless permission to import had been sufficiently given? In Britain, for instance, while the patent was conceived as continuing to apply to products deriving from the patentee, even after their sale to an independent owner, they were treated as bearing an implied licence allowing use and exportation unless that licence was expressly denied by conditions which were adequately notified to all purchasers down the chain of distribution.[23]

[22] Cf. J. S. Chard and C. J. Mellor, 'Intellectual Property Rights and Parallel Imports' (1989) 12(1) *World Economy* 69; L. Hancher, 'The European Pharmaceutical Market: Problems of Partial Harmonisation' (1990) 15 *European Law Review* 9; REMIT Consultants, Report to EC Commission, 'Impediments to Parallel Trade in Pharmaceuticals within the EC' (1992, OPOCE, IV/90/06/01); Rothnie, *Parallel Imports*, esp. chs. 8, 11; R. Rozek and R. Rapp, *Parallel Trade in Pharmaceuticals: The Impact of Welfare and Innovation* (1992).
[23] Interestingly, the Japanese Supreme Court has recently introduced an equivalent principle into Japanese patent law: *BBS Kraftfahrzeugtechnik v. Rashimekkusu* (1995 H-

At present this result follows simply from the various national patent laws of the States concerned. There is as yet no overarching law, operating at the European level, which imposes a common solution upon all of the countries concerned. It is true that the States of the EU are signatories of the Community Patent Convention (CPC), originally of 1975 and revised in 1989. However, that Convention has not been brought into effect and will only become operative if the European Commission brings off its new campaign in favour of its introduction – still a problematic manoeuvre. It provides principally for the creation of a unitary patent for the entire EU territory. But will the patent specification for this instrument have to be translated into an official language of each Member State? To do so would be impracticably costly, yet not to do so would be deeply offensive to some national sensibilities.

Even in its present State of suspended animation, the CPC has had a considerable effect as a model for voluntary harmonisation of the national laws concerned. The CPC, Article 28 deals with the issue of parallel importation to the extent that it states:

> The rights conferred by a Community patent shall not extend to acts concerning a product covered by that patent which are done within the territories of the Contracting States after that product has been put on the market in one of these States by the proprietor of the patent or with his express consent unless there are grounds which, under Community law, would justify the extension to such acts of the rights conferred by the patent.[24]

When this takes effect, national patent laws are required to adopt the same principle of Community-wide exhaustion:[25] hence the introduction of the legal formula into those national laws in advance of the CPC requirement. In any case, so far as the internal market of the EEA is concerned, the Article only formulates in particular language the principle derived by the ECJ from Articles 28–30 of the EC Treaty.[26] Whether this necessarily implies that there is no exhaustion of rights when the patented products are first marketed outside the EEA is a matter still awaiting judicial consideration.[27] Certainly most States

---

7(O) Case 3 No. 1988, Judgment of 1 July 1997). For the impact of the principle in EU trade mark law, see below, chapter 2.

[24] The text has not yet been amended to make the principle embodied in it operative throughout the EEA.

[25] CPC, Article 76.

[26] See above, p. 18. The formula is distinctive in two elements: first, it makes exhaustion turn upon *express* consent – an attempt to prevent courts from presuming consent merely from failure to obtain patent protection in a given State; and second, it leaves room for future exceptions to exhaustion to be defined.

[27] The largely equivalent formula which is introduced into the now operative Regulation for a Community Trade Mark, and the associated First Harmonisation Directive on national trade mark law, has been argued to have just this effect by the European Commission and several Member States: see the *Silhouette* case, discussed below in

would assume that this is the correct implication to make, because, in one or other version, that is the traditional understanding of their own national patent law.

Until that point is reached, the British approach is as follows: when goods to which a British patent applies are imported from (say) the United States or the Far East, their entry into Britain requires the consent of the British patentee. If that authorisation has not been given, expressly or impliedly, the act of importation will infringe the patent, as will subsequent sales and uses. The authorisation will be assumed to be given, when the marketing of the goods abroad has been by the British patentee; it can be countermanded only by notification that importation into Britain is not after all permitted.[28] The notice must be such as will alert a reasonable man that such a condition is operative, even if he does not know precisely its terms. Moreover, that notification must have been sufficiently given to each person who acquires the goods down the chain of distribution,[29] a matter which may be difficult to prove.

The present British approach is regarded by some as the best outcome because it honours the expectation of buyers generally that they take ownership without conditions; yet at the same time it allows conditions to be imposed at the right-owner's behest if they are made plain enough in advance. But those who want to block parallel imports and who, at the same time, understand the British position amongst the differing solutions around the world, will make it their business to give the necessary notice. So it can be doubted whether this form of solution does much more than add expense and uncertainty to the manner in which the parallel movement of patented products can be prevented. It is certainly not a solution which advocates of international exhaustion ought to accept, and so not an outcome which they would want to see if, for example, the TRIPs Agreement were to be revised so as to lay down an international law rule on the subject.

In the end, the issue should be resolved one way or the other as a matter of law. Global industry is likely to benefit most by having a clear rule under which to operate. The hard fact is that countries and industrial groupings remain intensely divided on the question whether the economic balance is broadly for or against adopting a rule of exhaustion. That is not surprising, given in particular that a rule one way or the other is a choice for a long period across widely differing

---

chapter 2. In my idiosyncratic view, the judgment of the ECJ in that case does not go so far as to establish such a proposition, though in future the Court may well be obliged to accept it.

[28] *Betts* v. *Wilmott* (1871) LR 6 Ch App 239.
[29] *Roussel Uclaf* v. *Hockley* [1996] RPC 441.

industrial and commercial conditions. In the meantime, the world has accepted the need for patent systems and their use is growing. They are above all incentive systems, and necessarily their inducement will be enhanced if patentees can engage in international price discrimination. It is for the proponents of a rule of international exhaustion to establish that the case for it ought to overrule this basic objective of all patenting.

2 The free movement of goods II: pharmaceuticals, trade marks and parallel imports

Belinda Isaac

Introduction

Consumers and retail stores buy and sell pharmaceutical products by reference to the brand name or trade mark of each product. Health care professionals can (and in some cases still do) prescribe or recommend medication by reference to a trade mark or brand name rather than the generic name of the compound, often because the ultimate consumer is more familiar with the brand name (as a result of advertising) than with any technical name for the product. The result is that the trade mark becomes a valuable shorthand means of identifying a product of a particular composition with a particular therapeutic effect originating from a specific manufacturing source. If the same product is sold in different markets at significantly different prices, should a third party be allowed to export goods from the low-price market to the higher one and sell the goods at a profit? Where products vary in their composition from one market to another or, if the brand name is different in one market compared to another market, should a third party still be entitled to redistribute the product and, if necessary, relabel or repackage the product, changing the brand name in the process? Should it matter whether the product was first sold within the European Economic Area (EEA) or not? These are just some of the questions that this chapter seeks to explore whilst considering the impact of trade mark law on the free movement of goods, and pharmaceuticals in particular.

This chapter will consider whether the owner of a registered trade mark should be permitted to rely upon the rights acquired by virtue of registration to prevent the free movement of goods either within the EEA or into the EEA. In addressing this question the emphasis will be on registered trade marks and the efforts of the European Court of Justice (ECJ) to strike a balance between the conflicting demands of proprietary rightholders and the principle enshrined in Article 28 (ex 30) EC, that is, the freedom of movement of goods. Although many of the comments expressed by the ECJ in relation to other forms of intellectual property rights are relevant when considering the exercise of trade mark rights, it is important to remember that the justification for trade mark protection is quite different from that of patents or copyright and consequently it cannot be assumed that the *rationes decidendi* of decisions involving patents and/or copyright will automatically apply to other intellectual property rights in the same fashion. Accordingly, this chapter will begin with a discussion of trade mark protection before considering the impact of the Treaty of Rome on national trade mark law. We will see that, in an effort to reach a compromise between the conflicting demands of trade mark owners and the establishment of a single market, the ECJ has developed the principle of 'exhaustion of rights'. Until now the exhaustion principle has only been applied in relation to the free movement of goods within the common market, but recently there has been significant debate over whether the principle should be applied internationally. The author will suggest that whilst the principle of international exhaustion may be a logical extension of trade mark philosophy, the realities of the current world market are such that even regional exhaustion may impose unrealistic burdens on manufacturers in the absence of true economic and legal parity.

The nature of intellectual property rights

Intellectual property rights such as patents, copyrights, registered designs and registered trade marks are generally speaking national rights that give the proprietor a measure of exclusivity in the subject-matter of protection and in so doing protect the owner of the right from the effects of competition. These rights are usually justified on the basis of different policy considerations. Patents are frequently justified on the basis that they provide incentives for research and development, whilst copyright is justified as a reward for authors and an incentive to create further works. Trade marks, however, are traditionally justified on the grounds that they act as an indication of the origin of the goods to which the marks are applied. They act as symbols embodying the goodwill of a particular trader and guarantee the quality of a trader's products. This guarantee is not absolute but it does provide an incentive for the trade mark owner to improve the quality of his goods so that consumers come to associate, and indeed expect, a particular level of quality with a particular trade mark. Trade marks also protect consumers against the use of confusingly similar marks by third parties seeking to trade off the reputation and goodwill established by the owner of the original mark.

The extent of the rights granted to the owner of the various intellectual property rights varies depending on the nature of the right in question and the basis for its justification. For example, the owner of a patent right has the exclusive right to exploit the material covered by the patent. Independent creation of the same invention will amount to an infringement. In relation to copyright, however, the holder only has a right to prevent, *inter alia*, unauthorised reproduction so that independent creation will not amount to infringement. Thus the scope of protection afforded by copyright is much narrower than that available under patents. To reflect this difference in scope the term of protection is much shorter for patents (twenty years) than for copyright (life of the author plus seventy years). Unlike patents and copyright, registered trade marks are not limited in time (provided that renewal fees are paid). However, the protection available to owners of registered trade mark rights is not as broad as that available to owners of patents. In general terms the protection available under trade mark law is predicated upon the existence or risk of confusion.

Intellectual property rights are limited in scope geographically. Thus trade mark owners must apply to register their trade marks in every jurisdiction where protection is required. A registration in the United Kingdom would not ordinarily enable the proprietor of the mark to take action, in say, France. A consequence of this geographic limitation is that it is possible for trade marks to be registered in the names of different organisations in different countries. Equally it is possible that a manufacturer may use and register different trade marks in relation to the same product in different markets.[1] One further consequence of the geographical limitation of a trade mark right is that, on the face of it, a trade mark owner may rely upon his registration to prevent the importation of goods bearing the same mark from another country, for example, Brazil.[2] Before considering how a trade mark owner might rely upon a registered trade mark in this way, we first need to clarify what a trade mark is and what rights are granted to the owner of a trade mark registration.

Registered trade mark rights

In the UK the law relating to registered trade marks is set out in the Trade Marks Act 1994 ('TMA 1994') which implements the EC Trade

---

[1] This may not extend from any desire by the manufacturer to partition markets but may simply reflect the fact that certain trade marks do not translate well into other languages, or that a third party has already registered the mark in the country in question so that the manufacturer has no alternative but to select a different mark if it is to market its goods in that territory.

[2] *Colgate-Palmolive v. Markwell Finance* [1989] RPC 497.

Mark Harmonisation Directive.[3] Section 1(1) of the TMA 1994 defines a trade mark as: 'any sign capable of being represented graphically which is capable of distinguishing goods or services of one undertaking from those of other undertakings . . . [trade marks can consist of] . . . words (including personal names), designs, letters, numerals or the shape of goods or their packaging'. Thus in relation to pharmaceutical products a trade mark may consist of the shape of a capsule or tablet, the colour of a capsule or tablet, the proprietary name of the product (but not its generic name), a logo, the shape or colour of the packaging of the goods and/or any text, provided in each case that the mark is distinctive and is capable of distinguishing the proprietor's products.

Although it is not necessary to obtain registration of a trade mark in the UK in order to acquire rights in the mark, it is not possible to take action for trade mark infringement unless the mark is registered.[4] Without a registration the owner of a trade mark will only be able to rely upon the common law action of passing off which, depending upon the circumstances, can be much harder to establish than an action for trade mark infringement since passing off requires a misrepresentation; and that can be difficult to establish if the goods are genuine.[5] For the purposes of this essay we will only consider the action of trade mark infringement and therefore references to trade marks will be to trade marks registered in accordance with the TMA 1994.

The rights afforded by registration are set out in Sections 9 and 10 of the TMA 1994. Section 9(1) states that: 'the proprietor of a registered trade mark has exclusive rights in the trade mark which are infringed by use of the trade mark in the United Kingdom without his consent . . .'. Section 10 sets out the infringement provisions. Subsection 1 states that: 'a person infringes a registered trade mark if he uses in the course of trade a sign which is identical with the trade mark in relation to goods or services which are identical with those for which it is registered'.

By virtue of Section 10(4) a person is considered to have 'used' the sign (that is, the offending mark) if, amongst other things, he offers or exposes goods for sale, puts them on the market, stocks them under the sign or imports or exports goods under the sign. Although, on the face of it, a trader in the UK buying goods from a proprietor of a UK-registered trade mark would technically infringe the registration by reselling the goods within the United Kingdom, the trade mark owner

---

[3] Directive 89/104/EEC [1989] OJ L40/1: hereafter referred to as the 'Directive'.

[4] If the unregistered mark is entitled to protection under the Paris Convention as a 'well-known' mark it may be possible to initiate action for trade mark infringement even in the absence of a registration under Section 56 of the TMA 1994.

[5] It may be possible to establish a misrepresentation where the imported goods are of a different quality: see *Colgate-Palmolive* v. *Markwell Finance* [1989] RPC 497.

would ordinarily be deemed to have consented (or granted an implied licence) to the trader in relation to the resale of the products unless the goods had been altered following the first sale. This implied licence is equivalent, in its effect, to a national doctrine of exhaustion of rights.[6] In other words, by consenting to the sale of the product within the United Kingdom the proprietor of the UK trade mark registration is said to have exhausted his rights.

From the definition of trade mark infringement under Section 10(1) of the TMA 1994, and the definition of 'use' under Section 10(4), it can be seen that the importation of goods into the UK that bear a trade mark identical to a trade mark registered in the UK in relation to identical goods, *prima facie* infringes the rights of the trade mark owner in the UK. In theory therefore a trade mark owner can seek to exercise its trade mark rights as a means of preventing the importation of such goods. If the goods in question are manufactured by the trade mark proprietor or with his consent (for example, by a licensee or an associated company) then the imported goods are often referred to as 'grey goods' or 'parallel imports'. This situation is quite distinct from that where the goods are manufactured without the consent of the registered proprietor, that is where they are 'counterfeit' or 'pirate' goods. In relation to pharmaceutical products parallel imports should not be confused with 'generic' goods, which may have the same formulation as a branded product but which are made by third parties and sold under the generic name of the formulation rather than the brand name. The packaging of generic products should be distinct from that of the branded equivalent. For the purposes of this chapter attention will be focused on genuine goods, that is parallel imports, and we will not therefore be considering what action a trade mark proprietor may take against the producer or importer of generic or pirate goods.

Parallel imports and the treaty of Rome

Parallel importation arises where goods are manufactured and sold in one country (Country A) at a higher price than that at which they are sold in another country (Country B) to which they are exported. A third party (referred to as a parallel importer) acquires the goods in Country B and exports them to Country A where they are sold at a profit but at a lower price than those sold by the original manufacturer (or his distributor). The parallel importer therefore makes his profit by exploiting the price differential that exists between different markets. The reasons

---

6 J. Rasmussen, 'The Principle of Exhaustion of Trade Mark Rights Pursuant to Directive 89/104 (and Regulation 40/94)' [1995] *EIPR* 174.

for the price differential are manifold and various and may, or may not, be within control of the product manufacturer: for example, they may be the result of government restrictions on pricing,[7] the increased costs of marketing and advertising in one country compared to another, the cost of transport and storage, differences in overheads, increased competition in one market compared to another or economies of scale. Whatever the reason, the effect of the parallel import trade is to redistribute the goods to the parallel importer's best advantage and at the cost of the original manufacturer or authorised distributor. In the long term, unless the manufacturer can stop the flow of grey goods the consequence will be to distort competition, to reduce price differentials wherever these exist and are within the control of the manufacturer, and to restrict the supply of the goods so that they are not exported to the cheapest markets (so far as this is possible). In extreme cases, the parallel trade may affect the ability of the manufacturer to conduct and invest in research and development if its profits are seriously undermined.[8] From a consumer perspective, the sale of parallel imports is often favourably regarded because the consumer can purchase the branded products more cheaply. Thus supermarkets, discount stores and consumer organisations are often vociferous in their support of policies that encourage the parallel import trade.[9] Such a view ignores, however, the fact that the cheaper goods may be of a different quality or are in some other respect different from the goods with which the consumer is familiar.[10]

As has been noted above, intellectual property rights are principally national rights and their owners are entitled to prevent certain activities from taking place within national boundaries. Such rights are, however, subject to international treaties that may be entered into by the State in question which may limit the scope of the rights granted. This is particularly true where States enter into free trade agreements designed to promote trade between signatory countries. In such circumstances

---

[7] See, e.g., S. Kon and F. Schaeffer, 'Parallel Imports of Pharmaceutical Products: A New Realism, or Back to Basics' [1997] *ECLR* 123.

[8] This was an argument put forward in *Glaxo Group Ltd & Others* v. *Dowelhurst* [2000] ETMR 415.

[9] See press comments following the ECJ decision in the *Silhouette* case (discussed below) on 16 July 1998; Case C-355/96 *Silhouette International Schmied* v. *Hartlauer Handelsgesellschaft* [1998] ECR I-4799.

[10] Whether the composition of two medicinal products was essentially similar was central to the issue of whether or not a marketing authorisation should be granted to a parallel importer in Case 201/94 *R* v. *The Medicines Control Agency ex parte Smith & Nephew Pharmaceuticals Ltd and Primecrown Ltd* [1996] ECR I-5819. This essay does not seek to address the regulatory issues relating to parallel imports and the sale of pharmaceutical products: for further information on this area see Kon and Schaeffer, 'Parallel Imports of Pharmaceutical Products'.

the ability of the rightholder to prevent imports may be curtailed. The most important free trade agreement governing rightholders in the UK is the Treaty of Rome which sought to establish, and subsequently regulate, the single market. Among its primary objectives the Treaty of Rome sought to eliminate restrictions upon the free movement of goods between Member States. This principle is embodied in Article 28 (ex 30) EC which states that: 'quantitative restrictions on imports and all measures having equivalent effect shall, without prejudice to the following provisions, be prohibited between Member States'.

Article 30 (ex 36) EC provides a derogation from the effect of Article 28 EC as far as intellectual property rights are concerned provided that the exercise of such rights does not constitute a means of arbitrary discrimination or restriction on trade between Member States. Article 30 EC states: 'The provisions of Articles 28 and 29 shall preclude prohibitions or restrictions on imports, exports or goods in transit justified on the grounds of public morality, public policy . . . or the protection of industrial or commercial property. Such prohibitions or restrictions shall not, however, constitute a means of arbitrary discrimination or disguised restriction on trade between the states.'

Thus, although Article 28 EC prohibits restrictions on imports or measures having equivalent effect, Article 30 EC provides an exception in relation to industrial and commercial property. This would, on the face of it, appear to enable a trade mark owner to prevent goods bearing an identical trade mark from being imported into a Member State without his consent. However, in *Centrafarm* v. *Winthrop*[11] it was held that: 'The owner of a trade mark cannot exercise his rights to prohibit the importation of products with the same trade mark and marketed in another Member State provided that the goods are marketed by the trade mark owner, or with the trade mark owner's consent. To do so would be incompatible with the free movement of goods provisions in the EEC Treaty.' Thus the ECJ and the EC Commission have interpreted the provisions of the Treaty of Rome as limiting the scope of national intellectual property laws in certain circumstances where they might conflict with policies expressed in the Treaty.

The ECJ's initial analysis of instances where intellectual property rights had been used as barriers to trade focused upon the 'existence' of the right and the 'exercise' of that right.[12] Cornish observes[13] that these terms have the appearance of being formulated only after the policy

---

[11] [1974] ECR 1183.
[12] See, e.g., the decision of the ECJ in Case 40/70 *Sirena Srl* v. *EDA Srl* [1971] ECR 69.
[13] W. R. Cornish *Intellectual Property: Patents, Copyright, Trade Marks and Allied Rights* (4th edn, London: Sweet & Maxwell, 1999) p. 43.

decision had been taken to give preference to Community policies over national rights. In subsequent decisions the ECJ sought to strike a balance between the conflicting demands of intellectual property owners and the desire for a single market and in so doing it developed the doctrine of 'exhaustion of rights'.

In applying the exhaustion doctrine to instances of alleged trade mark infringement the ECJ has considered the 'essential function' of a trade mark and has stressed that trade mark rights may only be exercised in a way that is consistent with this essential function. The essential function is said to be the guarantee of the identity of the origin of the marked product. This guarantee of origin means that the consumer can be certain that a trade-marked product which has been sold to him has not been interfered with by a third party so as to affect the original condition of the product. Thus the trade mark owner is only able to enforce his rights in his registered trade mark against commercial activities of a third party if such activities affect the essential function of the mark.[14]

The application of the exhaustion principle within the EEA

Since the decision in *Centrafarm* v. *Winthrop* in 1974 the ECJ has applied the doctrine of exhaustion of rights to a variety of situations involving the free movement of goods and trade mark rights. In order to appreciate the commercial impact of the application of the exhaustion rule to trade mark owners we will now turn to consider briefly some of the most significant decisions of the ECJ.

Parallel importation of identical products with identical marks

The *Centrafarm* v. *Winthrop* case established the principle that where goods are put on the market by one member of a group of companies it is not possible for another member of the same group to object to the importation of those trade-marked goods into a territory where it is the owner of a trade mark registration. Thus, even though trade mark registrations may be owned in different Member States by different companies within the same organisation, the trade mark proprietor is deemed to have consented to the marketing of the goods in question throughout the Community under the trade mark by the associated company.

---

[14] Case 102/77 *Hoffman-La Roche & Co* v. *Centrafarm* [1978] ECR 1139.

Identical products with different trade marks

The slightly later case of *Centrafarm* v. *American Home Products*[15] concerned sale of goods that were identical but were sold under different trade marks in the different markets. The trade mark owner was held to be entitled to take action to prevent the repackaging and subsequent resale in the Netherlands of goods under the mark Seresta that were originally sold in the UK under the trade mark Serenid. It was held that unless it could be shown that use of the two marks was intended artificially to partition the market, the owner of the Seresta trade mark was entitled to prevent the use of its mark on products originating from the UK under the Serenid name. However, when virtually the same issue came before the ECJ in *Pharmacia & Upjohn*[16] it was held that if it was 'objectively necessary' within the meaning of *Paranova* (discussed below) for the parallel importer to replace the original trade mark with that used in the State of import then this would be permissible, but not otherwise.

Conflicting trade mark rights

Where grey goods are imported into a market and there exists a registered trade mark in the name of an organisation completely separate from that of the organisation originally responsible for labelling the grey goods, the registered proprietor may take action relying on national laws to prevent the importation of such products. In such a situation there is no application of the exhaustion doctrine since there is no common origin of the products and no consent to the use of the trade mark, provided that there is no evidence of discrimination against imports.[17]

Repackaging and relabelling of goods

In the case of *Hoffman-La Roche* v. *Centrafarm* the trade mark owner took action to prevent Centrafarm from repackaging the product and reaffixing the trade mark. In that particular case, the trade mark owner sold its tablets in packets of twenty or fifty for individuals in the German market and quantities of 100 or 250 tablets for the use of hospitals in the German market, whereas in the UK the product was sold in packages containing 100 or 500 tablets at prices considerably below those of the German market. Centrafarm purchased supplies of the tablets in the

---

[15] Case 3/78 *Centrafarm* v. *American Home Products* [1979] 1 CMLR 326.
[16] Case 379/97 *Pharmacia & Upjohn* v. *Paranova* [1999] ETMR 937.
[17] Case 119/75 *Terrapin* v. *Terranova* [1976] ECR 1039 and more recently in Case C-9/93 *IHT* v. *Ideal Standard* [1994] ECR I-2789.

UK and repackaged them for sale in the German market using Hoffman-La Roche's trade marks on the outside of the packaging. The German subsidiary of Hoffman-La Roche took action against Centrafarm on the basis of trade mark infringement. Hoffman-La Roche argued that the repackaging of the product interfered with the essential function of a trade mark which was to indicate the origin of the product and to guarantee its quality. Whilst acknowledging the importance of the guarantee function of trade marks, the ECJ held that to prevent a product to which the trade mark had lawfully been applied in one Member State from being marketed in another after it had been repackaged constituted a disguised restriction on trade. It held that if it could be established that:

1. the use of the trade mark in this way would contribute to the artificial partitioning of the market;
2. repackaging cannot adversely affect the original condition of the product;
3. the proprietor of the mark received prior notice of the repackaging;
4. it is stated on the new packaging by whom the product has been repackaged;

then the trade mark owner would not be able to exercise its intellectual property rights to prevent the sale of the repackaged product. The effect of the *Hoffman-La Roche* decision was, in effect, to grant the parallel importer an implied licence to re-affix a registered trade mark belonging to a third party to repackaged products provided that these four requirements were satisfied.

The Trade Marks Directive

Article 7 of the Directive[18] states that:

1. The trade mark shall not entitle the proprietor to prohibit its use in relation to goods which have been put on the market in the Community[19] under that trade mark by the proprietor or with his consent.
2. Paragraph 1 shall not apply where there exist legitimate reasons for the proprietor to oppose further commercialisation of the goods, especially

---

[18] Directive 89/104/EEC [1989] OJ L40/1. The equivalent provision is Section 12 of the TMA 1994: '(1) A registered trade mark is not infringed by the use of the trade mark in relation to goods which have been put on the market in the EEA under that trade mark by the proprietor or with his consent. (2) Subsection (1) does not apply where there exist legitimate reasons for the proprietor to oppose further dealings in the goods (in particular, where the condition of the goods has changed or impaired after they have been put on the market).'

[19] This has been extended to cover the whole of the EEA in accordance with Annex XVII, point 4 of the EEA Agreement.

where the condition of the goods is changed or impaired after they have been put on the market.

Article 7 in effect codifies the jurisprudence of the ECJ concerning the doctrine of exhaustion developed over the previous twenty-five or more years. In the *Paranova* case,[20] the parallel importer went one step further than its counterpart in *Hoffman-La Roche*. Not only did it repackage the products, but it also included additional material in the repackaged product; for example, in one package containing a spray, Paranova replaced the spray with a product from a source other than that of the original manufacturer of the product. In relation to other products Paranova included new user information in the local language. The various trade mark owners of the products concerned took action against Paranova and the matter was referred to the ECJ. Although, on the face of it, the facts of the *Paranova* case are very similar to those of the *Hoffman-La Roche* case, in the intervening period since the *Hoffman-La Roche* decision had been handed down, the Directive had been adopted and thus clarification was also sought as to whether or not the exhaustion of rights principle, expressed in the *Hoffman-La Roche* case, was altered in any way by the Directive.

In the *Paranova* case, the plaintiff sought clarification as to whether the repackaging of goods and the inclusion of material of a different origin constituted a 'legitimate reason' within the meaning of Article 7(2) of the Directive to object to the repackaging or whether the application of Article 7 had to be interpreted in the light of previous jurisprudence of the ECJ, and in particular the decision in *Hoffman-La Roche*. The ECJ held that Article 7 was subsidiary to the Treaty of Rome and therefore must be interpreted in accordance with the provisions on the free movement of goods and in particular Article 30 EC. Accordingly, the Court affirmed its decision in *Hoffman-La Roche* indicating that a trade mark owner may only legitimately oppose the further marketing of a pharmaceutical product if the importer had repackaged it and re-affixed the trade mark and the four conditions set out in the *Hoffman-La Roche* case were not met. The ECJ thus reinforced its determination to apply the principle of exhaustion throughout the EEA in order to achieve its objective of a single market.

In the recent case of *Glaxo Group* v. *Dowelhurst*[21] the repackaging undertaken by the defendants was challenged on the ground that it was

---

[20] Joined Cases C-427/93, C-429/93 and C-436/93 *Bristol-Myers Squibb* v. *Paranova A/S, Boehringer & Others* v. *Paranova A/S, Bayer AG & Another* v. *Paranova A/S* [1996] ECR I-3457; [1996] ETMR 1.
[21] *Glaxo Group Ltd & Others* v. *Dowelhurst Ltd & Others* [2000] ETMR 415.

not 'necessary'. The requirement of necessity was said to be based on a passage in *Paranova* where the ECJ said that '[t]he power of the owner of trade mark rights protected in a Member State to oppose the marketing of repackaged products under the trade mark should be limited only insofar as the repackaging undertaken by the importers is necessary in order to market the product in the Member State of importation'.[22] The consequence of such a requirement, according to Laddie J, would be that importers would rarely be entitled to repackage and he was therefore of the view that this could not be what the ECJ meant. Accordingly he referred the case to the ECJ because he felt that the decisions of the ECJ were not entirely consistent and it was important that clarification was obtained. He also questioned the need for the parallel importer to give prior notice of the repackaging (the third condition laid down in *Hoffman-La Roche*), regarding it as an unnecessary precondition. In referring nine questions to the ECJ on the subject of repackaging Laddie J was no doubt hoping that the current ambiguities concerning when and in what circumstances repackaging may take place will be answered once and for all. The judgment of the ECJ will be awaited with interest. Whether the Court will be as exhaustive in its treatment of the subject as Laddie J was in his judgment, remains to be seen. In any event, it is hoped that the ECJ will make the most of the opportunity to reconsider the matter in detail.

The application of the exhaustion principle to non-pharmaceutical goods was confirmed in *Loendersloot* v. *Ballantine*,[23] a case involving the relabelling of Scotch whisky. In *Dior* v. *Evora*,[24] although Dior, the trade mark owner, did not object to the resale of grey goods within the EEA, it did object to the subsequent use of its trade marks and representations of its perfume bottles in advertising material produced by the parallel importer on the basis that the form of advertising material, and in particular its inferior quality, changed or impaired the condition of the goods given their luxury nature. Although the ECJ did not support Dior entirely, in that it did not allow Dior to exercise its intellectual property rights so as to restrict the further commercialisation of the products, it did recognise that in relation to luxury prestige brands the context of the sale of the goods (for example, the location of the goods and the form of advertising used to promote them, etc.), could have a detrimental effect on the reputation associated with the trade mark. Quite how such a detrimental effect can be demonstrated and in what circumstances

---

[22] *Paranova* at paragraph 56.

[23] Case C-349/95 *Loendersloot (Frits), trading as F. Loendersloot Internationale Expeditie* v. *George Ballantine & Son Ltd.* [1997] ECR I-6227; [1998] ETMR 10.

[24] Case C-337/95 *Christian Dior Parfums* v. *Evora* [1997] ECR I-6013; [1998] ETMR 26.

remains open to speculation. The decision does, however, indicate that the ECJ is willing to entertain exceptions to the application of the exhaustion principle, albeit that the exceptions are hard to identify.

Regional or international exhaustion?

During the course of its development from a proposal for a Directive to the adoption of the Directive, the wording of Article 7 was significantly altered. The Commission's initial proposal[25] contained a provision establishing international exhaustion. It stated that: 'The trade mark should not entitle the proprietor thereof to prohibit its use in relation to goods which have been put on the market [i.e. in or outside the Community] under that trade mark by the proprietor or with his consent.'

However, during the debate in the European Parliament an amendment was adopted to the effect that Community, and not international, exhaustion should be applied. In its amended proposal of 17 December 1985[26] the wording was altered to read: 'The trade mark shall not entitle the proprietor thereof to prohibit its use in relation to goods which have been put on the market *in the Community* under that trade mark by the proprietor or with his consent' (emphasis added). The explanation for the change of wording given by the Commission was that this amendment was necessary in order to avoid the requirement that Member States introduce the principle of international exhaustion into national law since at that stage not all Member States applied such a principle.

Despite the Commission's explanation there were, until recently, significant doubts as to whether the effect of Article 7 was indeed to introduce Community-wide exhaustion, or whether this was a minimum standard such that Member States could implement international exhaustion if they wished.[27] Decisions such as that of the EFTA Court in *Mag Instruments* v. *California Trading Co.*[28] have only served to fuel this debate. In that case the EFTA Court was asked to decide whether the owner in Norway of the trade mark Maglite could rely upon its trade mark rights to prevent the importation of genuine goods from the United States. The defendant relied on the defence of international exhaustion that was available under Norwegian trade mark law. The

[25] [1980] OJ C351/1.
[26] [1985] OJ C351/4.
[27] See, e.g., Rasmussen, 'Principle of Exhaustion' and A. Carboni, 'Cases Past the Post on Trade Mark Exhaustion: An English Perspective' [1997] *EIPR* 198.
[28] [1998] ETMR 85.

EFTA Court considered the provision of Article 7 of the Directive but held that, according to the EEA Agreement, it was for the EFTA States to decide whether or not to apply the principle of international exhaustion where goods originated from outside the EEA.

The dangers of introducing only a minimum requirement of Community-wide exhaustion were clearly illustrated in the case of *Pytheron International SA* v. *Jean Bowdon SA.*[29] In that case, Bowdon contracted to purchase a plant health product sold by reference to the trade mark Previcur N. The product was manufactured in Turkey and imported into Germany (a country which operated a principle of international exhaustion). The product was to be sent from Germany to France but Bowdon terminated the contract on the basis that importation into France would infringe the French trade mark (on the basis that France did not operate a policy of international exhaustion). The Court held that Article 7 of the Directive must be interpreted as preventing the application of any law that would enable a trade mark owner to prevent the importation of a genuine product if the product is lawfully imported into the Member State where it was lawfully acquired, before importing it into another Member State, and the packaging has not been changed. Thus if ever one Member State were allowed to operate a principle of international exhaustion it would become the gateway for all grey products to enter the Community, since once the products have lawfully been sold in that market other Member States would not be able to object to their importation.

When drafting the Directive, the Commission was therefore faced with a choice either to require Member States to introduce a principle of international exhaustion or to insist upon a standard of Community-wide (or rather EEA-wide) exhaustion which would effectively ring-fence Europe and its single market, leaving the Commission to negotiate reciprocity agreements with third-party States as it chose. As the Advocate-General noted in the *Silhouette* case,[30] considerations of commercial policy and concerns about possible lack of reciprocity were no doubt among the reasons why the original proposal for international exhaustion was not mentioned.

In any event, the debate was settled (to some extent at least) with the ECJ's decision in *Silhouette* v. *Hartlauer*[31] when it confirmed that under Article 7(1) of the Directive, Member States were obliged to apply the principle of EEA-wide exhaustion. In the case, Silhouette, an Austrian manufacturer of luxury fashion spectacle frames, sold a consignment of

[29] [1997] ETMR 211.
[30] C-355/96 [1998] ECR I-4799.
[31] [1998] ECR I-4799 at 4814.

its old stock to a Bulgarian company with the express stipulation that the frames be sold in the countries of the former Soviet Union and not in the EEA. The Bulgarian company sold the consignment to Hartlauer who began to market the frames in Austria in competition with Silhouette but at significantly lower prices. Silhouette issued proceedings for infringement, relying on Article 7 of the Directive. Hartlauer argued that no restriction on sale within Austria was actually made. As the Advocate-General noted in his Opinion: 'the Court is faced squarely with the question whether the Trade Marks Directive . . . requires Member States to oppose the import into the community of products placed on the market outside the EEA by [the proprietor] or with his consent'.[32]

The Advocate-General concluded from the legislative development of the Directive that it was clearly not intended that the principle of international exhaustion would apply. Basing his decision in part on the wording of the Community Trade Mark Regulation[33] (which used wording equivalent to Article 7), the legislative history of the Directive and the undesirable effects of leaving the question to the discretion of Member States, the Advocate-General's Opinion was that the principle of EEA exhaustion should apply. The ECJ concurred with the Opinion of the Advocate-General that Article 7 of the Directive provided for EEA-wide exhaustion, stating that it 'was the only interpretation which is fully capable of ensuring that the purpose of the Directive is achieved, namely to safeguard the functioning of the internal market'. Furthermore, it reasoned, if some Member States introduced international exhaustion whilst others implemented only Community-wide exhaustion, barriers to trade within the single market would be created which would be contrary to the whole object of the Directive.

Despite the attraction of arguments put on behalf of the Swedish Government that international exhaustion 'would bring substantial advantages to consumers and would promote price competition' and that regional exhaustion would enable trade mark owners to divide up markets and exploit price differentials, the Court emphasised that the exhaustion principle had been developed in the context of intra-Community trade and it was not therefore appropriate to apply the principle on an international basis.

Although the *Silhouette* decision left a lot of questions unanswered it did, for a while at least, settle the issue that trade mark owners within the EEA might, on the face of it, take action to prevent goods entering the EEA without their consent. There are, however, still a number of

---

[32] [1998] ECR I-4799 at 4809.
[33] Council Regulation 40/94/EEC on the Community Trade Mark [1994] OJ L11/1.

cate the fight against counterfeiting and piracy. The result of the two meetings was reported to the Internal Market Council in June 1999 when it was agreed that the Council would prepare a working document as a precursor to a possible change to the current trade mark exhaustion regime.

As Professor Cornish notes in his chapter,[39] the application of the exhaustion of rights principle is an extremely political issue and is one on which there is no universal agreement. Indeed, there are no international treaties that incorporate provisions relating to international exhaustion, largely because agreement cannot be reached on whether such a policy should be applied or not. The TRIPs Agreement, which was concluded in 1994 as part of the GATT Uruguay Round of negotiations, is not only silent on the subject, but also specifically states that '[f]or the purposes of dispute settlement . . . nothing in this Agreement shall be used to address the issue of exhaustion of intellectual property rights',[40] thus making it clear that the Agreement may not be construed as supporting the issue one way or the other. It is quite likely that when the Agreement comes up for renegotiation later in 2000 the subject of international exhaustion will be high on the agenda, given the recent discussions at the Internal Market Council of Ministers. The question then will be whether the principle of international exhaustion can be resisted and, if not, whether a special case can be made out to exclude its effect from any particular industry sector that is adversely affected by it, such as the pharmaceutical industry.[41]

From a purely philosophical point of view, is there any justification for distinguishing between goods sold outside the EEA and those sold within the EEA for the purposes of exhaustion of trade mark rights? If, as is frequently stated, the essential function of a trade mark is to indicate the manufacturing origin of the goods to which the mark is applied, then it is difficult to justify on the face of it the exercise of trade mark rights to prevent the flow of trade mark goods into the EEA where the mark has been applied with the consent of the trade mark owner. It is important to remember, however, that the concept of exhaustion was developed by the ECJ under the umbrella of the Treaty of Rome at a time when steps were being taken to realise legal and economic harmo-

---

[39] See above, chapter 1 and also W. R. Cornish, 'Trade Marks: Portcullis for the EEA' [1998] *EIPR* 172.

[40] Article 6 of TRIPs. See M. Blakeney, *The Trade Related Aspects of Intellectual Property Rights: A Concise Guide to the TRIPs Agreement* (London: Sweet & Maxwell, 1997) p. 42.

[41] This was one of the proposals put forward in the Commission's working paper. The main problem identified with this approach was the difficulty of defining the products that might fall within any exception.

nisation. The ECJ's primary objective then, as now, was to establish a single unified market with no internal barriers to trade. This point was emphasised by the Advocate-General in *Silhouette*,[42] where he stated that the Court's case law on the function of trade marks was developed in the context of the Community, not the world market, and he pointed to the decision of the Court in *EMI* v. *CBS*[43] to support the fact that case law developed under Articles 28 and 30 EC could not be transposed and applied to imports from third countries. Kobia also notes, in his article reflecting on the future expansion of the EU,[44] that one of the underlying reasons for the Community exhaustion principle and a prerequisite for its application in all countries of the Community is that they present homogeneous economic conditions. Expansion of the EU to include former Eastern Bloc countries raises the risk that branded goods will be sold more cheaply in those markets than in existing EU Member States with the consequence that there will be a flood of cheap imports from those countries. On the present interpretation of the Directive it would not be possible for trade mark owners to prevent such imports. This brings us back to the fact that parallel imports are primarily about cheaper prices and economic issues rather than purely intellectual property considerations.[45] The real question, therefore, is whether intellectual property laws should be relied upon to reduce the harm suffered as a result of economic differences in markets.

If the goods sold under the mark are universally of the same quality then there can be little justification (under trade mark law) for distinguishing between those sold in one market compared to another unless the circumstances surrounding the sale of the goods are such that they will injure the reputation of the trade mark owner. Assuming that there is no injury to the trade mark owner's reputation then the issue is purely economic and the exercise of trade mark rights is inappropriate. The economic issue should be addressed by other means.

Where, however, the goods sold under the trade mark differ in quality from one market to another, then applying a principle of international exhaustion may well lead to confusion amongst consumers and may well denigrate the reputation attaching to the trade mark. In these circumstances trade mark law can and should be relied upon to justify intervention. In such circumstances, it may be within the control of the proprietor to differentiate between these different quality products

---

[42] [1998] ETMR 286 at 300.
[43] Case 51/75 *EMI* v. *CBS* [1976] ECR 811.
[44] R. Kobia, 'Reflections on the Effects of Future Enlargements of the EU on Industrial Property: The Case of Trade Marks' [1998] *EIPR* 183 at 185.
[45] Rothnie, *Parallel Imports*, p. 7.

either by means of labelling or by using different trade marks for each product. This would certainly help to reduce the risk of consumer confusion by enabling consumers[46] to distinguish between the different products, or sources. If this is not possible (and, because of the requirement for single trade mark registration in order to obtain marketing authorisation under the centralised procedure,[47] the manufacturer may be obliged to sell the products under the same mark) then, in the interests of consumers, the trade mark owner should be entitled to rely upon its trade mark rights to prevent imports of products of differing quality. To do otherwise would be to besiege unsuspecting consumers with a host of conflicting symbols which they previously understood to signify goods of a particular manufacturer, and perhaps a particular taste, colour, shape or size but which can no longer be relied upon in the same way. Instead of reducing consumer search costs and reducing consumer risk, trade marks will just confuse them. Trade marks will not be seen as reliable indicators of quality and may well damage the reputation of the trade mark owner irreparably. Treating trade marks as though they only indicate manufacturing origin is far too simplistic a view of the role of a trade mark and as such it undermines its value.[48] This cannot be in the interests of trade mark owners or consumers.

Thus, until there is greater harmonisation of markets around the world (from both a legal and an economic perspective) the principle of exhaustion should, in this author's view at least, be applied only regionally. Where certain markets operate policies of government-controlled pricing (usually fixing the prices at low levels), and manufacturers are obliged to sell products in those markets, operating a principle of international exhaustion can cause significant damage to the businesses involved and to their respective trade marks.[49] Whilst in the context of new members of the EU this could be mitigated by a temporary derogation that could be included in any new accession treaty as Kobia suggests,[50] it is difficult to see how such a provision could be applied on an international scale.

---

[46] I.e. both health care professionals and end-users.
[47] Regulation 2309/93/EEC [1993] OJ L214/1.
[48] An observation shared by G. Tritton in 'Parallel Imports in the European Community' [1997] 1(2) *Intellectual Property Quarterly* 196 at 205.
[49] Case 187/80 *Merck* v. *Stephar* [1981] ECR 2063 is an example of such a case in the field of patents.
[50] Kobia,'Reflection on the Effects of Future Enlargements', 184.

3 The free movement of health care professionals in the European Community

Julian Lonbay

Introduction

Health care professionals across the EU prescribe and administer medicinal products every day.[1] As this is a critical task they are closely regulated and must be fully qualified in order to do so. This chapter seeks to explain the development of European Community law (hereafter EC or Community law) and policy as it attempts to tackle difficulties arising for free movement of individuals involved in the health care sector.[2] The difficulties are caused by differences in structures of the relevant professions,[3] differences in the modes of provision of health care[4] that are found in the fifteen Member States of the European Community (EC),[5] as well as the limited competence of the

---

[1] The number of professions with the power of prescription is growing. In the UK doctors, dentists and some nurses are acknowledged as permitted to prescribe medicines within their competence: Medicinal Products: Prescription by Nurses, Midwives and Health Visitors Act 1992. The blurring of traditional professional boundaries in the flexible health care market-place is not just a UK phenomenon. See generally WHO, *Nursing beyond the year 2000. A Report of a WHO Study Group*, Technical Report Series No. 842; M. Warner, M. Longley, E. Gould and A. Picek, *Health Care Futures 2010* (Pontypridd: Welsh Institute for Health and Social Care, 1998).

[2] Not all the health care professions can be dealt with for reasons of space, so the chapter concentrates on those most closely involved with prescribing and administering medicinal products, namely, doctors, pharmacists and nurses. Dentists and midwives, though involved with prescribing and administering medicinal products, are not included for reasons of space and because they are covered by sectoral Directives which are very similar to those dealing with the above-mentioned professions.

[3] See below, p. 46.

[4] For an overview of the then twelve Member State health care systems, see M. McCarthy and S. Rees, *Health Systems and Public Health Medicine in the European Community* (London: Faculty of Public Health Medicine of the Royal Colleges of Physicians of the UK and the Royal College of Physicians, 1992).

[5] The difficulties are not new: see Sir Abraham Goldberg, 'Towards European Medicine: An Historical Perspective' (1989) 23 *Journal of the Royal College of Physicians of London* 277 for a historical perspective. Free movement of health care professions in Europe also has its antecedents: L. Hurwitz, *The Free Circulation of Physicians within the European Community* (Aldershot: Avebury, 1990) at p. 6. C. Ludvigsen and C. Roberts, *Health Care Policies and Europe* (Oxford: Butterworth-Heinemann, 1996).

EC to act in this area.[6] After examining these issues the chapter sets out the methods used to liberate health care professionals and their patients from national boundaries. The application of internal market rules to health care activities is examined and the sectoral[7] and general Directives[8] on recognition of qualifications are analysed. The gaps left by these instruments are exposed in the context of the current revisions[9] and case law of the Court of Justice of the European Communities (ECJ).

Regulation of professionals

The medical profession, in common with many other health care professions, has long been regulated both by the State and as a matter of self-regulation. The two prime motives of State control are to ensure the safety of the final consumers (patients) and to control the costs involved, as the State is heavily involved in paying them. As we shall see, the European Community has a strictly limited role in relation to the provision of health care, which remains primarily a national responsibility. Whatever motives caused their creation initially, the structures created by national systems of regulation can, in fact, amount to barriers for migrant professionals coming from another Member State. The classic example is that of qualifications required in order to undertake medical and related activities. These qualifications are rooted in national systems of education. This means that, to take a simple example, in the United Kingdom national qualifications are required in order to be recognised as fit to practise. In other Member States the qualification requirements for practice are similarly couched in national terms. This clearly poses problems for the free movement of professionals. The EC rules regarding this are examined below.[10]

There are also considerable differences in the national regulatory environment for doctors, with some countries granting them monopolies over medical practice,[11] whilst others have rather restrained limitations, for example, in the Netherlands, where only a few nominated medical acts are reserved for doctors, and the protection for patients

---

[6] See below, pp. 47–8.
[7] See below, pp. 56–7.
[8] See below, pp. 57–8.
[9] The SLIM amendments: see below, p. 68.
[10] See below, p. 55.
[11] France and Belgium, for example: N. De Bijl and I. Nederveen-van der Kragt, 'Legal Safeguards Against Medical Practice by Not Suitably Qualified Persons: A Comparative Study in Seven EU Countries' (1997) 4 *EJHL* 5 at 10.

relies more on securing protection of the title of doctor.[12] Some countries have very 'tolerant' systems which allow for the practice of 'alternative medicine' by non-traditional medically qualified persons, for example in the UK, Germany and Ireland. However, certain procedures and prescription powers are reserved for qualified medical doctors who are often recognisable by their 'protected' titles, if not their reserved activities. The subsidiary nature of Community competence allows this variation in regulation, but it too obviously causes concerns regarding quality control and raises its own difficulties for free movement rights of the medical and allied professions.[13] Such variation in regulation allows practitioners in the UK, for example, to practise alternative and complementary medicine where such practice, say in Belgium or France, may lead to prosecution.[14] The Community so far has not dealt with complementary and alternative medical practitioners explicitly in its legislation.[15]

EC competence

The EC's competence is limited in the field of health care. The first mention of health (as a general matter, as opposed to health and safety at work) came in the Maastricht Treaty, which introduced a limited role for the Community in relation to public health with the introduction of Article 129 (now 152) EC.[16] This left health care matters primarily in the hands of the Member States.[17] As Article 152 (ex 129) EC states in paragraph 5: 'Community action in the field of public health shall fully respect the responsibilities of the Member States for the organisation and delivery of health services and medical care.'

The main role of the EC in public health matters is in encouraging co-operation between the Member States[18] and providing pump-priming

---

[12] *Ibid.*

[13] This is considered further below at p. 63.

[14] See, for an overview of complementary medicine: A. Vickers and C. Zollman, 'ABC of Complementary Medicine' [1999] 319 *BMJ* 1254.

[15] The European Parliament has called for studies to be undertaken: EP doc. A4–0075/ 1997. There are two Directives on homeopathic medicinal products. See generally COM(97) 362 and COM(98) 588.

[16] M. McKee, E. Mossiolos and P. Belcher, 'The Influence of European Law on National Health Policy' (1996) 6 *Journal of European Social Policy* 263.

[17] C. Altenstetter, 'The Effect of European Policies on Health and Health Care' in H. E. G. M. Hermans, A. F. Casparie and J. H. P. Paelinck (eds.) *Health Care in Europe after 1992* (Rotterdam: Dartmouth with Erasmus University, 1992) p. 30.

[18] E.g. Decision 1400/97/EC of the European Parliament and of the Council of 30 June 1997 adopting a programme of Community action on health monitoring within the framework of action in the field of public health [1997] OJ L193/11.

funds for tackling health scourges[19] such as AIDS[20] and cancer.[21] These 'incentive measures', leading the way by persuasion, allow the Member States to maintain their own methods of providing health care for their general populations and exclude from EC competence 'any harmonisation of the laws and regulations of the Member States'.[22] Nevertheless Article 152 (ex 129) EC allows in paragraph 1 that: 'A high level of human health protection shall be ensured in the definition and implementation of all Community policies and activities.'[23] In a similar fashion the EC also has limited competence to set out or control educational matters.[24] Articles 149 and 150 (ex 126 and 127) EC specifically exclude any harmonisation of content of education or vocational training.[25]

[19] Article 152 (ex 129) EC:

> 1. A high level of human health protection shall be ensured in the definition and implementation of all Community policies and activities.
>
>   Community action, which shall complement national policies, shall be directed towards improving public health, preventing human illness and diseases, and obviating sources of danger to human health. Such action shall cover the fight against the major health scourges, by promoting research into their causes, their transmission and their prevention, as well as health information and education.
>
>   The Community shall complement the Member States' action in reducing drugs-related health damage, including information and prevention.
> 2. The Community shall encourage co-operation between the Member States in the areas referred to in this Article and, if necessary, lend support to their action.
>
>   Member States shall, in liaison with the Commission, co-ordinate among themselves their policies and programmes in the areas referred to in paragraph 1. The Commission may, in close contact with the Member States, take any useful initiative to promote such co-ordination . . .

[20] Decision 647/96/EC of the European Parliament and of the Council of 29 March 1996 adopting a programme of Community action on the prevention of AIDS and certain other communicable diseases within the framework for action in the field of public health (1996 to 2000); Interim report from the Commission to the European Parliament, the Council, the Economic and Social Committee and the Committee of the Regions on the implementation of the programmes of Community action on the prevention of cancer, AIDS and certain other communicable diseases, and drug dependence within the framework for action in the field of public health (1996–2000) (Decisions Nos. 646/96/EC, 647/96/EC and 102/97/EC of the European Parliament and of the Council) COM(99) 463 final.

[21] The Europe against Cancer programme has been running since the mid-1980s. See Commission Recommendation 89/601/EEC concerning the training of health personnel in the matter of cancer [1989] OJ L346/7 for an example of its work. Other areas have also been targeted, e.g. rare diseases: see COM(97) 225 [1997] OJ C203/6.

[22] Article 152(4)(c) EC.

[23] See Resolution on the second report from the Commission to the Council, the European Parliament, the Economic and Social Committee and the Committee of the Regions on the integration of health protection requirements in Community Policies, COM(96) 407, [1998] OJ C104/148.

[24] See J. Lonbay, 'Education and Law: The Community Context' (1989) 14 *European Law Review* 363–87.

[25] See generally J. Lonbay, 'Education' in *European Union Law Reporter*, vol. IV (Bicester: CCH-Kluwer, 1997) 13001–564. This will be examined further below at p. 56 in the section dealing with mutual recognition of qualifications.

The internal market

The European Community has a functional competence to create an internal market.[26] The rules on the free movement of persons, services, goods and capital apply in the health care sector as elsewhere.[27] This sector is not immune from the effects of EC law, though it is to some extent sheltered from the market forces unleashed by the creation of the internal market, as the bulk of its provision lies in the public sector.[28] The idea of the internal market requires that pharmaceutical products, for example, being 'goods' in terms of Article 28 (ex 30) EC, should be able to move freely across borders.[29] The ECJ has thus protected individuals carrying their day-to-day medicines[30] from being prosecuted for illegal possession of medicines under State rules. In these cases, the ECJ[31] justified its ruling, in part, on the grounds that the prescribing authorities, both pharmacists and doctors, had had their qualifications co-ordinated in the Member States, thus eliminating much of the risk for cross-border private movement of medicines.[32] The general provisions of EC law should ensure that patients themselves are able to travel to seek medical care in the other Member States.[33] Equally, they should also allow doctors, nurses and other health care workers the right of free movement. Both issues are now considered in turn.

The free movement of persons: mobility of EC citizens and the right to health care

Introduction

EC citizens seeking to travel across national frontiers within the Community can only be prevented from doing so on health grounds in

[26] Article 14 (ex 7a) EC.
[27] Case C-96/85 *Commission* v. *France* [1986] ECR-1475.
[28] The so-called Beveridge (direct State provision) (UK and Nordic countries) and Bismark (State-supervised insured provision) models of health care provision: P. Kokkonen and M. Kekomäki, 'Legal and Economic Issues in European Public Health' in C. Normand and J. Vaughan, *Europe Without Frontiers: Implications for Health* (Chichester: John Wiley, 1993) at p. 39; see below, p. 50.
[29] See above, chapters 1 and 2.
[30] This applies to over-the-counter ordinary medicines (Case 215/87 *Schumacher* v. *HZA Frankfurt am Main-Ost* [1989] ECR 617) and to prescription medical products (Case C-62/90 *Commission* v. *Germany* [1992] ECR I-2575).
[31] *Schumacher* §20; *Commission* v. *Germany* §§16–18.
[32] Non-national prescriptions were also better being supplied abroad as the pharmacist there would understand the language of the prescription more easily. *Commission* v. *Germany* §§19–20.
[33] Joined Cases 286/82 and 26/83 *Luisi & Carbone* v. *Ministerio del Tesoro* [1984] ECR 377.

accordance with Directive 64/221/EEC.[34] This Directive limits the rights of States to prohibit travel to those who have a small number of particular medical conditions that are set out in the Annex of the Directive. Thus Member State discretion to prevent the cross-border movement of persons who are sick is severely curtailed.

Workers and the self-employed have full travel and residence rights.[35] The more recent Directives, implementing a right of residence more widely, require that migrants should 'avoid becoming a burden on the social security system of the host Member State during the period of residence' and the right of residence is conditional in that they must be 'covered by sickness insurance in respect of all risks in the host Member State'.[36] They also require that migrants should have sufficient income to avoid needing any 'social assistance'.[37] Over 2 million people have taken advantage of the rights bestowed by these Directives.[38]

Provision of medical services

There is one major distinction to be emphasised with regard to the health care sector – it is mainly a public-sector-funded activity and is closely linked to national social insurance/security regimes, dealt with below. This has implications for the application of the principles of the EC Treaty.[39] A 1997 project assessing patient mobility observed that 75

[34] Directive 64/221/EEC, Council Directive of 25 February 1964 on the co-ordination of special measures concerning the movement and residence of foreign nationals which are justified on grounds of public policy, public security or public health [1964] OJ 56/850; OJ spec. edn 1963–4, 117.

[35] Under Title III (Free Movement of Persons, Services and Capital) of the EC Treaty, especially Articles 39–55 (ex 48–66) EC and related Directives.

[36] Council Directive 90/365/EEC of 28 June 1990 on the right of residence for employees and self-employed persons who have ceased their occupational activities [1990] OJ L180/28, Article 1.

[37] For example Council Directive 93/96/EEC of 29 October 1993 on the right of residence for students [1993] OJ L317/59 as amended by Decision 95/1/EEC [1995] OJ L1/1. This Directive gives the right of mobility to students with 'sufficient resources' 'to avoid becoming a burden on the social assistance system of the host Member State during the period of residence', provided that the student is enrolled 'in a recognised educational establishment for the principal purpose of following a vocational training course – and that he is covered by sickness insurance in respect of all risks in the host Member State' (Article 1). See also Directive 90/365/EEC [1990] OJ L180/28, Article 1. Council Directive 90/364/EEC of 28 June 1990 on the right of residence [1990] OJ L180/26 has similar provisions.

[38] Report from the Commission to the Parliament and the Council on the implementation of Directives 90/364, 90/365 and 93/96. The Report can be found on the Europa website at http://europa.eu.int/comm./dg15/en/people/right/resid.htm.

[39] It does not permit the total exclusion of this sector from the rigours of the free movement principles under the exceptions permitted by Articles 39(3) and 46. See Case 131/85 *Gül* v. *Regierungspräsident Düsseldorf* [1986] ECR 1573.

to 80 per cent of health care expenditure was covered by public systems of health care.[40] This effectively removes the bulk of this sector from the free provision of services rules of the EC.[41] The ECJ has defined services as those provided against remuneration and not State-funded services for the public good.[42]

Social security regimes

The social security regimes of the Member States are largely left untouched by Community law.[43] It is within these regimes that health care entitlements are established in most of the Member States. The role of Community law is to co-ordinate the national social security regimes[44] in order to prevent disadvantages arising to those EU citizens[45] exercising their rights of free movement. There are three main schemes of co-ordination: for migrant workers and frontier workers (the E106 scheme);[46] for those temporarily in another Member State where their health condition 'necessitates immediate care' (the E111

[40] J. Hermesse, H. Lewalle and W. Palm, 'Patient Mobility within the EU' (1997) 7 *European Journal of Public Health* (Supplement 3) 4. Gooijer notes that the health care sector is much sheltered from the forces of competition by its public nature: W. J. Gooijer, 'Introduction' in Hermans, Casparie and Paelinck, *Health Care in Europe after 1992*, p. 215.

[41] Articles 49ff (ex 59ff) EC.

[42] Case C-263/86 *Belgian State* v. *René Humbel and Marie-Thérèse Edel* [1988] ECR 5365; Case C-159/90 *Society for the Protection of Unborn Children Ireland* v. *Stephen Grogan* [1991] ECR I-4685. Advocate-General Tesauro, in his Opinion in the *Decker* and *Kholl* cases, distinguished *Humbel*, which dealt with public instruction, from medical practice, as medical treatment was supplied for consideration which the insured had made with health insurance contributions: Opinion at §41. However, one could make a similar argument regarding one's tax contributions to education.

[43] Article 136 (ex 117) EC provides for co-operation but not harmonisation of social security. The main co-ordinating regulations were adopted, however, using Article 42 (ex 51) EC. As the ECJ stated in Case C-70/95 *Sodemare SA and Others* v. *Regione Lombardia* [1997] ECR I-3395 at §32, Member States have freedom to choose how to provide medical and social care. In that case, Italy's exclusion of profit-based firms from receiving contracts for the provision of old people's homes was acceptable. It also stated at §27: 'as the Court has already held in case 238/82 *Duphar and Others* v. *Netherlands State* [1984] ECR 523, paragraph 16, and Joined Cases C-159/91 and Case C-160/91 *Poucet and Pistre* v. *AGF and Cancava* [1993] ECR I-637, paragraph 6, Community law does not detract from the powers of the Member States to organize their social security systems'.

[44] R. Leidl and G. Rhodes, 'Cross-border Health Care in the EU' (1997) 7 *European Journal of Public Health* (Supplement 3) 1.

[45] Article 17 (ex 8) EC provides that all nationals of the Member States are also EU citizens. Non-nationals are not protected by the co-ordination regime. There are also several other exclusions. See Hermesse, Lewalle and Palm, 'Patient Mobility' at 6; T. Hervey, *European Social Law and Policy* (London: Longman, 1998) pp. 88–9.

[46] The frontier worker has a double entitlement, being allowed to choose health care in the State of residence as well as in the State where s/he works (using form E106).

scheme);[47] and the system of pre-authorised care (the E112 scheme).[48] Hermesse, Lewalle and Palm assessed the system and found that the expenditure under the schemes in 1993 amounted to just 0.13 per cent of national expenditure on health care.[49] Of the cost of cross-border health care treatment, 60 per cent went on the pre-authorisation scheme, 25 per cent on the E111 scheme and 16 per cent on the E106 scheme.[50] The pre-authorisation scheme allows Member States to share the cost of expensive treatments, and is much used by Luxembourg, as it would be uneconomic for them, given their size, to establish all the necessary health care facilities. The main advantages of EC facilitation of cross-border health care provision could be to allow the national health care regimes to seek lower cost health care abroad, or from the patients' point of view, to seek shorter waiting lists elsewhere.[51] Several authors expect EC Centres of Excellence to emerge where particularly difficult or expensive treatments can be focused, allowing a sharing of scarce resources.[52]

The result of the EC social security co-ordination regime is that Community workers and the self-employed travelling or working in another Member State will be covered by that State's health care protection system. In other words, they will have the right to the same level of care as the local population.[53]

However the pre-authorisation system under the social security rules was bypassed in the recent *Decker* case[54] where the ECJ ruled that the Luxembourg pre-authorisation system breached Article 30 (now Article

---

[47] The well-known form E111 facilitates the entitlement. This regime covers business travellers and tourists alike. Hermesse, Lewalle and Palm, 'Patient Mobility'. W. P. M. M. Van der Ven, 'Introduction' in Hermans, Casparie, and Paelinck, *Health Care in Europe after 1992*, p. 233 at p. 235.

[48] The medical care has to be authorised by the State of residence, using form E112.

[49] The sum spent was 1,102.7 million Ecus: Hermesse, Lewalle and Palm, 'Patent Mobility', 6.

[50] There are also other regimes, for example for transport workers (E110) and the unemployed (E119) who are seeking work. See McKee, Mossiolos and Belcher, 'The Influence of European Law' at 274.

[51] See Leidl and Rhodes, 'Cross-border Health Care'.

[52] Hermesse, Lewalle and Palm, 'Patient Mobility'; H. D. C. Roscom-Abbing, 'European Community and the Right to Health Care: An Agenda for the Future' in Hermans, Casparie, and Paelinck, *Health Care in Europe after 1992* p. 23 at p. 29; W. J. Van der Eijk, *et al.* 'Europe 1992 and the Consequences for Health Care' in Hermans, Casparie, and Paelinck, *Health Care in Europe after 1992*, p. 172 at p. 183.

[53] This system is eased in practice by a system of 'entitlement' forms such as E111 and others mentioned above at p. 51

[54] Case C-158/96 *Raymond Kholl* v. *Union des Caisses de maladies* [1998] ECR I-1931 and Case C-120/95 *Nicolas Decker* v. *Caisse de maladie des Employés Privés* [1998] ECR I-1832 noted by A. P. van der Mei, 'Cross-border Access to Medical Care within the EU: Some Reflections in the Judgments in *Decker* and *Kholl*' (1998) 5 *Maastricht Journal of European and Comparative Law* 277, and P. Cabral, 'Cross-border Medical Care in the

28) EC as it was liable to curb the import of spectacles,[55] which could not be justified. This follows the classic *Dassonville* case law of the ECJ on Article 28 EC whereby State measures that might hinder the import of products are prohibited.[56] The *Decker* ruling creates a new bypass around the EC Social Security Regulations as these explicitly allow for a Member State authorisation procedure.[57] The new Court-led route to reimbursement would, however, only allow reimbursement to the level available in the State of residence.[58] It is clear that reimbursement can still be limited to those pharmaceutical products available under national health insurance schemes.[59] The EC pre-authorisation scheme allows for a system of full reimbursement.[60]

The ECJ in the *Kholl* case allowed that Member States could argue in defence of their measures that the prohibition of open access to non-national health care facilities was necessary if it was 'indispensable for the maintenance of an essential treatment facility or medical service on national territory'.[61] Equally the Court allowed Member State-justified restrictions on this right of open access if they could show the risk of 'seriously undermining the financial balance of the social security system'. It seems clear from this that patients escaping national waiting lists by seeking treatment abroad could only be blocked if the State could show that the additional costs incurred would deprive the home State of resources necessary to maintain the facilities for which a waiting list had already grown. Neither of these two defences was able to help in the actual cases before the Court.[62] Essentially Member States can, and do, contain health care costs by limiting the supply of health care. Opening access to the health care systems of other Member States, at

---

European Union – Bringing Down a First Wall' (1999) 24 *European Law Review* 387; R. Giesen, case note in (1999) 36 *Common Market Law Review* 841.

[55] Case C-120/95 *Nicolas Decker* v. *Caisse de maladie des Employés Privés* [1998] ECR I-1832 at §36.

[56] Case 8/74 *Procureur du Roi* v. *Dassonville* [1974] ECR 837.

[57] See above, p. 51.

[58] §29 of *Decker*. This has been criticised on the grounds that it would mean in some cases that only the wealthier EC citizens could benefit from this Treaty-based right: Cabral, 'Cross-border Medical Care' at 393; van der Mei, 'Cross-border Access to Medical Care' at 293–6.

[59] Case 238/82 *Dulphar* [1984] ECR 523 still applies. This case allowed States to exclude pharmaceutical consumption on cost grounds: van der Mei, 'Cross-border Access to Medical Care' at 294.

[60] See Hermesse, Lewalle and Palm, 'Patient Mobility'. The Government in Germany announced that it could not comply with the ECJ's rulings, and that it would seek to apply the exceptions set out in the Court's ruling: *Financial Times* 6–7 June 1999.

[61] *Kholl* §52, where the Court cites Case 72/83 *Campus Oil* v. *Minister for Energy* [1984] ECR 2727.

[62] The third defence of 'quality' is dealt with below, p. 64.

the expense of the home State, could potentially undermine this control, even if reimbursement was at home State levels.[63]

One can see from this brief summary that those who are not economically active have limited rights of mobility dependent on having health care insurance and sufficient resources, though the *Decker* and *Kholl* cases indicate that they should also have a right to travel to receive health care. One can observe that the EC's free-market policy does not grant a general right to travel and residence.[64] Havinghurst states[65] that the right to travel, constitutionally established in the United States, has led to downsizing of welfare benefits, particularly in the sunshine belt, by States seeking to avoid an influx of poor people. The EC regime excludes this 'negative' competition by limiting the right to travel to those with sufficient means, and by specifically insisting on health insurance coverage for those granted the right to residence who are not economically active. The ECJ's recent opening of the doors in the *Decker* and *Kholl* cases does not alter this aspect of the 'frontierless zone', but it does show that EC citizens, and the rights accruing to them, can still be dependent on nationally controlled resources which are not available to all citizens equally. It also casts doubt on the likelihood of achieving the perceived benefit of European Centres of Excellence, as Member States are arguably free to reject such notions in order to maintain their own health care systems. Common sense may nevertheless lead to a pooling of resources from which all parties would benefit.

Although the preliminary barriers of nationality[66] and residence[67] requirements have been removed by the ECJ's interpretation of the

---

[63] Giesen, case note, at 847 ff. Again it is clear that reimbursement here is to be at home State levels.

[64] A policy much criticised: see D. O'Keeffe, 'Comments on the Free Movement of Various Categories of Persons' in H. G. Schermers *et al.* (eds.) *Free Movement of Persons in Europe* (Dordrecht: Martinus Nijhoff, 1993) at pp. 515ff. Another permitted differential treatment affects third-country nationals who are generally excluded from EC mobility rights on account of their citizenship. The Amsterdam Treaty revisions and adoption of the Schengen Acquis by most Member States (but not the UK, Ireland and Denmark) seek to help overcome this difficulty in part. The Schengen Agreements, deal, *inter alia*, with the EU external frontiers, removal of internal borders and third-country nationals, and are now part of the EU framework post Treaty of Amsterdam. See J. Lonbay, 'Free Movement of Persons, Recognition of Qualifications, and Working Conditions' (1992) 41 *ICLQ* 714 at 718 and (1995) 44 *ICLQ* 705 for a brief explanation of the Schengen Agreements themselves.

[65] C. C. Havinghurst, 'American Federalism and American Health Care: Lessons for the European Community' in Hermans, Casparie and Paelinck, *Health Care in Europe after 1992*, p. 37 at p. 42.

[66] Case 2/74 *Reyners v. Belgium* [1974] ECR 631.

[67] Case 33/74 *Van Binsbergen v. Bestuur van der Bedrijfsvereiniging voor de Metaalnijverheid* [1974] ECR 1299.

Treaty articles[68] on free movement of persons, these are not the only barriers that need to be addressed in order to establish a proper single market for health care workers.

The facilitation of the free movement of health care professionals

The free movement rules and qualifications

The fundamental freedom of movement of persons is expressly recognised in Article 6 (ex 3c) EC and, in the context of professional mobility, Article 47(2) (ex 57(2)) EC allows for the 'co-ordination' of rules regulating the take-up and pursuit of self-employed activities. Article 47(3) (ex 57(3)) provides that: 'In the case of the medical and allied and pharmaceutical professions, the progressive abolition of restrictions shall be dependent upon co-ordination of the conditions for their exercise in the various Member States.'

We see that the medical and allied and pharmaceutical professions are singled out for co-ordination before restrictions on free movement are lifted. The medical and allied professions certainly cover those professionals concerned with human life and health.[69] In *Auer*, a case involving a veterinary surgeon, the Commission argued that this involvement with human life and health was what caused the professions to be singled out in Article 47 (ex 57) EC and they were supported in this by Advocate-General Warner.[70] The allied professions are generally considered to be those whose activities would be covered by national health insurance laws, persons who carry out therapeutic treatment independently on their own responsibility, and those undertaking medical treatment under the jurisdiction of medical practitioners, who are mainly nurses.[71] Others potentially included by this definition would be alternative and complementary therapists, hospital attendants, social workers and medical technicians. For the reasons stated above,[72] this chapter looks at doctors, pharmacists and nurses in particular.

---

[68] Articles 39, 43 and 49 EC. Member States cannot prevent doctors, dentists or veterinary surgeons who are established in another Member State from maintaining their existing practice: Case 96/85 *Commission* v. *France* [1986] ECR 1734; Case C-351/90 *Commission* v. *Luxembourg* [1992] ECR I-3945.

[69] Case 136/78 *Ministère Public* v. *Auer* [1979] ECR 437.

[70] See generally D. Vaughan, *Law of the European Communities Service*, vol. III, part 16, issue 43, p. 1313 (Butterworths, 1998).

[71] Nurses themselves can now practise on their own authority in some Member States.

[72] See above, n. 2.

Mutual recognition provisions

The powers of co-ordination of activities of the self-employed and the creation of rules on mutual recognition of diplomas granted by the EC Treaty have been exercised in a series of legislative phases – the transitional, sectoral and then the general Directives – and we are now entering a fourth phase led, in part, by the ECJ. The EC legislation covers health care professionals in a variety of ways and leaves exposed some odd gaps. Questions relating to control of content of education, training and control of professional practice are not fully resolved. The rights of EU health care professionals to settle and work in other Member States are not always smoothly dealt with by Community law or national competent authorities.

The initial general phase for implementing mutual recognition of qualifications in the European Communities[73] involved the thirty-five transitional Directives[74] which have now been reformed to become the third general system Directive.[75] This Directive is not the most relevant for the medical and health care sectors. The second phase of legislative activity in the Community development of the law in this area brought forth the sectoral Directives. The medical and other health care professions were amongst the first to have their systems regulated at the EC level as required by Article 47 EC.[76] The next sections examine the sectoral Directive systems that have been put in place for doctors, pharmacists and nurses and the general Directive systems for mutual recognition of qualifications, where relevant.

The sectoral Directives

The sectoral Directives co-ordinate minimum common standards of education and training for the professions covered and then list the diplomas which meet these common standards for each Member State. Those holding the relevant diplomas will benefit from automatic

---

[73] For a general overview see J. Lonbay, 'The Mutual Recognition of Qualifications in the EC' in R. Hodgin (ed.), *Professional Liability: Law and Insurance* (2nd edn, London: LLP, 1999) pp. 12 ff.

[74] The initial Directives did not involve mutual recognition provisions but rather recognition of experience.

[75] Directive 99/42/EC establishing a mechanism for the recognition of qualifications in respect of the professional activities covered by the Directives on liberalisation and transitional measures and supplementing the general systems for the recognition of qualifications [1999] OJ L201/77.

[76] See above, p. 55. The Treaty of Rome, from its inception, made provision for this eventuality in Article 47 (ex 57). Article 47(3) indicates: 'In the case of the medical and allied and pharmaceutical professions, the progressive abolition of restrictions shall be dependent upon the co-ordination of the conditions for their exercise in the various Member States.'

recognition of the qualifications. The sectoral Directives thus ensure common minimum standards and allow automatic recognition. This makes life easier for the competent authorities of the Member States who merely have to ensure that the migrant holds the relevant diplomas, and satisfy themselves on the other requirements of good character and so on, without an elaborate assessment of the competence or knowledge of the migrant. However, the downside is that the common minimum standard is set out in an EC Directive that is hard to amend and keep updated, and those States with higher standards worry about levels of training in the other Member States. The Advisory Committee structure[77] set up to support the system has also suffered from an insufficient number of meetings and lack of follow-up.[78]

The general Directives

The sectoral Directive system provides the benefit of automatic recognition of qualifications, but the price is paid in terms of flexibility. One has to agree that the activities carried out by the profession are the same across the fifteen Member States. The general assumption of equivalence can be erroneous: for example, both Italy and Austria have had to introduce 'dentists' as a result of the EC sectoral dentists' Directives. If the Member States cannot agree on the scope of activities of the professions the Directives can be limited to a particular set of activities, as in the case of pharmacists.[79] However, in many sectors there is insufficient parallelism in the relevant professions, and the pressure for establishing a widely available scheme quickly[80] has led to the adoption of a more generally flexible regime of Community law.[81]

The general Directive system[82] allows a systematic assessment of qualifications and knowledge and also permits compensation measures

[77] See below, p. 67.
[78] European Commission, *Positions and Replies adopted by Professional Associations and Member States in Reply to Commission Questions on the SLIM Project for the SLIM Team on the Mutual Recognition of Diplomas*, DGXV – E2/ZPS D(96) XV/E/68572/96 (21 October 1996).
[79] See below, p. 69.
[80] The sectoral Directives took a long time to negotiate. The architects' Directive, for example, took seventeen years.
[81] See Lonbay, 'Mutual Recognition of Qualifications' for a more general view.
[82] The general Directives are: Council Directive 89/48/EEC on a general system for the recognition of higher education diplomas awarded on completion of professional education and training of at least three years' duration [1989] OJ L19/16 and Council Directive 92/51/EEC on a second general system for the recognition of professional education and training to supplement Directive 89/48/EEC [1992] OJ L209/25 as amended.

to be imposed on the migrant,[83] if necessary, within a structured and time-controlled process.[84] In other words, the system does not provide an automatic recognition of qualifications. The benefits are that Member States do not have to agree collectively as to what are the parallel professions, and there is no stultifying EC-based reform process for amending professional requirements. Other advantages over the general treaty regime outlined below include a relatively speedy recognition system for migrants with well-established procedures of assessment.[85] Where 'the matters covered by the education and training he [the migrant] has received as laid down in Article 3 (a) and (b), differ substantially from those covered by the diploma required in the host Member State',[86] then the host State can require either an adaptation period or an aptitude test normally at the migrant's choice. These are commonly called the 'compensation mechanisms' and are set out in Article 4. The current SLIM reforms[87] will implement the *Vlassopoulou* doctrine[88] of recognising post-qualification professional experience before compensation measures can be imposed. The general Directives cover regulated professions which include many of the professions allied to the medical profession. For example, in the first three years, 1991–94, over 1,450 physiotherapists[89] used the general Directive system.[90] This chapter does not have the space to deal with the impact of the general Directives on all these professions.[91]

---

[83] These are either additional time for training, or further professional experience or an aptitude test.

[84] The general system Directives cover 'regulated' professions. This has been widely interpreted and includes many health care related professions: Case C-164/94 *Georgios Aranitis* v. *Land Berlin* [1996] ECR I-135. The second general Directive 92/51/EEC also includes the concept of 'regulated education and training' to extend its scope beyond the 'regulated professions'. The SLIM initiative reform would add the concept of 'regulated education and training' to the first general Directive 89/48/EEC. See below, p. 68.

[85] For a fuller introduction and analysis of the general system, see Lonbay, 'Mutual Recognition of Qualifications'.

[86] Article 4 of Directive 89/48/EEC.

[87] See below, p. 68.

[88] See below, n. 93 and accompanying text.

[89] Physiotherapists fall under both the general Directives because of the differences between Member States in the way that they are trained.

[90] European Commission, *Report to the European Parliament and the Council on the State of Application of the General System for the Recognition of Higher Education Diplomas* COM(96) 46 (15 February 1996) at p. 28. See also *Report from the Commission to the Council and the European Parliament on the Application of Directive 92/51/EEC*, COM(2000) 17 (3 February 2000).

[91] In the UK there are at least fifteen health care professions covered by the first general Directive 89/48/EEC ranging, for example, from chiropodists, art therapists and speech therapists to orthoptists.

The EC Treaty

The Treaty of Rome provides for the fundamental right of free movement of workers and the self-employed. The EC Directives, both sectoral and general, were created in order to try and make it easier for such mobility to be achieved. The right of mobility accrues to EU nationals by virtue of the EC Treaty itself. Thus, if none of the mutual recognition Directives is able to facilitate the cross-border mobility of the migrant, then he or she can rely on the Treaty rights themselves. These rights have been widely interpreted by the European Court of Justice. They include procedural rights, such as the right to both a reasoned decision and judicial review of such a decision,[92] and the right to have one's knowledge and experience taken into account when assessing whether one's education, training and professional experience are equivalent to that locally required for entry into the profession in question.[93] Additionally, the EC Treaty can be used to help interpret the various Directives. However, the application of the case law does not have well-established national procedures, structures or temporal guarantees, and this causes considerable difficulties for applicants.

The medical profession

General doctors   The medical profession was fairly involved in the creation of the medical sectoral Directives, both through the ordinary EEC decision-making process and through their European organisations.[94] The first Directive, 75/362/EEC,[95] dealt with the diplomas, certificates and other evidence of formal qualifications in general medicine, specialised medicine available in all Member States, and specialised medicine available in two or more Member States. Each Member State was required to recognise the qualifications listed in the Directive

[92] Case 222/86 *UNECTEF* v. *Heylens* [1987] ECR 4097.

[93] Case C-340/89 *Vlassopoulou* [1991] ECR I-2357. It is this interpretation of the EC Treaty by the ECJ that is being brought into the horizontal Directives under the SLIM proposal: COM(96) 22, COM(97) 638.

[94] These include the Standing Committee of European Doctors (CP) (created in 1959), European Union of Medical Specialists (UEMS: see http://www.uems.be) (which has produced a Charter on training (1992) and on continuing medical education for specialists (1994), and a European Accreditation Council for Continuing Medical Education), the Permanent Working Group on European Junior Hospital Doctors and the European Medical Association (EMA) amongst others. For a caustic view of the activities and a plea for diversity, see S. Brearly, 'Harmonisation of Specialist Training in Europe: Is it a Mirage?' (1995) 311 *BMJ* 297.

[95] [1975] OJ L167/1, now repealed and consolidated in Council Directive 93/16/EEC to facilitate the free movement of doctors and the mutual recognition of their diplomas, certificates and other evidence of formal qualifications, as amended: [1993] OJ L165/1. This consolidating Directive incorporates, *inter alia*, the 'general practitioners'' Directive 86/457/EEC relating to specific training in general medicine [1986] OJ L267/26, and has itself been amended several times.

and give effect to such qualifications as though they were the equivalent national qualification. Directive 75/363/EEC[96] provided for the co-ordination of the medical training courses. These Directives are now repealed and consolidated in Council Directive 93/16/EEC.[97] Recommendation 75/367[98] provided for admission to clinical training posts to be opened to nationals of other Member States, though this is now a binding requirement of Community law by virtue of the development of the case law by the ECJ.[99]

Article 2 of Directive 93/16/EEC requires that Member States recognise the diplomas listed in Article 3[100] that have been awarded in accordance with Article 23. Article 23 of Directive 93/16/EEC sets out the basic knowledge of sciences that trainees should receive as well as knowledge of the structure, functions and behaviour of healthy and sick persons, together with adequate knowledge of clinical disciplines and practice. This is designed to provide the trainee with a 'coherent picture of mental and physical diseases from points of view of prophylaxis, diagnosis and therapy and of human reproduction'.[101] In addition, clinical experience with appropriate supervision is required[102] and general course length is prescribed – medical training should comprise at least a six-year course or 5,500 hours of theoretical instruction at university level.[103]

General practitioners For general practice medicine (as opposed to hospital doctors), Member States have had to institute additional minimum levels of training since 1 January 1990.[104] The GPs' Directive[105] followed on from the *Van Broeckmeulen* case,[106] where the ECJ held that the Netherlands was not entitled to prevent a Belgian-trained

[96] [1975] OJ L169/14, now repealed and consolidated in Directive 93/16/EEC as amended.
[97] Council Directive 93/16/EEC.
[98] Council statements made on adopting the texts concerning freedom of establishment and freedom to provide services for doctors within the Community: [1975] OJ C146/1.
[99] Case 83/293 *Gravier* [1989] ECR 593; generally Lonbay, 'Education and Law' and Case 19/92 *Kraus* [1993] ECR 1.
[100] Article 3 lists the diplomas by home State title.
[101] Directive 93/16/EEC, Article 23(1)c.
[102] *Ibid.*, Article 23(1)d.
[103] *Ibid.*, Article 23(2).
[104] Council Directive 86/457/ EEC of 15 September 1986 on specific training in general medical practice [1986] OJ L267/26. These provisions are now incorporated in Council Directive 93/16/EEC, Article 30. See COM(96) 434 for a review of the GP provisions in Directive 93/16/EEC.
[105] Council Directive 86/457/EEC on specific training in general medical practice [1986] OJ L267/26.
[106] Case 246/80 *Van Broeckmeulen* v. *Huisarts Registratie Commissie* [1981] ECR 2311.

Dutch doctor from practising medicine on the grounds that Dutch GPs had to follow special courses in general practice medicine, which van Broeckmeulen had not done. As the doctors' Directives[107] did not recognise general practice as a speciality, the Dutch could not disallow van Broeckmeulen from practising in the Netherlands as a GP. They were entitled, however, to impose higher requirements for nationals training in the Netherlands.[108]

Since January 1995 the exercise of general medical practice under national social security regimes[109] has been conditional on possession of a qualification, in accordance with Directive 93/16/EEC,[110] subject to acquired rights.[111] The initial training mentioned in Article 23 of Directive 93/16/EEC must be completed prior to undertaking training as a general practitioner.[112] The courses must last at least two years and be supervised by competent authorities and are to be practically based (rather than theoretical). Furthermore they must entail the personal participation of the trainee in professional activities and responsibilities

[107] At that time these were Directives; 75/362/EEC and 75/363/EEC; see above, nn. 95 and 96.

[108] This was confirmed in Case C-93/97 *Fédération Belge des Chambres II Syndicales de Médecins ASBL* v. *Flemish Government, Government of the French Community, Council of Ministers* [1998] ECR I-4837.

[109] There is not yet a requirement for all GPs. See Article 40 of Directive 93/16/EEC and European Commission, *Report on Specific Training in General Medical Practice*, COM(96) 434 final (9 September 1996). The medical profession's view is that it should become mandatory as soon as possible: *ibid.*, at p. 10.

[110] Article 36(1) made possession of the Article 30 qualification necessary. See above, n. 104.

[111] Cf. Joined Cases C-69/96 to C-79/96 *Garafolo et al.* v. *Ministero della Sanità and Unità Sanitari Locale (USL) no. 58 di Palermo* [1997] ECR I-5603.

[112] Council Directive 93/16/EEC, Article 31(1)(a). Article 31(3) does not make an Article 3 qualification, as such, a condition for obtaining an Article 30 qualification. In Case C-93/97 *Fédération Belge des Chambres II Syndicales de Médecins ASBL* [1998] ECR I-4837 the ECJ took a hands-off view of the requirements of Article 31 of Directive 93/16/EEC by distinguishing between successfully completing 'six years' study within the framework of the training course referred to in Article 23' and being awarded the diploma 'referred to in Article 3'. The ECJ stated:

Directive 93/16 does not thus impose the requirement of possession of a basic diploma referred to in Article 3 in relation to participation in the professional activity referred to in Article 31(1)(d) thereof.

Since Directive 93/16 does not make possession of a basic diploma referred to in Article 3 a precondition for commencing specific training in general medical practice but only imposes that requirement when the diploma, certificate, or other evidence of formal training in specific general medical practice is awarded, and since that is a minimum requirement, Directive 93/16 leaves the Member States free to decide whether the trainee must already hold the basic diploma referred to in Article 3 at an earlier stage. §§36–7.

The European Commission *Report on Specific Training in General Medical Practice* indicates at p. 8 that the professions wished to have this training only after completion of the initial diplomas.

for the persons with whom he/she works.[113] The effect, in some Member States, is that a doctor with only Article 3 qualifications and no acquired rights is unable to practise medicine.[114] The European Commission's Report[115] suggested that the Article 30 qualifications should be included in Article 5 dealing with all the other 'specialist' qualifications. This would be a neat solution. It is to these specialist qualifications that we now turn.

Specialist doctors   Specialised medical training is dealt with in Article 24 of Directive 93/16/EEC, which specified that it should commence on completion of the medical training mentioned in Article 23. Articles 26 and 27 specify the duration of such training for the various types of speciality. The specialist training qualifications are listed in Articles 5 and 7 of Directive 93/16/EEC. The specialities listed in Article 5 are recognised by all the Member States and automatic recognition follows for the holders of the relevant diplomas.[116] The specialities listed in Article 7 are common to two or more Member States and are recognised automatically by those States listed in Article 7, by virtue of Article 6. Article 8 requires EU citizens coming from Member States which do not train in a speciality referred to in Articles 4 or 6, who wish to acquire a specialist diploma, to submit to the training required in the host State, subject to recognition (even if only partial) of the training that the migrant has so far undertaken.

As the ECJ pointed out in *Commission* v. *Belgium*,[117] Member States are obliged to act in accordance with the Directive and thus are not free to abolish specialities recognised in the Directive until the Directive itself has been amended. They must also remunerate trainee specialists,[118] but only those listed in Articles 5 and 7.[119] In *Carbonari*[120] this was confirmed and the ECJ also indicated that the full-time nature of specialist training must be respected else the 'authorities of the other Member States can no longer have faith in the equal value of the legislation of the Member State in question in the field of training in specialised medicine, which thus undermines the objective of the "recognition" and "co-ordination" Directives . . .'.[121]

---

[113] Article 31(1)(d).
[114] European Commission, *Report on Specific Training in General Medical Practice* at p. 6.
[115] *Ibid.* at p. 15.
[116] Article 4 of Directive 93/16/EEC.
[117] Case 306/84 *Commission* v. *Belgium* [1987] ECR 675.
[118] Articles 24 and 25 with Annex 1 of Directive 93/16/EEC.
[119] Case C-277/93 *Commission* v. *Spain* [1994] ECR I-5515.
[120] Case C-131/97 *Annalisa Carbonari and Others* v. *Università di Bologna et al.* [1999] ECR I-1103.
[121] *Ibid.*, §43. Italy was similarly castigated for 'wrecking' the dentists' Directives in Case

However, the provisions of Directive 93/16/EEC do not mean that the training to be achieved for the national medical specialities is harmonised. As the Advisory Committee on Medical Training (ACMT)[122] noted in its fourth report on specialist training,[123] the types of speciality 'vary a great deal', as does 'the content and duration of specialist training for what is nominally the same speciality'.[124] The Directive contains no definition of the scope of activities of doctors,[125] nor does it harmonise medical training.[126]

Safeguards Directive 93/16/EEC allows that host Member States can request information regarding good character or good repute of would-be migrant doctors if these characteristics are required of its own doctors.[127] Article 11(3) provides that:

If the host Member State has detailed knowledge of a serious matter which has occurred, prior to the establishment of the person concerned in that State, outside its territory and which is likely to affect the taking up within its territory of the activity concerned, it may inform the Member State of origin or the Member State from which the foreign national comes.

The Member State of origin or the Member State from which the foreign national comes shall verify the accuracy of the facts. Its authorities shall decide on the nature and extent of the investigation to be made and shall inform the host Member State of any consequential action which they take with regard to the certificates or documents they have issued.

This formula is also used in Article 12 regarding disciplinary and criminal offences. The Council Statement[128] on Article 12 at the time of its adoption indicates that for acts committed outside its territory 'the host Member State may not suspend or withdraw the right of establishment' unless the host State or State of origin has in fact imposed such a penalty.

These provisions are regarded as being too weak and are not, in fact,

---

C-40/93 *Commission v. Italy* [1995] ECR I-1319, A.-G. Léger at §24, and pharmacists' Directive: Case C-307/94 *Commission v. Italy* [1996] ECR I-1611.

[122] See below, p. 67.
[123] ACMT, *Fourth Report and Recommendations on the Conditions of Specialist Training*, adopted on 14–15 November 1996; XV/E/8306/4/96–EN final (30 June 1997).
[124] *Ibid.* at p. 51.
[125] This became clear in the *Bouchoucha* case where the ECJ held that the definition of medical acts fell within national competence. Thus France was entitled to reserve the act of osteopathy to medical doctors, frustrating the attempts of Bouchoucha to act as an osteopath in France using English qualifications: Case C-61/89 *Marc Gaston Bouchoucha* [1990] ECR 3551 at §12.
[126] 'These Directives were the result of the failure to achieve harmonisation across the Community about the content of medical training . . .': Hurwitz, *Free Circulation of Physicians* at p. 15.
[127] Article 11 of Directive 93/16/EEC. There are less onerous provisions regarding doctors providing services: see Articles 17–18.
[128] [1975] OJ C146/1.

being complied with in many cases.[129] As we have seen, the medical Directives do not harmonise training but rather co-ordinate recognition of diplomas, whilst laying out minimum standards. These minimum standards are enforceable[130] but there can be considerable variations in length and details of required training, as we have noted above.[131] There is no effective pan-EU assessment procedure for checking training standards. This has led to fears regarding quality control.[132] These fears are seemingly not shared by the ECJ, which apparently trusts the mutual recognition Directives to provide uniform care as regards migrant professionals.[133] It could be argued that this might make sense in the context of the sectoral Directives where, as we have seen, minimum training standards are established and some level of Community safeguard procedures is in place. However, it surely cannot make sense in the context of the general Directives where Community law does not provide a minimum guarantee of proficiency, but rather allows Member States to impose 'compensation' mechanisms. It is submitted that the ECJ goes too far in the *Decker* case where Directive 92/51/EEC is used to draw the conclusion that 'an optician in another Member State provides guarantees equivalent to those afforded on the sale of a pair of spectacles by an optician established in the national territory'.[134]

Since the beginning of the 1970s there has been an overall increase in the number of physicians practising in every Member State: coupled with the declining birth rate, this is leading to a surplus of physicians, particularly in Italy, Greece and Belgium.[135] In 1985, Italy had 322 physicians per 100,000 inhabitants, whilst Ireland trailed with 129 physicians per 100,000 inhabitants, the rest of the Member States falling between these two figures.[136] At this time, the United States had

---

[129] H. Roscam Abbing, 'Main Issues and Findings of the Symposium', Quality of Medical Practice and Professional Misconduct in the European Union, Symposium (Amsterdam, 1997). The symposium considered that an EC-wide database could help, pp. 54–5. The United States operates such a system. See Roscam Abbing, 'The Right of the Patient to Quality of Medical Practice and the Position of Migrant Doctors within the EU' (1997) 4 *EJHL* 347 at 357, and 'Quality of Medical Practice and Professional Misconduct in the European Union' (1997) 4 *EJHL* 273; E. Segest, 'Consumer Protection and the Free Movement of Medical Practitioners in the European Union' (1997) 4 *EHJL* 267.

[130] See Case 306/84 *Commission* v. *Belgium*.

[131] See above, pp. 63ff.

[132] Roscam Abbing, 'Right of the Patient to Quality of Medical Practice' at 352.

[133] See particularly *Kholl* at §47. See also A.-G. Tesauro in *Decker* and *Kholl* at §52. The Council has, however, called for improvements: Council Resolution of 24 July 1997 [1997] OJ C241/1. Roscam Abbing, 'Right of the Patient to Quality of Medical Practice' at 359.

[134] See *Decker*, esp. §§42–3.

[135] Hurwitz, *Free Circulation of Physicians*, pp. 38–9.

[136] *Ibid.*, p. 40. Later statistics put the Italian figures at 419 per 100,000, with Ireland at

170 physicians per 100,000 inhabitants and Japan 120 per 100,000 inhabitants.[137] By 1991, the Italian figure had reached 510 doctors per 100,000 inhabitants.[138] The UK by 1993 appears to have had the lowest density of doctors at 164 per 100,000 inhabitants, as against Italy's 535 per 100,000.[139] A lot of Italian doctors are underemployed, providing emergency on-call services, for example.[140]

One of the results of the oversupply of doctors is that the actual training and post-training practice can be limited. In Italy, for example, there is allegedly too limited an opportunity for surgeons to practise surgery.[141] Moreover, it is more difficult for migrant physicians to find positions when medical jobs are few and far between and underemployment is common.[142] This would at least partially explain why the UK is a popular destination country for migrant doctors.[143]

Medical Directives in the UK   The impact of the medical profession Directives was significant in the UK[144] which, prior to the reform instigated by the Calman Report,[145] did not recognise specialists as such but rather consultants.[146] The UK criteria for awarding specialist medical accreditation were admitted in the High Court to be in breach of the doctors' sectoral Directives. The Calman Report recommended that a certificate in specialist training should be introduced. Holders of such certificates would be indicated on the Medical Register. This

131 per 100,000; Statistical Office of the European Communities, DG34/E-2/13728/MDS/ml/9411P025 (28 November 1994).

[137] Hurwitz, *Free Circulation of Physicians*, p. 40.

[138] Statistical Office of the European Communities, DG34/E-2/13728/MDS/ml/9411P025 (28 November 1994).

[139] Committee of Senior Officials on Public Health: Statistics on the number of doctors and dentists 11/95, FL/fl – csp\statisti\9602p005 XV/E/2 XV/E/8270/96 (20 February 1996).

[140] F. Auxilia and S. Castaldi, 'Health Care Labour Market' in Normand and Vaughan, *Europe Without Frontiers*, p. 86 at p. 89.

[141] Hurwitz, *Free Circulation of Physicians*, p. 45.

[142] *Ibid.* at p. 46.

[143] The UK also benefits from having a widely spoken world language, and from being a gateway to the medical markets in the United States.

[144] They were influential not just in the UK. Indeed, both Italy and Austria had to introduce the new profession of 'dentist'.

[145] Report of the working group on specialist medical training, *Hospital Doctors: Training for the Future* (London: Department of Health, 1993). In turn this review was prompted by challenges to the UK implementation of the medical Directives by, among others, the European Commission.

[146] An acknowledged failure of the UK to implement the Directives properly was illustrated in a case brought by Anthony Goldstein, a London rheumatologist, in a High Court writ against the Health Secretary: *R* v. *Secretary of State for Health, ex parte Goldstein* [1993] 2 CMLR 589 (*The Times* 5 April 1993). Case C-148/96P(R) *Anthony Goldstein* v. *Commission of the ECs* [1996] ECR I-3883 outlines some of the voluminous litigation on this matter.

would allow certification of the migrant specialist doctors from the EC/ EEA in accordance with Directive 93/16/EEC. The changes were introduced by the European Specialist Medical Qualifications Order 1995,[147] which came into force in January 1996. This established the Specialist Training Authority (STA),[148] which now awards the Certificate of Completion of Specialist Training (CCST).[149] This is the certificate required under Articles 5 and 7 of Directive 93/16/EEC to allow automatic recognition of specialist qualifications within the EEA. The award of the CCST allows for registration on the Specialist Register (maintained by the GMC) and shows eligibility for appointment as a consultant.[150]

There is no doubt that the EC Directives on medical professions have increased the numbers of doctors moving between the Member States. Britain has been the most popular destination. The figures for 1998 (final figures are not yet available)[151] show that over 1,576 non-UK EU national doctors trained in the EEA[152] used the medical Directives to become recognised as able to practise in the UK.[153] The largest provider to the UK was Germany (411), followed by Greece (291), with Italy and Ireland both providing just under 200 doctors each. The next largest recipient of non-nationally trained doctors was Greece, to where 219 EU national doctors trained in the EEA migrated. Of these, 156 were trained in Italy and 43 in Germany. Since December 1976, when the Directives came into force, the UK has accepted over 18,696 EC

---

[147] European Specialist Medical Qualifications Order 1995, SI 3208/1995, as amended notably by SI 1997/2928 and the European Specialist Medical Qualifications Amendment Regulations 1999 SI 1999/1371.

[148] Its membership includes representatives from all the UK medical Royal Colleges, the Faculties of Public Health Medicine and Occupational Medicine, two representatives of the General Medical Council (GMC), two deans of post-graduate medicine and two lay persons appointed by the Secretary of State for Health. Its website contains much useful information: www.sta-mrc.org.uk.

[149] The STA also ensures that the training regimes provided by the Royal Colleges conform to the EC sectoral medical Directives.

[150] Senior House Officers are the second largest category of hospital doctors in the UK, and the ranks of consultants are primarily selected from this pool of doctors. See generally, Sir Charles George (Chairman, Education Committee) *Recommendations on Senior House Officer Training*, General Medical Council: http://www.gmc-uk.org/.

[151] Committee of Senior Officials on Public Health: Statistical Tables relating to the migration of doctors, nurses responsible for general care, dental practitioners and midwives in the Community during 1998, FVA/mw – j:\csp\statist\1998\en-8245 XV/ E/8245/3/99–EN (4 November 1999).

[152] Only forty EFTA nationals used the Directives in 1998.

[153] Committee of Senior Officials, 1998, statistical table 1. This is down on 1997 when 1,836 doctors migrated to the UK, Committee of Senior Officials on Public Health: Statistical Tables relating to the migration of doctors, nurses responsible for general care, dental practitioners and midwives in the Community during 1997, FVA/mw – j:\csp\statist\8130en98 XV/D/8130/6/98–EN (4 November 1999).

doctors, by far the highest number of any of the Member States. The nearest Member State in terms of numbers of medical migrants is the Netherlands, which received 1,838 over the same period.

In the UK, the proportion of doctors in the workforce trained in the UK itself is in decline. In 1996, only 76 per cent of doctors working in the UK qualified in the UK.[154] Of the roughly 10,000 GMC registrations per annum, only 4,000 are UK graduates with 1,500 from the EEA and 4,500 from non-EEA countries.[155] This has led to an increasing unease regarding the dependence on overseas sources[156] in the UK and a corresponding increase in the number of student places in medical faculties has been made available.[157]

The Advisory Committee on Medical Training   An Advisory Committee on Medical Training was established by Decision 75/364/ EEC.[158] The ACMT consists of experts from each Member State, one representing the medical profession, one from the academic community and one representing competent national health authorities. The Committee was designed as a vehicle for the exchange of information on training methods, content, level and structure and as a forum for discussion and consultation and to keep under review advances in medical science and teaching. It has issued numerous influential reports on issues relating to medical training. The profession considers that the Committee is insufficiently supported and meets too infrequently.[159]

The Committee of Senior Officials on Public Health[160] was also set up to adapt the Directives to changing conditions. The speed of change, however, has made keeping the Directives up to date difficult. An amendment in 1997[161] allowed the Commission to update the lists of specialists and the minimum duration of their training covered by

---

[154] 'Planning the Medical Workforce' Medical Workforce Standing Advisory Committee: Third Report, December 1997, p. 24.

[155] *Ibid.*, p. 61.

[156] NHS Executive, Specialist Workforce Standing Advisory Group Recommendations: Higher Specialist Training Numbers, 1997/98, EL(97)14; 'Planning the Medical Workforce', Medical Workforce Standing Advisory Committee: Third Report, December 1997.

[157] See the letters columns of the *BMJ*: [1997] 314 *BMJ* 1278.

[158] Council Decision 75/364/EEC of 16 June 1975 setting up an Advisory Committee on Medical Training [1975] OJ L167/17.

[159] Royal College of General Practitioners, response to SLIM questionnaire, above, n. 78.

[160] Council Decision 75/365/EEC of 16 June 1975 setting up a Committee of Senior Officials on Public Health [1975] OJ L167/19.

[161] Directive 97/50/EC of the European Parliament and of the Council of 6 October 1997 amending Directive 93/16/EEC to facilitate the free movement of doctors and the mutual recognition of their diplomas, certificates and other evidence of formal qualifications [1997] OJ L291/37.

Directive 93/16/EEC, subject to the usual comitology[162] restraints. However, this in itself has not resolved the issue as Member States have failed to implement speedily the resulting Commission Directives.[163]

Directive 93/16/EEC has itself been amended,[164] and is now the subject of further amendments under the current SLIM proposals dealt with below. There is a good case for arguing that simple updating amendments should be in the form of Regulations, thus avoiding the implementation problem. The SLIM proposals suggest that Member States notify the Commission which would publish a 'notice' in the Official Journal.[165]

The SLIM reforms   The SLIM reforms are part of an overall updating to simplify legislation in the internal market (SLIM).[166] As mentioned above in the area of mutual recognition, the thirty-five transitional Directives have already been updated and consolidated under the scheme.[167] There are current plans to reform the Advisory Committees[168] established under the sectoral Directive systems. The ACMT and the Advisory Committee on the Training of Nurses (ACTN) and other Advisory Committees allow three members (and substitutes) for each country. This makes ninety members in each Committee. Even without the proposed EU enlargement eastwards, the size of meetings needs trimming if only to save costs.[169]

Furthermore, the Treaty of Rome itself has been amended since the institution of the Committees to exclude all harmonisation of training or education systems at the Member State level,[170] thus diminishing the potential role of the Advisory Committees on Training. The initial proposal suggested that there be only two members per State: one from the profession and one from an educational establishment, with one of

---

[162] Decision 87/373/EEC [1987] OJ L197/33.

[163] Commission Directive 98/21/EC (8 April 1998); Commission Directive 98/63/EC (3 September 1998); Commission Directive 99/46/EC OJ L139/26 (2 June 1999). The Commission has recently (January 2000) referred the Netherlands, Ireland, Spain and Portugal to the ECJ for failing to implement Directive 98/21/EC and issued them with reasoned opinions in relation to Directive 98/63/EC.

[164] For the amending Directives see above, n. 163.

[165] COM(96) 22, COM(97) 638, Article 4.

[166] SLIM was initially launched in March 1996: further, see *Communication to the Council and European Parliament on the SLIM initiative*, COM(96) 559 (6 November 1996).

[167] Directive 1999/42/EC: see above, n. 75 and accompanying text.

[168] The six Advisory Committees cover doctors, nurses, midwives, dental practitioners, veterinary surgeons and pharmacists. Part of the reform proposal would repeal the decisions setting up the Committees: COM(99) 177.

[169] The professions have felt that the Committees met too infrequently.

[170] See above, n. 25 and accompanying text.

them acting as an alternate.[171] The term of members would be extended from the current three to six years,[172] and the appointments procedures would be streamlined.

The pharmaceutical profession

It is not proposed here to go into as much detail with the pharmaceutical profession as with the medical profession. This is partly for reasons of space, but also because the EC's mode of dealing with the pharmaceutical profession largely follows the classical sectoral Directive line, which has already been outlined above. The main distinction for the pharmaceutical profession is that their Directives[173] do not deal extensively with establishment rights,[174] largely because several Member States do not allow automatic rights to establish pharmacies.[175] Directive 85/432/EEC does not disallow States from having competitive exams for those seeking to control new pharmacies.[176] Nor does it exhaustively define the activities of pharmacists, but rather it sets out the minimum conditions for access to a minimum range of defined activities. These are set out in Article 1(2) of the Directive and include:

[171] The experts from the Competent Authorities are already represented in other Committees: Committee of Senior Officials on Public Health; Pharmaceutical Committee; and the ad hoc Group of Senior Veterinary Officials.

[172] The Decisions establishing the Advisory Committees would be repealed: Proposal for a Council Decision repealing Decisions 75/354/EEC, 75/454/EEC, 76/688/EEC, 78/1028/EEC, 80/156/EEC and 85/434/EEC setting up advisory committees for the training of nurses responsible for general care, dental practitioners, veterinary surgeons, midwives, pharmacists and doctors. Doc. No. 599PC0177, COM(99) 177; http://europe.eu.int/eur-lex. This is resisted by the Member States who do not wish to abolish the Committees without first seeing the shape of their replacements.

[173] Council Directive 85/432/EEC of 16 September 1985 concerning the co-ordination of provisions laid down by law, regulation or administrative action in respect of certain activities in the field of pharmacy [1985] OJ L253/34; Council Directive 85/433/EEC of 16 September 1985 concerning the mutual recognition of diplomas, certificates and other evidence of formal qualifications in pharmacy, including measures to facilitate the effective exercise of the right of establishment relating to certain activities in the field of pharmacy, as amended by Council Directive 85/584/EEC of 20 December 1985 amending the Directives, on account of the accession of Spain and Portugal; Council Directive 90/658/EEC of 4 December 1990 amending certain Directives on the mutual recognition of diplomas consequent upon the unification of Germany. The latter Directive introduces special arrangements for recognition of the diplomas etc. of the former German Democratic Republic.

[174] A. C. Oostermann-Meulenbeld, 'Quality Regulation on Professional Health Care Practice in the European Community' (1993–4) *Legal Issues in European Integration* 61 at 67.

[175] See generally Articles 2 and 3. The Greek derogation in Article 3 will be withdrawn if the SLIM initiative reform is adopted. Doc. 13378/99, CODEC 729. Some States, e.g. Luxembourg, require periods of professional experience: see Article 5.

[176] Article 1(3).

the preparation of the pharmaceutical form of medicinal products,

the manufacture and testing of medicinal products,

the testing of medicinal products in a laboratory for the {of medicinal of medicinal products, [*sic*]},

the storage, preservation and distribution of medicinal products at the wholesale stage,

the preparation, testing, storage and supply of medicinal products in pharmacies open to the public,

the preparation, testing, storage and dispensing of medicinal products in hospitals,

the provision of information and advice on medicinal products.

The ECJ has recognised the role of these Directives in guaranteeing minimum qualification levels for the key activities of pharmacists, which added to the reasoning for allowing individuals to have their own drugs transported across borders.[177] Article 2 of Directive 85/433/EEC sets out the minimum training required for the award of pharmaceutical diplomas.

The nursing profession

The sectoral nurse Directives follow the same general pattern as for doctors (though they do not deal with specialists) and pharmacists: that is to say, the first Directive co-ordinates the training, and the second causes Member States to recognise (mutually) the diplomas that result from the co-ordinated training. The sectoral nurse Directives themselves will not receive complete treatment here for the same reasons as for the pharmaceutical Directives, explained above. However, the sectoral nurse Directives only cover the activities of the general care nurse.[178] The growth in the specialisation of nurses, which is clearly evident,[179] has not been taken into account by the development of new Directives or amendments to the existing ones to take account of the new specialities. There are no sectoral Directives for the specialised nurse, let alone any speedy machinery allowing such a potential Directive to be adjusted in the light of developments in the nursing profession.[180] Many specialised nurses have a 'general care' qualification before becoming a specialist nurse, but others, who might be termed 'branch nurses', have no such general care

---

[177] Case 215/87 *Schumacher* v. *HZA Frankfurt am Main-Ost* [1989] ECR 617 §§9–20; Case 62/90 *Commission* v. *Germany* [1992] ECR I-2575 §§16–20; see also Advocate-General Jacobs at §19.

[178] Article 1(1) of the sectoral nurse Directive 77/452/EEC [1977] OJ L176/1 reads: 'This Directive shall apply to the activities of nurses responsible for general care.'

[179] The Netherlands, Portugal, Italy, Spain, Belgium and Sweden are all planning to introduce new categories of post-basic specialised nurses. See J. Lonbay, *Study of Specialist Nurses in the EC Europe* (MARKT/D/8031/2000 Brussels, 1 August 2000).

[180] For example, as per the doctors' Directive 93/16/EEC as amended [1993] OJ L165/1; see above, pp. 59ff.

qualification. The direct entry branch nurses who are not trained in general care can, however, also undertake post-registration training in nursing specialities in some of the Member States. The structural divergences of the nursing professions in the different Member States can lead to some levels of a given nursing profession finding themselves locked out from utilising the general system Directives, because their 'base profession' is covered by the sectoral nursing Directives. This follows from the operation of Article 2 of Directive 89/48/EEC which reads:

This Directive shall apply to any national of a Member State wishing to pursue a regulated profession in a host Member State in a self-employed capacity or as an employed person.

This Directive shall not apply to professions which are the subject of a separate Directive establishing arrangements for the mutual recognition of diplomas by Member States [emphasis added].

Article 2 of Directive 92/51/EEC has a similar provision. Such a branch nurse, moving to a Member State that has no similar branch nursing, might find that the nursing diploma mentioned in the sectoral nurse Directives is required in order to work in the host State. In this situation, the migrant branch nurse will need to rely on the case law of the ECJ, as the general horizontal Directives (89/48/EEC and 92/51/EEC) are not available by virtue of Article 2 of each Directive, mentioned above. This means that types of nurse other than the general care nurse, for example, those who have specialised after having qualified as a general care nurse (the post-basic specialist nurse) or those who have never qualified as a general care nurse but have directly entered a 'branch' nurse profession,[181] are not fully covered by the sectoral nurse Directives. These are left to be covered by the third-wave measures (the general or 'horizontal' Directives)[182] or, in some cases, by general EC law. Because of the lacunae in the nursing Directives mentioned above, all three modes of EC law potentially apply, i.e. the sectoral Directives, the general Directives and the case law of the ECJ itself. As the *Study of Specialist Nurses in Europe*[183] shows, the number and variety of such branch nurses are diminishing across the European Union.

In 1996, the Commission proposed[184] a solution to this difficulty by suggesting the amendment of Article 2 of the horizontal Directives in

---

[181] This left out very large numbers of nurses with primary qualifications that permitted them to undertake specific nursing tasks, e.g. the psychiatric nurses trained not in general care but in psychiatric issues.

[182] Directives 89/48/EEC and 92/51/EEC.

[183] Lonbay, *Study of Specialist Nurses in Europe*. The study outlines the fundamental modes of regulating nurses in each Member State and how the mutual recognition Directives are applied. The comments in this chapter are entirely those of the author, and do not reflect the position of the European Commission on any issue.

[184] COM(96) 22 (8 February 1996) Article 8.

interpose any rules regarding access to the professions, nor the number of training places for the professions. This means that manpower planning is in national hands. Just as the ECJ has allowed the medical consumer to plunder the national health care larders by opening cross-border access to health care in *Decker* and *Kholl*, so under the mutual recognition Directives, in principle, qualified professionals in the health care sector can choose in which country to work, thus potentially under-mining national manpower planning controls. There is no principle of EC law requiring Member States to limit the number of students admitted to medical faculties.[195] The ACMT in its second Report of Specialist Training in 1982 called for regulation of the number of trainee specialists, a call reiterated in its fourth Report in relation to selection of trainees.[196] A quota examination system was introduced in Italy in 1986 to cap medical student numbers. There have been some attempts in other countries to limit entrants. However, EC-engendered mobility could undermine such national constraints. Again we can see that the internal market imperative can override national-based control systems and the Member States are too concerned about competence to allow the EC to take a guiding role. They do, however, like the 'centralising' sectoral system of mutual recognition of professional qualifications, though they do not allow sufficient resources for the central control mechanisms to work effectively, and have resisted the Commission's hints that it is perhaps unnecessary and should be dismantled.

The medical, allied and pharmaceutical professions were singled out in Article 47 EC for co-ordination. Many of the allied professions are, in fact, covered by the general system Directives without prior co-ordina-tion. No disaster has followed. The numbers of professional migrants are growing, and there has been a beneficial learning curve for the national competent authorities applying the EC Directives. This has occurred even under the general system Directives (i.e. without the Advisory Committee structure), achieved in part by the role of co-ordinators,[197] and in part through the efforts of the professions them-selves.

The sectoral co-ordinating Directives establish minimum standards

---

[195] Joined Cases 98, 162 and 258/85 *Bertini* v. *Regiona Lazio* [1986] ECR 1885. See generally K. Poulton, 'Health Service Workforce Planning in Europe' in Normand and Vaughan, *Europe Without Frontiers*, p. 79.

[196] ACMT, *Fourth Report and Recommendations on the Conditions of Specialist Training*, p. 41. Formally, the issue of *numerus clausus* (a cap on student numbers) is beyond the ACMT remit. *Ibid.* at p. 49.

[197] The general system Directives have a system of national co-ordinators to help implement the system.

without harmonising training in any detail. This has led to fears of lower standards in some countries, and to concerns about evasion of national controls.[198] The ECJ itself is perhaps overly enthusiastic regarding the guarantees offered by the general system Directives,[199] and perhaps also over-generous to Member State regulation of professions, particularly when nationals might seem deliberately to be evading domestic controls.[200] But the ECJ has also had a major beneficial impact, for example, with the *Vlassopoulou* case, now being incorporated in the SLIM reform to the mutual recognition system.[201]

One of the undoubted difficulties of the current system of mutual recognition of professional qualifications is the gaps it leaves. These were illustrated in the nursing sector above. Where professions are very different, or do not exist in the same way, or even at all, then migrants can be forced out of the Directive systems, and must rely on the general case law of the ECJ. This is an uncertain fate and provides a route filled with delays and difficulties. The European Commission, in its Communication on *The Strategy for Europe's Internal Market*,[202] promises a review of the whole system of recognition of professional mobility and will hopefully tackle these issues.

---

[198] The fears were noted by the Council in 1997: Council Resolution of 24 July 1997 on migrant doctors within the Community [1997] OJ C241/1.

[199] See above, p. 64.

[200] Case C-61/89 *Marc Gaston Bouchoucha* [1990] ECR 3551.

[201] See above, p. 58.

[202] COM(99) 624 final/2 (29 November 1999).

4 EC competition law, pharmaceuticals and intellectual property: recent developments

Leigh Hancher

Introduction

The application of the EC competition rules to the pharmaceutical sector has been the subject of considerable commentary and analysis in recent years. This is partly due to the intrinsic importance of the subject from a practical as well as a more theoretical or academic perspective, but is perhaps also to be attributed to the fact that the organisation and practices of the pharmaceutical industry have produced a rich seam of European legal problems, often raising many novel issues. Indeed the doctrines applicable to parallel imports have largely been developed through the application of the rules on free movement (Articles 28–30 (ex 30–6) EC) and competition (Articles 81–2 (ex 85–6) EC) to this complex legal sector.

This chapter cannot attempt to cover the many and varied aspects of the application of EC competition law and principles in full. Instead it focuses on several key recent developments in the case law of the European Courts, with a view to determining whether it is possible to explain or continue to explain these developments by peculiarities in the underlying policies on which the relevant EC rules are based. This contribution will therefore look in some detail at the development of the case law with respect to parallel imports. This is of course only one aspect of EC pharmaceutical law. Important matters relating to the development of the centralised authorisation procedure are not covered here, nor are issues relating to product safety and efficacy or advertising rules,[1] or the many facets of the sector which are now subject to increasingly complex bodies of secondary law. The law on parallel imports is singled out because it is based upon a certain paradoxical situation and as such produces a variety of tensions which find their reflection in both policy and law.

Parallel trade in pharmaceuticals is well established as a phenomenon,

---

[1] For an overview, see the series of volumes entitled 'The Rules governing Medicinal Products, the European Union' (http://dg3.endra.org/endralex/index.htm).

even though it seems difficult to quantify with any degree of exactness. For some it has its origins in the fact that it is a product of national regulations on pricing and profit controls and/or controls on reimbursement through social security schemes. Thus the process is driven by the ease of exporting certain products from low-priced countries into higher priced countries, thereby undercutting existing suppliers of the same products in the Member State of importation. For others it is attributable to the practices of an industry which seeks to maximise the benefits of national regulatory divergence: parallel importing therefore promotes overall efficiency by curbing excessive profits. It is probably fair to say that the truth of the matter lies somewhere between these two poles: the industry must continue to live with a scattergram of national policies on pricing and profit controls, but is of course able to react to this situation in a number of ways, even if it cannot necessarily control it. Price divergences have been further fuelled by currency movements. Exchange rate movements alone account for a 40 per cent price gap between Germany and Italy for SKB's Seroxat (paroxetine), even though the brand was introduced at a common launch price in 1993. Obviously the introduction of the Euro has tempered the impact of currency fluctuations, at least as between those Member States whose currencies are now fixed to the Euro. However, certain countries who are not members remain net importers of parallel products.

The recent case law to be reviewed here indicates that the ECJ has been unwilling to reverse its previous pro-internal market and hence pro-parallel import approach, especially in the field of intellectual property law. Intellectual property rights are of vital importance to the research-based industry. At the risk of oversimplification, the Court has taken the attitude that once the holder of a patented product or the owner of a trade mark or copyright puts its product on the market of Country A as well as that of Country B, its rights are 'exhausted' in the sense that it cannot rely upon these rights to prevent trade in the products between Country A and Country B. This chapter will not examine the implications of the Court's judgment in the *Silhouette* case[2] for the future of the doctrine of international versus European exhaustion.

Article 28 EC and industrial property rights

Article 28 EC prohibits all measures which have equivalent effect to quantitative restrictions on the free movement of goods, including in principle national intellectual or industrial property right laws. Never-

---

[2] Case C-355/96 *Silhouette International Schmied* v. *Hartlauer Handelsgesellschaft* [1998] ECR I-4799. See above, chapter 2

theless Article 30 EC provides that Article 28 EC shall not preclude prohibitions or restrictions on imports which are justified by the protection of industrial and commercial property as long as these rights do not constitute a means of arbitrary discrimination or a disguised restriction on trade between Member States.

The early case law of the Court firmly established the principle that the owner of an industrial or commercial property right could not invoke it in order to prevent the importation and sale of goods which had been placed on the market with his consent in another Member State. That principle was first laid down in *Deutsche Grammophon* v. *Metro*[3] in relation to copyright, in *Centrafarm* v. *Winthrop*[4] in relation to trade marks and *Centrafarm* v. *Sterling*[5] in relation to patents. The so-called principle of exhaustion of rights was prompted by the desire to eliminate any risk of the use of intellectual property rights to establish artificial divisions within the common market. The principle balanced the idea that the owner could hold or enjoy the national rights in question – i.e. that the rights in question continued to exist in national law – against the idea that the exercise of those rights was controlled by Community law. As with any principle, its limits were quickly put to the test.

In *Merck* v. *Stephar*[6] the Court upheld a strict interpretation of the principle of exhaustion, and found that even where a Member State did not provide patent protection, the mere consent to placing of the product on that market was sufficient to establish exhaustion.

In 1996 the Court was offered the opportunity to reverse its judgment in *Merck* and to reconsider the issue of consent in *Merck* v. *Primecrown*.[7] Merck argued that in fact pharmaceutical companies did not choose where to market their products, but that they were under an ethical and sometimes even a legal obligation to supply their products to a market. They could not discontinue existing supplies to a market and were forced to put up with national price controls. The Advocate-General strongly recommended that the Court should reconsider the earlier *Merck* v. *Stephar*[8] judgment and that the patent holder should be able to prevent parallel imports from Member States (Spain and Portugal) where the patent holder could not have obtained protection. The Court maintained its approach to the matter of consent.

[3]   Case 78/70 *Deutsche Grammophon* v. *Metro* [1971] ECR 487.
[4]   Case 16/74 *Centrafarm* v. *Winthrop* [1974] ECR 1183.
[5]   Case 15/74 *Centrafarm* v. *Sterling* [1974] ECR 1147.
[6]   Case 187/80 *Merck* v. *Stephar* [1981] ECR 2063.
[7]   Joined Cases C-267/95 and C-268/95 *Merck* v. *Primecrown* [1996] ECR I-6285.
[8]   Case 187/80 *Merck* v. *Stephar* [1981] ECR 2063.

Patents

A major flaw in the Court's approach to the doctrine of exhaustion has resulted from the fact that in several EC Member States, full patent protection for pharmaceutical products has not always been available. This was originally the case in Italy, but was also true for the newer Member States – Spain and Portugal. Hence imitation, and eventual exportation to high-priced markets, was an attractive possibility as products marketed in these countries could not benefit from full protection. The original manufacturers argued that, logically, they could not 'exhaust' patent protection rights which they did not enjoy in the first place, and so they should be entitled to exercise their patent rights to prevent cheaper imitations reaching other markets.

In the *Primecrown*[9] case, in 1996, the Court rejected this line of reasoning, and ruled that the original manufacturers had 'consented' voluntarily to putting their products on the market in the knowledge that full patent protection could not be obtained. While acknowledging the problems created by national price differentials as being the fuelling force for parallel trade, the Court firmly placed responsibility for resolving them with the Commission and the Council. It resolutely refused to water down the rights of free movement as guaranteed by the European Community treaties. The judgment has however been criticised as failing to take on board the realities of the situation confronting the industry, which are of course that national price regulation still divides the common market.

The Court's insistence on a strict application of the exhaustion doctrine has led the research-based industry to lobby for strict safeguards in the accession treaties with the Eastern European countries who have also traditionally denied strong patent protection to pharmaceuticals. The precedent of such safeguard measures in the earlier accession agreements with Spain and Portugal indicates that a transitional period preventing importation of non-patented products is possible, but that these safeguard measures must be properly drawn up to be effective in practice.

Trade marks

Litigation has also arisen with respect to trade marks, and the rights of the original manufacturer to defend its trade mark where parallel importers have repackaged a product sold under a particular trade mark

---

[9] Joined Cases C-267/95 and C-268/95 *Merck* v. *Primecrown* [1996] ECR I-6285.

in Country B to resell it under the trade mark current in Country A. Once again the doctrine of exhaustion is of importance here. Has the manufacturer exhausted his trade mark rights by putting the product on the market under different trade marks in the first place? The answer to this question lies in the nature of the specific subject-matter of the trade mark right. The Court has recognised that trade marks have as an essential function a guarantee to the consumer or end-user of the identity of the trade-marked product's origin.[10] Hence the Court has recognised that a trade mark owner can oppose any use of the trade mark which is liable to impair the essential function of the trade mark. Nevertheless, in its early case law, the Court added an important proviso: it was still necessary to consider whether the exercise of that right could constitute a disguised restriction on trade within the meaning of the second sentence of Article 30 EC.[11]

Three cases decided in 1996 – *Paranova*,[12] *Eurim-Pharm*[13] and *Rhône-Poulenc*[14] – raised the issue of whether the trade mark holder could rely upon the EC Trade Marks Directive[15] to prevent importation of repackaged products. Article 7(1) of this Directive enshrines the principle of exhaustion of rights but Article 7(2) introduces an exception so that the owner of the trade mark may oppose further marketing of a repackaged product 'where there exist legitimate reasons for doing so especially where the condition of the goods is changed or impaired'. The Directive has led to a number of competing interpretations, ranging from a narrow concept of exhaustion, where only if the imported product was in the very form in which it had been marketed could the trade mark owner not oppose its use, to a broader approach, whereby the trade mark owner could only oppose the use if the product was put on the market and was substantially changed.

In these cases the parallel importers had repackaged the goods, either by removing the blister packs from their original external packs and placing them in new packs or by severing the blister strips and repackaging them. The key issue before the Court in these 'repackaging cases' was whether any of these actions impaired or changed the conditions of the products. However, the Court was also asked to address the relevance of the trade mark owner's intention to partition markets. In essence, it was asked to determine whether this test should be a

---

[10] Case 3/78 *American Home Products* [1978] ECR 1823.
[11] Case 102/77 *Hoffman-La Roche* [1978] ECR 1139.
[12] Joined Cases C-427/93, C-429/93 and C-436/93 *Bristol-Myers Squibb* v. *Paranova* [1996] ECR I-3457.
[13] Joined Cases C-71/94, C-72/94 and C-73/94 *Eurim-Pharm* [1996] ECR I-3603.
[14] Case C-232/94 *MPA* v. *Rhône-Poulenc* [1996] ECR I-3671.
[15] [1989] OJ L140/1.

subjective or an objective one: was it necessary to demonstrate that the trade mark owner actually planned this result, or was it sufficient to demonstrate that this was the inevitable result of its action in using different marks in the first place?

The Court took a strict approach to the question of intention.[16] The trade mark owner could not oppose repackaging of the product in new external packaging when the size of packet used by the owner in the Member State where the importer purchased the product could not be marketed in the Member State of importation by reason, in particular, of a rule authorising packaging only of a certain size or a national practice to the same effect. The power of the owner of trade mark rights protected in a Member State to oppose the marketing of repackaged products under the trade mark should be limited only in so far as the repackaging undertaken by the importer was necessary in order to market the product in the Member State of importation. It was not up to the importer to demonstrate that the trade mark owner had deliberately sought to partition the markets between Member States. It held that an adverse effect on the original condition of the product refers to the condition of the product inside the packaging. Only if the action of the parallel importer affected or was likely to affect the product itself, could the trade mark owner oppose the repackaging as an infringement of its legitimate trade mark rights. It expressly stated that 'trade mark rights are not intended to allow their owners to partition national markets and thus promote the retention of price differences which may exist between Member States'.[17]

There will be no artificial partitioning where action by the trade mark owner is needed to safeguard the essential function of the mark. In this sense the Court reformulated the requirement of intention: where reliance by the owner of the trade mark right was justified by the need to safeguard the essential function of the trade mark, the resulting partitioning could not be regarded as artificial. Article 7(2) had the same effect as Article 30 EC. Hence subjective intention is irrelevant.

The Court did however seek to ensure that the trade mark owner could exercise some degree of control over how products were repackaged. The parallel importer must indicate who has repackaged the product; he must indicate on the packaging who manufactured the product; and he must not wrongly attribute any responsibility for any

---

[16] For a discussion of the earlier case law and the question of subjective versus objective intention, see F. Castillo de la Torre, 'Trade Marks and Free Movement of Pharmaceuticals' [1997] *EIPR* 304.

[17] Joined Cases C-427/93, C-429/93 and C-436/93 *Bristol-Myers Squibb* v. *Paranova* [1996] ECR I-3457, §§42–5.

additional articles added to the packaging to the trade mark owner. He must give the trade mark owner advance notice of the product being put on sale, and the owner can require that he is supplied in advance of sale with a specimen of the repackaged product.[18]

A further development in this line of case law concerns the right of a parallel importer to affix different trade marks to parallel imported products. Once again, the original trade mark owner may have been compelled for reasons of national law to register its product under different marks in different Member States. This may be because certain similar marks had already been registered at national level or because of simple language differences. Again the basic question arises, should the trade mark owner be allowed to take advantage of a situation that has arisen as a result of circumstances outside his control and rely on his trade mark in order to exclude parallel imports even though the exclusion of such imports is not necessary on grounds of trade mark protection? The Advocate-General recently concluded in Case C-379/97 *Upjohn* v. *Paranova* (Opinion of 19 November 1998) that a similar approach should be taken where the affixing of different trade marks is an issue. The factors which led the trade mark owner to use different marks in the importing and exporting States are not relevant. Nevertheless the Advocate-General has raised the question of when it might be necessary for parallel importers to rebrand products in order to import and market them lawfully in another Member State. In principle, if various practices or rules in the Member State of import have the effect that the importer cannot market the products under the mark they bear in the State of export, the trade mark owner will not be able to rely on the trade mark rights to prevent importation of identical goods. Indeed there may be an even greater necessity for the importer to rebrand in order to avoid confusion with other marks currently used in the State of import.

The circumstances which led the original trade mark owner to use different marks should be regarded as historical and, according to the Advocate-General in *Upjohn*, there is no good reason for the Court to use them as defining criteria for determining the lawfulness of subsequent conduct. The decisive test, according to the Advocate-General, who based himself squarely on the Court's approach in the recent repackaging cases, is whether in a given case prohibiting the importer from rebranding would constitute an obstacle to effective access by him to the markets of the importing Member State. The Court has

---

[18] Joined Cases C-427/93, C-429/93 and C-436/93 *Bristol-Myers Squibb* v. *Paranova* [1996] ECR I-3457.

followed this approach in its subsequent ruling handed down in October 1999.[19]

Licensing and access to data

A parallel importer cannot simply purchase products in Member State B and re-import them into Member State A: products can only be marketed if the person responsible for placing them on the market has obtained a valid marketing authorisation from the relevant national licensing authorities. Although a new centralised Community marketing authorisation procedure was introduced in 1993[20] this only applies to a limited range of products, including products derived from bio-technology and highly innovative products. In all other cases a national marketing authorisation must be obtained, albeit that the procedures for granting these authorisations have been extensively harmonised by a series of Community Directives. Furthermore, in order to facilitate the licensing of parallel imports as well as generic products, the Community legislative framework makes provision for accelerated, simplified licensing procedures which allow applicants to 'piggy-back' on the detailed data and information.

A parallel importer can invoke a simplified licensing procedure if he can establish that his product is identical to the product authorised and marketed in the country of importation. This will usually be fairly straightforward where the parallel product in question has been produced by one and the same manufacturer, albeit in a different country.

In a case referred by the English High Court to the European Court, a parallel importer, Primecrown, challenged a decision to revoke its parallel import licence for the UK market in respect of a Ditropan product, the original UK marketing authorisation for which had been held by Smith and Nephew. The UK Medicines Control Agency (MCA) had revoked the parallel import licence upon discovering that the product sourced by Primecrown in Belgium had not been manufactured by the original product approval holder for the UK market, i.e. Smith and Nephew. The European Court ruled that it was not necessary for the purposes of the parallel licensing procedure for the parallel product to be identical in all respects. The national licensing authority need only establish that the product is effective and not harmful. This will be demonstrated by evidence that the parallel product is manufactured according to the same formulation, using the same active ingredi-

---

[19] Case C-379/97 *Pharmacia & Upjohn SA, formerly Upjohn SA* v. *Paranova A/S* [1999] ECR I-223 at §43.
[20] Council Regulation 2309/93 [1993] OJ L214/1.

ents, and has the same therapeutic effects as the original product.[21] This ruling has been criticised on the grounds that the Court seems to have applied a quasi-exhaustion approach to the data involved: once the product has been put on the market, the first marketer can no longer prevent the data from being used by others.[22] More recently in its ruling in the case of *Rhône-Poulenc* (December 1999)[23] the Court has ruled that a parallel importer may still rely on the special accelerated licensing procedure for parallel imports even though the products' market authorisation in the country of import had been withdrawn from the market of importation but *not* from the markets of other Member States. It was not relevant to the application of Articles 28 and 30 EC to the case in hand that the original manufacturer had brought out and marketed an improved version of the product in the country of importation.

With regard to generic products, that is products which are no longer under patent, applicants can benefit from a so-called abridged procedure which exempts them from providing the results of pharmacological and toxicological tests or the results of clinical trials, if it can be demonstrated that the generic version of the product is essentially similar to a product authorised in the country concerned by the application and

1. the original manufacturer has consented to the original data being used for the purposes of the generic application; or
2. by detailed reference to published scientific literature establishing that the product is safe and effective; or
3. that the generic product is essentially similar to a product which has been authorised within the Community for not less than six years and is marketed in the Member State where the application is made. This period can be extended to ten years for so-called high-technology products.[24]

In other words, if the originator does not consent to the use of its confidential data or there is insufficient published literature to guarantee the safety and efficacy of the product, then the applicant must wait for up to ten years before the licensing authority can make use of the originator's confidential data. The idea behind this approach is to strike a balance between the innovator's rights by preventing access to his data

---

[21] Case C-201/94 *R* v. *Smith & Nephew Pharmaceuticals Ltd and Primecrown Ltd* [1996] ECR I-5819.

[22] See generally S. Kon and F. Schaeffer 'Parallel Imports of Pharmaceutical Products: A New Realism, or Back to Basics' [1997] *ECLR* 123.

[23] Case C-94/98, *R* v. *The Licensing Authority established by the Medicines Act 1968 (represented by the Medicines Control Agency) ex parte Rhône-Poulenc Rorer Ltd, May & Baker Ltd* [1999] ECR I-8789.

[24] Council Directive 87/21 [1987] OJ L15/36.

for six to ten years and the public interest in stimulating price competition from generic products. Disputes have arisen, however, as to how essential similarity is to be established, and whether or not published literature must provide a similar level of information to that which would have been obtained from original tests and trials. In a 1995 case the European Court interpreted the published literature test very strictly and held that the published literature must yield the same degree of detail. Obviously this will occur only very rarely, and many commentators believe that the effect of the 1995 ruling is to kill the published literature exception altogether.[25]

As the originator will only rarely give consent to use the original test and trial data, generic applicants will have to wait for the six-to-ten-year period to expire. But what happens in a case where the original manufacturer has added new indications to its original product – does the ten-year protection period run from the date these new indications were added or from the date the original product was first marketed? The UK MCA has taken the line that the ten-year period will only be extended in cases where a new marketing authorisation is required. If the original authorisation is only varied to include the new indications then no additional period of data protection will be granted. In Case C-368/96 *Generics (UK) Ltd*,[26] the ECJ was asked to rule on a reference submitted by the English High Court concerning the UK licensing authority's refusal to grant a marketing authorisation to Generics for products which had originally been licensed by research-based companies in 1981 but for which new indications had been subsequently developed. The licensing authority had however granted an authorisation for two other products which were subsequently marketed by the original licence holder in different dosages and routes of administration. These licences were subsequently challenged. The innovative pharmaceutical companies considered that the so-called abridged procedure may be applied only if the applicant can show that the composition of the product for which it has applied for a marketing authorisation is comparable to the original product which has been authorised for not less than ten years, and, in addition, that each therapeutic indication, dose, etc. for which the marketing authorisation has been applied for has been authorised for not less than ten years. Generics took the opposite view, arguing that the abridged procedure may be applied as long as the composition of the product for which a marketing authorisation is requested is essentially similar to the original product. The UK licensing authority sought to apply a compromise position: the abridged pro-

---

25 Case C-440/93 *Scotia Pharmaceuticals* [1995] ECR I-2851.
26 Case C-368/96 *Generics (UK) Ltd* [1998] ECR I-7967; [1999] 2 CMLR 181.

cedure could be applied so long as any additions or changes did not constitute major therapeutic innovations.

The Court focused its appraisal on the concept of 'essential similarity' in Article 4 of the Directive and ruled that, having regard to the purpose of the Directive, which was to safeguard public health, the concept of an essentially similar medicinal product could not be interpreted in such a way that the abridged procedure could amount to a relaxation of the requirements of safety and efficacy which must be met by medicinal products. The Court took note of the minutes of the meeting of the Council at which Directive 87/21 was adopted and of the criteria to be applied in determining the concept of essential similarity. On the basis of these criteria, it followed that as long as essential similarity could be demonstrated, the applicant could receive an authorisation for all therapeutic indications concerned. The Court rejected the argument – put forward by the innovative companies and the Commission – that any major therapeutic innovation should be given independent protection. In any event the Court found that not only did the actual wording of the Directive preclude such an interpretation but also that the concept of a major therapeutic innovation was too imprecise to guarantee legal certainty. It further rejected the argument that the tests laid down in the Directive were themselves invalid on the grounds that they infringed the principles of protection of innovation, non-discrimination, proportionality and respect for the right to property. With regard to the last of these principles, the Court observed that the principle of a right to property was not absolute, but must be viewed in relation to its social purpose. The provisions at issue were in accordance with the objectives of general public importance pursued by the Community. This judgment can therefore be seen as a significant victory for generic companies.

Competition law (Articles 81–2 EC)

Even if the parallel trader can take advantage of weak patent protection to obtain supplies of imitation products in some countries, the more usual source of trade is through wholesalers supplied through official distribution channels by the original manufacturers in low-priced Member States. The most obvious defensive strategy for such manufacturers is in turn to try to limit the available supplies to the volumes required to serve the relevant national markets or to attempt to persuade wholesalers not to supply parallel traders. Both these tactics can involve the risk of infringement of the Community competition rules, and with it the risk of a heavy fine. In this respect, pleas to the effect that the internal market is divided along national lines as a result of national pricing rules and that original manufacturers should be able to defend their position accordingly have fallen on deaf ears at DGIV – the Community's competition directorate. This argument was run – without success – by Organon in 1995 to defend its attempts to limit supplies of cheap contraceptive drugs from finding their way from the UK into the Netherlands.[27] It has similarly been rejected by the Spanish competition authorities in relation to an attempt by Glaxo to introduce dual pricing systems for the Spanish market. The EC Commission is presently considering the *Glaxo* case.

A similar fate befell Bayer in its attempts to stem the flow of parallel imports of its product 'Adalat' which could be purchased on the French market at up to 50 per cent less than the UK market price. A straightforward ban on export by wholesalers can lead to breach of Article 81(1) (ex 85(1)) EC which prohibits, *inter alia*, anti-competitive agreements between manufacturers and distributors. Bayer's approach was more subtle. Wholesalers were requested to provide regular information on their onward supplies. No contractual agreements were entered into, however. The Commission took action against this strategy, claiming that a quasi-contractual agreement existed between Bayer and the suppliers, and that these bilateral arrangements infringed Article 81(1) EC. It should be noted that the Commission could not have condemned Bayer's apparent plan to control supplies as an abuse of a dominant position under Article 82 (ex 86) EC, as it found that Bayer only held a relatively small share of the relevant market.[28] Bayer has challenged the Commission's decision on the ground that its behaviour was purely unilateral, and so could not be caught by Article 81(1) EC.

The President of the European Court has so far agreed with Bayer and has suspended the Commission decision in interim proceedings in 1996. At the time of writing (February 2000), the Court still has not handed down its eagerly awaited judgment. If the Court adopts the same approach in its final ruling, this will certainly provide a useful signal to original manufacturers as to the legitimate scope of measures to monitor and eventually source supplies through particular distribution channels.

In the meantime the research-based industry has attempted to persuade the Commission to advocate the adoption of a block exemption regulation to cover industry agreements which sought to limit parallel trade. This proposal was submitted to the second 'Bangemann Round Table' in early 1998, a forum established by DGXV (now DG Enter-

---

[27] Case IV/M.555 [1995] OJ C65/4.
[28] [1996] OJ L201/1.

prise) of the Commission to examine the implications of parallel trade in pharmaceuticals and to investigate potential solutions. DGIV – the Commission's competition directorate – originally indicated its unwillingness to agree to a block exemption, and suggested a compromise based on individual exemptions and the eventual promulgation of guidelines. At the same time, however, it is clear that the Commission is of the view that a solution to the problem of parallel imports should be based on a strategy which is compatible with the principles of the common market rather than one which would lead to further distortions of competition. The Commission itself seems to favour a piecemeal approach which would be based on the setting up of an 'observatoire' to collect more rigorous data on how parallel imports affect the pharmaceutical industry, as well as increased efforts towards harmonising national price and profit control regulation on the basis of therapeutic similarities between products. A possible solution put forward by the Commission in the early Bangemann rounds was to encourage Member States to deregulate those segments of the market where in its view price regulation is no longer justified – for example in the over-the-counter (or self-medication) and generic (or out-of-patent) segments of the market. It should be noted, however, that Member States remain in principle free to determine selling methods of pharmaceutical products pursuant to Article 28 EC provided that imported products are not discriminated against (see, for example, *Commission* v. *Greece*[29]). The Commission's Communication of 25 November 1998 (COM(98) 588 final) on the Single Market in pharmaceuticals confirms that, despite the fact that the various parties involved, the Member States and the Commission have deliberated on the issue of pricing in three Bangemann round tables, little real consensus has been reached. The Commission's compromise is to persist with the market segments approach and to promote deregulation in the over-the-counter market as well as to stimulate competition in the 'out-of-patent' or generic market. As far as 'in-patent' medicines are concerned, the main thrust of policy would be to execute adequate stimulation for the research-based industry. The communication has been widely criticised by the industry – generic as well as research-based – and by the pharmacy profession. No further concrete action has resulted from the document.

Conclusion

The question of whether the European Commission should take a positive or a negative attitude to parallel importing is a much debated

[29] Case C-391/92 *Commissie* v. *Griekenland* [1995] ECR I-1621.

one. The Commission appears equivocal, accepting to a certain extent that the practice is an important stimulus to intra-brand competition, but at the same time expressing a certain sympathy towards the claims of the research-based industry that it must continue to receive adequate rewards to fund expensive research into new forms of treatment. At the same time, in so far as the cause of parallel imports is to be attributable to national divergence in price regulation, the Commission has little political or legal means, or even hope of either, to attack the problem at source.

Parallel imports continue to proliferate and so do the legal issues, most notably on matters of intellectual property law protection. The various cases which have come before the Court in recent years were seen as offering the Court the possibility of re-assessing its hitherto somewhat narrow if not strict approach to the use of patent, copyright and trade mark protection by the industry in its attempts to curtail the flux of low-priced drugs into higher-priced markets. It was argued that this was an outdated approach, governed by the dictates of market integration as opposed to the recognition of the legitimate role of intellectual property law. Given the relative success of the single market exercise, it was anticipated that the Court might change direction and give more weight to the latter factors. The Court did not react as some had clearly hoped, and confirmed its established approach.

The more recent case law reviewed here confirms that the Court is still set on its earlier course, but it could be argued that the reasons underpinning that continuity have nevertheless changed. Although the earlier case law centred on the overriding goal of removing barriers to trade and to securing a common or single market, the latest case law, especially the ruling in *Upjohn* in October 1999,[30] combines an emphasis on the need to secure market access for those importing pharmaceutical products into markets which still remain subject to a high degree of divergent national regulation with a strict emphasis on the principles of legal certainty. This latter principle is especially important in situations where minimal harmonisation has occurred, as is the case with certain aspects of the market authorisation procedure or with respect to trade mark law. The Court has proved reluctant to allow the respective Directives to be interpreted in such a way that subjective criteria could have a role to play and could be used to continue to partition markets along national lines. Note, however, that this has caused conflicting interpretations of the *Upjohn* rulings in the national courts. This approach is particularly evident in its interpretation of

[30] Case C-379/97 *Pharmacia & Upjohn SA v. Paranova A/S* [1999] ECR I-223.

Article 7 of the Trade Marks Directive, discussed above, and in its interpretation of Article 4 of the Directive 87/21 on the abridged licensing procedures. Both lines of cases certainly encourage parallel importing and with it intra-brand competition. As the Court itself has repeatedly emphasised, a solution to the source of parallel importation – continued divergent national price regulation – must be tackled by the Commission and the Council. In the interests of legal certainty as well as market access, it will not itself tolerate any special exemptions from the fundamental principles of free movement and competition.

Part II

European drug regulation

5 Data protection and abridged applications for marketing authorisations in the pharmaceutical industry

Ian Dodds-Smith

Introduction: research data in the pharmaceutical sector

Know-how is important to all businesses but particularly to the pharmaceutical industry. Industrial know-how has been described as 'substantial technological information relating to the whole or a part of a manufacturing process or a product, or to the development thereof, which is not in the public domain . . .'.[1] It is implicit in the description that the information has value.

Traditionally, patents have been the main method by which the pharmaceutical industry has been able to protect the fruits of its research and the industry has devoted a lot of effort, both in the United States and in Western Europe, to successful lobbying for patent term restoration. This was seen as necessary due to the delay in being able to exploit the products derived from research as a consequence of the need for national marketing authorisations. Within the European Community, the need for marketing authorisations was harmonised in 1965[2] and the time taken to obtain authorisations, when added on to the time taken to develop the product in the first place and generate the requisite data relating to efficacy and safety, often left companies with insufficient time to make adequate profits before the patent expired. Such profits are required not only to recoup the cost of investment in the product in question but also to cover the significant amount of unsuccessful product development that is a fact of life for all research-based companies. In general, the industry's case for protection was accepted as

---

[1] Commission discussion paper, 86/EM-1 on 'Treatment of Know-How Licensing under the Competition Rules'.

[2] Council Directive 65/65/EEC on the approximation of provisions laid down by law, regulation or administrative action relating to proprietary medicinal products OJ spec. edn 1965–6, 20.

being a strong one and in the European Community there came into being the principle of Supplementary Protection Certificates.[3]

However, whilst the European Court of Justice has noted that Supplementary Protection Certificates were aimed at 'the shortcomings of the system for protecting pharmaceutical research, which arise from the need to obtain marketing authorisations in order to make use of the innovation',[4] the Commission has long also recognised that in many commercial sectors know-how that is not patentable can have an economic value equal to or greater than that of patents. The pharmaceutical industry is no exception. The economic value of know-how increases as the development and exploitation of know-how becomes more complicated and costly. The Commission noted in 1986:

The large sums spent by industry on research and development are not necessarily directed at or likely to lead to patentable inventions. Research and development effort is mostly directed at problem-solving, and examples from several industrial sectors suggest that only about a quarter of research and development results end up in patent applications. Non-patented results can be a major determinant of firms' competitive advantage. With the pace of technological change, the possession of immediate access to the latest technology is the key to success in the market. This is especially the case in high-technology sectors.[5]

These considerations led the Commission to consider less favourable treatment of know-how licences than patent licences as unjustified under competition rules. However, the European regulatory process no longer provides any real protection for know-how *per se*, despite having added considerably to the cost of developing sufficient know-how to access the market quickly.

The pace of technological change in the pharmaceutical sector has been matched by the increasing sophistication of the regulatory control of the industry's activities. The costs of conducting research of a type capable of demonstrating (to the extent that any pre-marketing experience can demonstrate) the safety and efficacy of products has risen steadily and, although the figures quoted for the cost of researching new products vary significantly, they are undoubtedly in the hundreds of millions of pounds. Recent regulatory initiatives to harmonise the controls over clinical research in the EU can but add to the costs, and

---

[3] Regulation 1768/92 concerning the creation of a supplementary protection certificate for medicinal products [1992] OJ L182/1. For further details on the Supplementary Protection Certificate, see chapter 8 below.

[4] Case C-350/92 *Kingdom of Spain* v. *Council of the European Union* [1995] ECR I-1985 at §15.

[5] Commission discussion paper, 'Treatment of know-how licensing under the Competition Rules'.

the costs are also likely to rise as a result of demands for data relating not only to establishing efficacy and safety but also to cost effectiveness. Such pharmaco-economic data relate to clinical effectiveness relative to other treatment options and the relationship between the incremental benefit and cost, either generally or in specific patient groups. Such data are increasingly required before products will be reimbursed under State health systems. Recent initiatives in the UK under which new technologies are appraised by the National Institute for Clinical Excellence ('NICE') are based on the assumption that such data will be generated when pre-marketing trials are carried out.[6]

As the cost of research and the time required to bring it to fruition increases, so also does the attraction of finding a short cut to satisfying the demands of the regulatory process. Under European legislation, the abridged application for marketing authorisations constitutes such a short cut, and the rules have become the most litigated area of European pharmaceutical law. To the generic companies, they provide a means of accessing the market at very low cost once any patent has expired. To the research-based companies, they appear to be a mechanism for transferring for no cost to a potential competitor the fruits of expensive research that was never capable of patent protection. Not only is the research-based company faced with a competitor but with one who starts with a lower cost base to recover when pricing his products. Therefore, far from 'non-patented results' providing a competitive advantage, the 'playing field' is skewed in the other direction. Some changes have been made to the rules and others are the subject of lobbying, but the lay observer would find it hard to understand how a sophisticated market such as the European Community could enact law in such an important area that is so poorly drafted and ill-thought out in principle. The uncertainties it has created for regulatory authorities, and for both research-based companies and generic manufacturers, are the antithesis of the clear regulatory framework that all businesses need if the benefits that each type of company can bring to public health are to be exploited efficiently.

The basic legal framework

Directive 65/65/EEC sets out the basic framework for the grant of marketing authorisations at a national level. Article 4 notes that in order to obtain an authorisation to place a product on the market, the person seeking to market it must apply to the competent authority of

[6] See SI 1999/220 and SI 1999/260; Memorandum of Understanding of Appraisal of Health Interventions (NICE, August 1999).

the Member State concerned. His application must be accompanied by various particulars and documents, including (according to Article 4.8) the results of physico-chemical, biological or microbiological tests; pharmacological and toxicological tests (essentially animal data directed at safety); and clinical trials (demonstrating in humans efficacy in the relevant indication and a favourable benefit-to-risk ratio for that indication).

The only abridged procedure (i.e. the procedure that did not require the full testing data set out in Article 4) in the Directive as originally adopted, concerned circumstances where adequate data existed in the public domain. The full results of pharmacological and toxicological tests and clinical trials were not required where the application was for a product that had an 'established use' that could be substantiated by providing a list of published references. Such references would arise initially from the summaries of testing experience published by the innovator itself but also from the post-marketing studies and epidemiological research carried out and published by the medical and scientific community as a whole.

The extent to which research data are confidential to the company lodging them was not addressed in the Directive (and is still not directly addressed). However, most research-based companies would have assumed that the data submitted would only be used by the competent authorities to assess safety and efficacy, and thereby to discharge their duty of protecting public health; it was not contemplated that such data could be utilised directly by the authorities to make good the deficiencies in another person's application, thereby relieving that other person of the difficulties and cost of generating the same data himself. However, in 1984 the European Commission recognised the concept of indirect use of such data. It noted[7] that certain national authorities 'tended not to be too demanding' in their assessment of the adequacy of 'published references', even where data on safety and efficacy were incomplete (normally because the innovator had only published some of the results from its tests and trials and, even then, in limited detail). Of course, the competent authorities normally had the comfort of knowing that the full data lodged with the authority by the innovator had been deemed a sufficient basis for grant of an authorisation. The Commission noted:

This practice seriously penalises the innovating firm which has had to meet the high cost of clinical trials and animal experiments, while its product can be copied at lower cost and sometimes within a very short period. Protection of a medicinal innovation by means of a patent is not, in fact, always possible or effective, as for example in the case of a natural substance or of a substance

---

[7] COM(84) 437 final.

which is already known but on which additional research has been carried out with a view to a new therapeutic use.

The Commission argued that it was time to re-establish the normal principle for exemption, namely that the second applicant has the consent of the holder of the original authorisation to cross-refer to the research data that has already been lodged by the innovator with the competent authority. It, therefore, put forward a proposal to amend Article 4.8 of Directive 65/65/EEC.

The proposal to amend Directive 65/65/EEC

The proposal to amend the abridged procedures involved a tightening of the published literature exemption and a balancing provision that would allow the competent authorities to use data lodged by the innovator after the expiry of an adequate time during which the innovator could recoup the investment that he had made in carrying out the successful research underlying the application (and, by implication, the cost of research that did not result in marketable products). In this way, the approach had regard to the public interest because, just as the technology subject to patents ultimately becomes available for exploitation by others on the expiry of the patent, the Commission saw the danger of know-how being kept confidential for ever, rather than only for such period as could be justified as necessary to protect innovation. In order to avoid a company having the market in a particular product to itself in perpetuity, the Commission proposed that ten years after the product was first authorised in a particular country, a second applicant ought to be able to obtain an authorisation to market a copy of that product by cross-referral to the same data, even in the absence of consent. Clearly, within that period the innovator could always expressly consent to cross-referral to its data. After ten years, the Commission viewed the public interest as having shifted to the avoidance of repetitive testing in animals and humans.

On 22 December 1986, Directive 87/21 was enacted.[8] The second recital to Directive 87/21 noted that experience had shown that it was advisable 'to stipulate more precisely the cases in which the results of pharmacological and toxicological tests or clinical trials do not have to be provided . . . while ensuring that innovative firms are not placed at a disadvantage'. The fourth recital noted that there were 'reasons of public policy for not conducting repetitive tests on humans or animals

---

[8] Council Directive 87/21/EEC amending Council Directive 65/65/EEC on the approximation of provisions laid down by law, regulation or administrative action relating to proprietary medicinal products [1987] OJ L15/36.

without over-riding cause'. In its note on implementation, the Commission declared the Directive to be a harmonising measure with the primary aim of protecting innovation.[9] However, the Directive, as adopted, did not prove to be harmonising, either as to the protection period or as to the interpretation of its core provisions.

The provisions of Directive 87/21/EEC

The revised Article 4.8 of Directive 65/65/EEC provided three ways in which a second or subsequent applicant did not need to provide the results of pre-clinical or clinical research.

First, under Article 4.8(a)(i), he could show that he had the consent of the person marketing the original product to allow the competent authority to use the existing data on file for the purpose of assessing his application for an 'essentially similar' product. Such a route to a copy authorisation had always been possible, although it was not expressly mentioned in the legislation. At a practical level, it simply avoids the need for the applicant to obtain the data from the originator and present it with the second application. If the applicant is the originator, it avoids the need to refile data the authorities already hold.

The second possibility, under Article 4.8(a)(ii), was to present detailed references to published scientific literature demonstrating that the constituent or constituents of the product 'have a well established medicinal use, with recognised efficacy and an acceptable level of safety'. However, those references also had to be 'presented in accordance with the second paragraph of Article 1 of Directive 75/318/EEC'. Directive 75/318 sets out in detail the types of tests and trials that must be submitted to meet the requirements of Article 4 of Directive 65/65/EEC and specifies the information that must be available from those tests and trials. In its preparatory memorandum, the Commission had indicated that, following the adoption of Directive 75/318/EEC, the published literature exemption should already have been of very limited application as Article 1 of that Directive had required bibliographical evidence to correspond 'in like manner' to the detailed requirements for safety and efficacy in the Annex to that Directive. The published literature exemption would be of limited application because published literature seldom contains all such details. On one view, therefore, the tightening of the published literature exemption was achieved merely by re-emphasising in Article 4.8(a) the need for published literature to satisfy the detailed requirements of Directive 75/318. Another view,

---

[9] Note from the Services of the Commission on the consequences of the Entry into Force of Directive 87/21/EEC:III/B/6 of 29 July 1987.

however, was that by emphasising the need for a product to have a 'well established medical use', rather than just an 'established use', the Commission intended the exemption to apply only after the therapeutic profile of a product had become well established through long use. Given the proposal for ten-year 'market exclusivity' discussed below, the inference was that the requirement for well-established medical use would not be met for at least ten years – but that was not stated in the Directive.

The third possibility, under Article 4.8(a)(iii), was to await the expiry of the protection period proposed by the Commission in respect of an 'essentially similar' product. During the negotiations on the Commission's original proposal, various changes were made concerning the protection period that were not helpful to the research-based industry. The basic period of protection was fixed at six years and not ten years for all products. An exception was made for a product derived from biotechnology or which had been given the status of a high-technology product because of an added element of innovation or novelty. Both categories were seen as justifying ten years' protection. The sister Directive adopted at the same time (Directive 87/22/EEC) had proposed a more favourable regulatory regime for biotech and high-tech products that involved centralised assessment. Member States were not allowed to change the ten years' protection period for these products but were given more freedom in relation to the other products. A Member State could increase the period of protection to ten years for all products 'where it considers this necessary in the interest of public health' (which clearly emphasised the link between encouraging innovation and improving public health). Alternatively, a Member State could decide not to apply the six-year period beyond the expiry of a patent protecting the original product. The majority of Member States have accepted the need to grant protection independent of the patent position.[10]

However, the period of protection was finally set to run from the first authorisation anywhere in the European Community of an essentially similar product, rather than from the first authorisation in the country where the second application was being made (as had been the Commission's proposal). The burden was upon the second applicant to establish that his application concerned a product which had been authorised within the Community 'in accordance with Community provisions in force' for the required period. The second applicant also

---

[10] Ten-year protection has been given by the UK, France, Germany, Belgium, Italy, the Netherlands and Sweden. All the rest offer six years except Spain, Portugal and Greece which will not protect data beyond the life of a patent covering the product.

had to demonstrate that the 'essentially similar' product was marketed in the country of application. In the absence of such marketing there were clearly no data available to the competent authority against which it could assess the safety and efficacy of the product covered by the further application. Although the concept of an essentially similar product was present in both Article 4.8(a)(i) and (iii), the term was not defined in the Directive. Not surprisingly, this has created many difficulties.

It should be noted that, whilst the provisions of Article 4.8(a)(iii) have commonly been referred to as creating a period of 'market exclusivity', this description is inappropriate. The provisions do not create any monopoly in a particular product in the way that a patent excludes others from the market. The originator only maintains any exclusivity so long as the second applicant is not prepared to spend the time and money generating the data himself. If he does so, there is no difficulty in him entering the market, provided there is no subsisting patent. The application of the abridged provisions is expressly declared in the new Article 4.8 to be 'without prejudice to the law relating to the protection of industrial and commercial property'. The fact that a product is authorised following an abridged application does not, therefore, guarantee that it will not be the subject of patent infringement proceedings. The generality of this saving provision is such that one company sought to argue that, since research data on file were 'industrial and commercial property', the competent authorities in the UK should not be entitled to use the data on file without consent, even after the expiry of the ten-year period. This submission was accepted at first instance but an appeal was successful and the subsequent appeal by the innovator to the House of Lords was dealt with in peremptory fashion. This was perhaps not surprising given that the innovator's submission would effectively have undermined the whole purpose of the imposition of a data protection period.[11]

The published literature exemption: the Scotia litigation

Article 4.8(a)(ii)

Given that the amendment to the abridged procedures had arisen from an over-relaxed approach by the competent authorities to use of published literature, it was surprising that it became the first area for litigation following the adoption of Directive 87/21. This was par-

---

[11] *R* v. *The Licensing Authority, ex parte SmithKline & French Laboratories Ltd* [1989] 1 All ER 578.

ticularly so as the product at the centre of the litigation was as a natural product, containing gamolenic acid derived from evening primrose oil. This was precisely the type of situation where patent protection was unavailable and the Commission's preparatory materials had noted the importance of protecting the interests of the innovator. Evening primrose oil had been freely available in the UK for many years as a food supplement in the health food market. However, researchers at a small company called Scotia thought it might be effective in the treatment of atopic eczema and undertook a full testing programme of animal studies and clinical trials, albeit only after the competent authorities had made it clear that no exemption from safety testing was appropriate simply because the product had been used in the unregulated health food market as a dietary supplement. In 1988 the product was granted a marketing authorisation in the UK under the name Epogam®. Further research in the treatment of mastalgia followed and led to the grant in 1990 of an authorisation for a product with that indication under the brand name Efamast®.

The authorisation of Epogam® in the UK represented the first authorisation for the product for a medicinal purpose anywhere in the Community. Medical texts had hypothesised that various extracts of the evening primrose plant might have medicinal properties but nobody had undertaken research in accordance with European Community standards to demonstrate efficacy for any particular medicinal use. Scotia's investment was not much short of £20 million and was predicated on the basis that the data would be protected from cross-reference for ten years. It was, therefore, very concerned when, in 1992, an authorisation was granted to a generic company called Norgine for both the eczema and mastalgia indications. It transpired that Norgine had submitted its application only two years into the ten-year protection period but that it sought an authorisation pursuant to the published literature exemption under Article 4.8(a)(ii), rather than under Article 4.8(a)(iii). It relied upon the published summaries of Scotia's research results that the company or academic researchers who had worked on the product for Scotia had published in medical journals. Where data had not been published that met the requirements of the Annex to Directive 75/318, Norgine argued that the UK authorities could have regard to the long period of apparently safe usage of the product as a food supplement. On the basis that safety was not an issue, the company did not submit any expert report on toxicology. This was seemingly contrary to Directive 75/319/EEC which requires the data supplied pursuant to Directive 75/318/EEC to be supported by an expert report for both the toxicology element of the dossier and the clinical trial element.

Scotia sought judicial review in the High Court in England on the basis of a breach of European law by the UK authorities and obtained permission to bring its case. Having obtained permission (which will not be granted unless the Court is satisfied that the applicant's case is properly arguable) the company then applied for, and obtained, an injunction suspending Norgine's authorisation (and therefore its right to market) pending the outcome of the substantive hearing.

The High Court proceedings: well-established medicinal use

At that hearing the UK authorities sought to defend their position by saying that, despite the relatively short period of marketing of Epogam® and Efamast®, it was for the authorities to decide whether a product had a well-established medicinal use. As this was a matter of scientific judgement, it was argued that under the limited supervisory function of the courts in judicial review under English law, the Court was not in a position to set aside the judgement of the authority that the uses of the product were well established. As regards the lack of detailed research results in the published literature for certain of the tests and trials required by Directive 75/318, it was argued that the UK authorities had a discretion to waive any such requirement (and with it the requirement for an expert report) if, in its scientific judgement, the authority considered the availability of such data to be unnecessary in order for it to be satisfied that the product was safe and efficacious for the requested indications.

Scotia submitted extensive expert evidence (including evidence from certain academics who had previously sat on the committees advising the Licensing Authority in the UK) to the effect that by no stretch of the imagination could the use of gamolenic acid in the treatment of atopic eczema or mastalgia be considered as well established. On the contrary, such evidence demonstrated that the medicinal use of the products was controversial. Scotia had sought to utilise its UK authorisation for Epogam® as a basis for a multi-State application elsewhere in the EU, but some of the Member States to whom an application was made expressed themselves dissatisfied with the evidence. The UK authorities submitted no expert evidence and indeed it was not obvious from the documents disclosed by the Licensing Authority that the issue had been considered at all before Norgine's application had been granted. Interestingly, in Ireland the National Drugs Advisory Board subsequently rejected an application from Norgine made on the same basis, on the grounds that the product did not have a well-established use. However, the strategy adopted by the Licensing Authority in the UK was successful in that the Court, whilst expressing some misgivings about the matter, said that it must be a matter of scientific judgement and the Court could not substitute its judgement for that of the competent authority.[12]

The High Court proceedings: the availability of detailed research data in the literature

The Court accepted,[13] however, that it was plain on the face of the record that certain classes of animal data required by Directive 75/318 were missing from the published literature and those requirements were unqualified, in the sense that they did not incorporate any discretion to waive the requirements if the competent authority believed that relevant criteria were met. Moreover, in relation to the clinical data, although there were summaries in the literature, the data were found to be insufficiently detailed to meet the requirements of Directive 75/318. The absence of an expert report from a toxicologist was also noted as a *prima facie* breach of European law. However, the Court thought it appropriate to refer certain questions to the European Court. These focused upon the issue of whether there was any general discretion to waive the requirements of the Directive.

The European Court proceedings

In his Opinion of February 1995,[14] Advocate-General Léger set out a detailed review of the background to the abridged procedure and noted that the amendment to Directive 65/65/EEC addressed the 'social and economic context' of regulatory procedures rather than the direct protection of public health through the assessment of a product's safety and efficacy. Nevertheless, by encouraging the development of new medicines the measure would help achieve the primary objective of safeguarding public health. He noted that the second recital to Directive 65/65/EEC had referred indirectly to the protection of innovation but

---

[12] The traditional reluctance of the English court to enter into a fact-finding exercise in judicial review was subsequently an issue in a reference to the European Court in litigation concerning regulatory action taken against a hypnotic called Halcion® marketed by Upjohn. The European Court found that there was no rule of European law that required a specific approach to judicial review provided that the remedy remained a real one. See Case C-120/97 *Upjohn Limited* v. *Licensing Authority (established by the Medicines Act 1968 and others)* [1999] ECR I-223.

[13] *R* v. *Department of Health and Social Security and Norgine Ltd, ex parte Scotia Pharmaceuticals Ltd*, QBD Divisional Court 23 July 1993 (unreported).

[14] Case C-440/93 *R* v. *1. Licensing Authority of the Department of Health and 2. Norgine Ltd, ex parte Scotia Pharmaceuticals Ltd* [1995] ECR I-2851, Opinion A.-G. Léger.

that Directive 87/21 was directly concerned with that aim by reducing the discretionary margin enjoyed by national authorities. This was achieved, he said at paragraph 20 of his Opinion, by imposing both 'a stricter limitation on access to that type of procedure' and 'a highly specific and very strict definition of the conditions to be satisfied in order for the abridged procedures to be used'. He noted that the terms of the published literature exemption were highly restrictive and consistent with a legislative intention that minimal use should be made of the possibility in order that innovation should be protected. He also noted that in every case involving the abridged procedure, the application must concern a medicinal product that was a generic of the established product. He viewed the third exemption (essential similarity after a period of protection) as entirely consistent with the objective of recognising the economic context because it allowed the applicant for a generic copy to use the data lodged by the innovator only after that person had had adequate time to recoup the costs attaching to the development of his product and make a profit.

Although outside the strict terms of reference from the English court, the Advocate-General expressed the view that the published literature exemption should never have been used in the first place because the product was not well established. He viewed this as a question of law and not of fact or scientific judgement. He suggested that any other approach carried with it the risk of undermining the purpose of Directive 87/21. For similar reasons, he rejected the contention of the UK that the competent authorities had a general discretion to waive any requirements of Directive 75/318 and (as regards expert reports) Directive 75/319.

The European Commission's position was equivocal; whilst expressing some doubts about the correct position, it decided that the competent authorities were entitled to a limited discretion when deciding whether to apply the requirements of Directive 75/318 to a particular case. But at the hearing it said that it could not extend that discretion to a waiver of the requirement to present any expert report on toxicology at all.

In November 1995 the European Court itself[15] rejected the arguments advanced by the UK and found that the competent authorities had no discretion to waive the requirement for detailed data just because literature rarely provided such data. The Court found that this would run counter to the protection of public health and would also undermine the main aim of Directive 87/21 to protect innovation. The Court

---

[15] Case C-440/93 [1995] ECR I-2851.

emphasised that the abridged procedure 'in no way relaxes the requirements of safety and efficacy which must be met by medicinal products'
and that, in the case of the published literature exemption, it was
necessary for the applicant not only to demonstrate that the results of
the tests and trials listed in Directive 75/318 could be found in the
published literature, but also to present expert reports substantiating the
existence of the grounds for using published references described in
Article 4.8(a)(ii). In practice, therefore, the European Court was
requiring experts to substantiate that the product had a well-established
medicinal use.

Related proceedings in Ireland

Proceedings in Ireland were commenced by Scotia against Norgine in
April 1993, Scotia having been granted an authorisation for Epogam®
in the treatment of atopic eczema in 1990. Ireland has a six-year data
protection period, but an authorisation was granted to Norgine's
product in 1992. The relevant Directives had not been properly transposed into Irish law but the Court accepted that the Directives had
'direct effect'. However, although Norgine's application had been made
on the basis of the published literature exemption, the National Drugs
Advisory Board ('NDAB') had decided that the exemption was not
applicable because the use was not well established and had assessed the
application under the 'essentially similar' head of Article 4.8(a)(iii).
Unbeknown to Norgine, it had used, as a comparator product, a
product containing gamolenic acid the authorisation for which had been
granted more than six years before Norgine applied. That product had
been licensed in 1979 in the treatment of multiple sclerosis and surprisingly was still in force (parallel licences in the UK having been surren-
dered in the absence of efficacy data to EU standards). The NDAB
argued that safety could be established by reference to this comparator
and that efficacy could be established by reference to the published
literature reporting Scotia's clinical trials in atopic eczema. As regards
such trials, therefore, the same lack of detail in the published literature
was an issue between the parties.

When the basis of assessment became apparent (and the case points
to the need for some transparency in the process by which abridged
applications are approved), Scotia amended its application to argue that
an abridged application under the 'essentially similar' head of Article
4.8(a)(iii) was inapplicable. The comparator relied upon by the NDAB
had been licensed on the basis of toxicological data falling well short of
the requirements of Directive 75/318 and without submission of any

expert reports at all. As that authorisation had not been granted 'in accordance with Community provisions in force' there were no proper data available for assessment in substitution for the toxicological data that Scotia had submitted. The NDAB did not contend that it could refer to those Scotia data. As regards the clinical data, Scotia pointed to the absence of adequate detail and made the same case as had been made in the UK (although the issues were currently the subject of the reference to the European Court).

The Irish court expressed surprise that the competent authorities felt able to assess an application on a different basis to that upon which it had been put forward by the applicant, but for the purposes of the case it was prepared to assume that the NDAB had a discretion to decide whether an application could succeed on a different basis. Nevertheless, it found that the absence of safety data for the comparator, consistent with the requirements of the Directives at the time Norgine made its application, rendered that comparator invalid. The Court avoided any detailed analysis of the quality of the comparator data by making a finding based upon the disclosed documents that the NDAB had never in fact looked at the comparator file. The inference from all the evidence (which included cross-examination of relevant officials on their affidavits) was that the NDAB had assumed that gamolenic acid from evening primrose oil was safe and had relied substantially upon the published literature relating to Scotia's product.

Despite the pending reference to the European Court, the Irish court also found no difficulty in concluding that the clinical data were insufficiently detailed to meet the requirements of Directive 75/318. It also found that Article 4.8(a)(iii) did not contemplate the use of published literature. It found such literature inadmissible under that head of exemption on the basis that it could not be right that the condition precedent to use of published data under Article 4.8(a)(ii) – well-established medicinal use – could be avoided by using the same data under the 'essentially similar' head of exemption. The Court also found that the expert report requirements were mandatory and had been breached by the NDAB. Interestingly, the Irish court anticipated the later decision of the European Court by emphasising that the requirements for proof of safety and efficacy could not be relaxed under the abridged procedures, which simply provided that an authorisation could be granted when the particulars were available from a source other than the applicant, as long as the access conditions created by the Directive were in each case met.

Finally, the Court found that the NDAB was in breach of its general obligation to treat companies similarly placed in a consistent fashion.

The Board had sought safety data from Scotia in 1986 (rather than treat the relevant requirements as having been met by the prior authorisation of the evening primrose oil product now viewed as a valid comparator for Norgine's product) but had not sought such data from Norgine. The Court, therefore, ordered Norgine's authorisation to be quashed.[16]

German litigation concerning Epogam®

Outside the UK and Ireland, Norgine only obtained approval for its product elsewhere in the EU in Germany where an authorisation was granted in January 1994 on the basis of published literature. Additional authorisations were granted on a similar basis to other generic companies. Scotia applied to the Berlin Administrative Court for interim relief suspending the authorisations pending a full hearing. In its judgment of November 1995,[17] Scotia's applications were dismissed on the grounds that it had no standing to challenge a failure by the authorities to apply the abridged procedures properly. Scotia successfully appealed against that decision but the Court then held that data protection did not apply to a product unless it was authorised for prescription only. Although, to the extent that German medicines law drew any distinction, that distinction was not reflected in the requirements of Directive 87/21/EEC, as a final decision on appeal was unlikely to be available much before the expiry of the protection period in the EU (September 1998) Scotia abandoned their challenge on commercial grounds.

The decision of the Irish court and the subsequent decision of the European Court in relation to the ambit of the published literature exemption might reasonably have been viewed by research-based companies as likely to end any controversy concerning use of published literature as a basis for obtaining copy authorisations. However, within a relatively short period, similar issues arose in the Netherlands in relation to a product called Taxol. The Taxol litigation also raised the meaning of 'well-established medicinal use' which had not been resolved by the reference in the *Scotia* case to the European Court for the reasons described above. However, it was this litigation that finally encouraged the Commission to propose an amendment to the Directive that substantially clarifies the law.

---

[16] *Scotia Pharmaceuticals Ltd* v. *NDAB and Minister for Health and Norgine Ltd*, Barron J, 30 June 1995 (unreported).
[17] *Scotia* v. *The Federal Republic of Germany*, Berlin Administrative Court, 22 November 1995, A284.95, A323.95 and A460.95.

The Taxol litigation in the Netherlands

Bristol-Myers Squibb (BMS) obtained a marketing authorisation for Taxol in the Netherlands in September 1993. The active ingredient of Taxol is paclitaxel, a compound obtained from the bark of the yew tree. Paclitaxel was developed for use in oncology and BMS was able to satisfy the European authorities that the product was of significant Community interest within the meaning of Directive 87/22. As such, the application could benefit from the concertation procedure for assessment by the Committee for Proprietary Medicinal Products[18] (CPMP) and, if granted, the underlying data would have ten years' protection. BMS ultimately obtained indications in ovarian and breast carcinoma, but in October 1995 Yew Tree Pharma BV applied for an authorisation for its generic copy (Yewtaxan) using the published literature exemption, BMS having published summaries of much of its data.

The competent authorities in the Netherlands argued that the access criterion of 'well-established medicinal use' was already met because Taxol had quickly become standard therapy in its indications. Although the product had only been marketed for a relatively short time, its launch had been very successful and the authorities contended that the considerable level of prescription meant that the innovator had received an adequate payback on its investment much more quickly than would otherwise have been the case. The authorities saw no basis for treating 'well-established medicinal use' as established with the expiry of a particular period from first authorisation; rather curiously they referred to the need to inject into the assessment of whether the access condition was met some consideration of whether the product was 'of major relevance to society'. Many read into this comment the suggestion that the more important the product (and the more costly it might be to meet all relevant clinical needs in the community) the slower national authorities under budgetary pressures would be to protect the innovation of the originator.

As regards the question of the level of detail in the literature, the competent authorities in the Netherlands were adamant that a single and detailed publication had contained sufficient information. Whilst accepting that the public interest in encouraging the publication of results without this undermining the proper protection of innovation was a 'complicating factor', the authorities relied substantially on the single publication, saying:

[18] Created by Second Council Directive 75/319/EEC on the approximation of the provisions laid down by law, regulation or administrative action relating to proprietary medicinal products [1975] OJ L147/13.

BMS has made a major contribution to the state of the medical science. In 1996 the Journal of Clinical Oncology published a study of Nabhoetz et al. of paclitaxel. Without such publication it is unlikely that Yewtaxan would have been authorised or at any rate not without Yew Tree itself being required to do extensive clinical trials.

The matter first came before the courts on the application by BMS for an interlocutory injunction. The District Court of Utrecht issued its decision on 28 May 1997. Curiously, there was no reference at all in the judgment to the *Scotia* decision, despite the fact that this was by now supposedly the controlling authority within the European Community and BMS had inevitably relied upon it considerably. The Court found that the period of registration was not decisive if a product was 'sufficiently established' and extensive use for over eighteen months could meet the criterion of 'well-established medicinal use'. Despite the existing jurisprudence from the European Court, the Court found that a literal interpretation of the Directives, with the result that detailed references would be required, would rob the published literature exemption of any practical significance. However, Yew Tree's success was short lived.

On 22 April 1998 the substantive hearing took place and the District Court (which was a panel of three that included the judge who had ruled on the application for an interlocutory injunction) found that the *Scotia* judgment was directly applicable. It found[19] that the level of detail required in the published literature was lacking and this was consistent with the intention of the legislature that the bibliographical procedure was to be used 'by way of a rare exception only'. The Court decided that, given this finding, it was unnecessary to consider whether the access criterion of well-established medicinal use was met. It was probably significant that the European Commission took an active interest in the case, and its view that the generic application was invalid became known to the Court and probably carried considerable weight. Nevertheless, although it quashed the generic authorisation, Yew Tree appealed and the Court suspended its decision pending the outcome of that appeal. In the face of a substantial delay, a commercial settlement took place between BMS and Yew Tree and the appeal was vacated.

---

[19] Rechtbank Utrecht (Utrecht District Court) 22 April 1998, no. AWB 97/2552 BESLU, *Bristol-Myers Squibb BV* v. *Het College ter Beoordeling van Geneesmiddelen (Medicines Evaluation Board) and Yew Tree Pharmaceuticals BV* [2000] 1(5) *Jurisprudentie Geneesmiddelenrecht* 10.

Amendment of the published literature exemption

However, the European Commission rightly found the situation unsatisfactory. It was only a matter of time before the concept of 'well-established medicinal use' would be back before the European Court and relatively quickly the Commission proposed an amendment to the legislative provisions controlling the published literature exemption. The Commission was also aware of the fact that the strictness of the *Scotia* judgment was causing considerable difficulties to Member States in the context of approving products that contained compounds, which unquestionably satisfied the definition of well-established medicinal use. Much of the literature relating to such 'old substances' did lack detail and attempts by the CPMP to adopt a pragmatic approach to whether it was justified to subject all such old substances to the full rigours of current safety (animal) testing had foundered on the realisation that such an approach was inconsistent with the European Court's decision in the *Scotia* case. This was becoming a particular problem in the context of the mutual recognition procedures under which a company with an authorisation in one Member State could seek a comparable authorisation in another Member State, effectively by submitting the same dossier and asking the second Member State to recognise the validity of the assessment report of the first. In April 1996 the CPMP had sought comments on a proposal entitled 'Non-clinical testing of substances with long-term marketing experiences (old substances)'.[20] This document noted:

Non-clinical tests for old substances are often incomplete or not in accordance with today's state of the art. In order to obtain a better understanding of the inherent risks with such products and avoid procedures that delay the mutual recognition of old substances in the EU, it is necessary to state the minimum requirements of non-clinical testing. Well-presented results of clinical trials as well as post-marketing experience gained by widespread clinical use in humans . . . contribute to the avoidance of unnecessary tests in animals. Protection of animals should be taken into consideration when requesting non-clinical testing of old substances. Studies that do not agree with the current state of the art (e.g. GLP[21]-conformity) should be judged for credibility; subsequent demands that could lead to a 'blind' repetition of animal experiments should be avoided.

The Commission clearly recognised that the language of the original amendment to Directive 65/65, as interpreted by the European Court,

[20] CPMP/SWP/799/95 Rev. 4 of 18 April 1996.
[21] GLP is an acronym for Good Laboratory Practice.

satisfied nobody and had not achieved the harmonisation in assessment that had been sought. The Commission proposed to amend the Annex to Directive 75/318 by clarifying what constituted adequate evidence of safety and efficacy from literature sources. New sections were inserted in Part 3 of the Annex relating to pre-clinical research and Part 4 relating to clinical trials that make clear that the documentation submitted by the applicant must cover all aspects of the safety and efficacy assessments respectively and 'must include or refer to a review of the relevant literature, taking into account pre- and post-marketing studies and published scientific literature concerning experience in the form of epidemiological studies and in particular, of comparative epidemiological studies'. It is noted that 'particular attention must be paid to any missing information and justification must be given why demonstration of an acceptable level of safety [or of efficacy] can be supported although some studies are lacking'.

Whilst these provisions encourage a broad approach to demonstration of safety/efficacy, the recitals to the Directive note the 'increased speed of innovation and publication of innovation as well as the increasingly stringent requirements foreseen by Community pharmaceutical legislation for new medicinal products'. The possibility of discouraging innovative companies from publishing results of research as quickly as possible is noted and, therefore, the need to define the access condition of 'well-established use' for a bibliographical application is accepted. In consequence, the Directive lays down the factors that have to be taken into account in order to establish a well-established medicinal use. These are said to be 'the time over which a substance has been used, quantitative aspects of the use of the substance, the degree of scientific interest in the use of the substance (reflected in the scientific literature) and the coherence of scientific assessments'. Although different substances may, therefore, reach the threshold for well-established use after different periods, the legislation goes on to state that 'the period of time required for establishing a well-established use of a constituent of a medicinal product must not be less than one decade from the first systematic and documented use of that substance as a medicinal product in the EU'.

One can observe only that, had the original legislation been more clearly drafted and the obvious analogy been made between the ten-year period proposed by the Commission for an adequate protection period and the concept of 'well-established medicinal use', a great deal of frustration and cost would have been avoided for many companies and regulatory authorities. The Commission is to be applauded, however, for recognising that industry and regulators alike require clarity and certainty in the application of provisions of this nature and that the public interest in publication and in innovation could be effectively protected only by better defined legislation. It is to be hoped that the Commission will also ultimately recognise the inherent ambiguities and unfairness in the provisions surrounding the concept of 'essential similarity' under Article 4.8(a)(iii). To date, however, the Commission's approach has been ambivalent.

Article 4.8(a)(iii): the 'essentially similar' exemption

Introduction

It has been seen that where the conditions applicable to use of the published literature exemption cannot be met, in the absence of consent from the innovator to cross-refer to the data already lodged with the competent authority, the second applicant must either conduct his own tests and trials to demonstrate safety or efficacy or await the expiry of the protection period granted pursuant to Article 4.8(a)(iii). On the expiry of that period, the second applicant may require the competent authority to cross-refer to existing data on file from the innovator, provided he can demonstrate that his product is 'essentially similar' to a product already authorised for the applicable period in the EU 'in accordance with Community provisions in force' and that it is marketed in the country of application. If the product were not marketed in the country of application, the data required for assessment would not be available to the competent authority.

Rationale for Directive 87/21/EEC

The preparatory materials for the Directive referred to above emphasised the need to stipulate more clearly when abridgement of data particulars was allowed in respect of registration of copies of established products, so that the innovator was not prejudiced. Clearly, therefore, a balance is sought to be struck between competing interests. Although protection of public health is central to all the Directives, the protection of innovation is linked to public health; a Member State is given the option of extending the basic six-year period of protection to ten years 'where it considers this necessary in the interests of public health' (Article 4.8(a)(iii)).

Whilst seeking to protect innovation, the Commission also sought to define a long-stop date after which (as the Court of Appeal in *R* v. *Licensing Authority, ex parte SmithKline & French Laboratories Ltd* noted)[22] 'the balance swings towards the public interest, and the licensing authority will be entitled to use the originator's confidential data without the originator's consent, thus preventing further unnecessary tests on animals and humans'.

In the *Scotia* case, Advocate-General Léger reviewed the background to the amendment to the abridged procedures[23] and noted the various means by which the legislature had sought to address the economic context in which authorisations were granted. He expressed the view that protecting the interests of innovative firms was implicit in the second recital to Directive 65/65, which noted that regulatory control to protect health must be achieved by means which will not hinder the development of the pharmaceutical industry or trade in medicinal products. The pursuit of what he called the 'specific intermediate objective' of allowing innovators to profit from their investment was, he said, central to the new abridged procedures and an 'overriding economic necessity'. He added that this 'must be regarded as being complementary, essential and necessary to the attainment of the ultimate objective' of promoting the interests of public health.

Protection periods

However, the Commission had even had difficulty in getting agreement on the period of protection that was appropriate. Its original proposal of ten years for all products was ultimately dropped and in its place ten years was to be mandatory only for products of biotechnology or high technology products assessed by the CPMP through the Community procedure of concertation, established by the sister Directive 87/22/EEC.[24] For all other products, six years was to be the basic protection period, although, by way of derogation, not only could this be increased to ten years by Member States, but also it could be reduced so as not to apply beyond the date of expiry of a patent protecting the original product (now, as extended by any Supplementary Protection Certificate). Few countries do not provide at least six years' protection. The UK, Germany, France, the Netherlands, Belgium, Sweden and Italy have chosen a ten-year protection period; Ireland, Luxembourg, Denmark, Austria and Finland six years; and Spain, Portugal and Greece do not protect beyond the life of the patent. Nevertheless, the lack of harmonisation has been of increasing concern to industry and to

---

[22] [1990] 1 AC 64 at 84E.
[23] Case C-440/93 [1995] ECR I-2851 at §§18, 22, 23 and 37 in particular.
[24] [1987] OJ L15/38.

the Commission because of the potentially disruptive effect on the mutual recognition process.

The fact that the Commission dropped its proposal that the protection period should run from the date of first authorisation in the country of application immediately reduces the protection afforded to many research-based companies. This was highlighted by the outcome of a judicial review commenced in the UK by Monsanto plc surrounding the analgesic product Tramadol.[25] Tramadol had been developed by a German company in the 1960s and was out of patent. However, the data required to register it in Germany had not been as comprehensive as those ultimately required under EU pharmaceutical legislation. Monsanto licensed the product but realised that to gain approval in the UK further test and trial data would be required. This was developed at some cost but the application in 1990 to the Medicines Control Agency (MCA) was rejected and it was only granted in 1994 after substantial further research (costing about £17 million) had been conducted. Monsanto then established an important market for the product in the UK and, within a year of it obtaining its authorisation, applications for generic copies were prepared and the first was granted in 1996 for an identical product. These relied upon the existence of the German authorisation more than ten years before and the marketing of the 'essentially similar' product in the UK as country of application. There was no dispute about the test of 'essential similarity' – the products were identical. The authorisations were granted by the MCA under Article 4.8(a)(iii), with cross-reference to the Monsanto data on file.

Monsanto argued that the fact that the MCA had rejected the data supporting the German licence (indeed, even a dossier supplemented by Monsanto) demonstrated that the requirement of Article 4.8(a)(iii) that the ten-year authorisation must have been granted 'in accordance with Community provisions in force' was not met and, therefore, the Monsanto data were protected from cross-reference. It was accepted that the generic companies would not have been able to obtain authorisations unless and until Monsanto (or some other company) had incurred the considerable costs of research in obtaining first authorisation in the UK. However, the Court found that the legislation expressly contemplated the 'discrimination' and 'unequal treatment' that Monsanto alleged. Once the first authorisation was granted in a Member State on a full dossier, that opened up the potential for abridged applications if the

[25] *R* v. *Licensing Authority Established under the Medicines Act 1968, ex parte Monsanto plc* [1997] Eu LR at 42.

product had been authorised for the required period anywhere else in the EU, and it did not matter that the company applying in the UK was a different company from that which had had the benefit of the ten-year protection period.

Moreover, the Court found that the competent authority in one Member State could not be expected to examine whether the authorisation of the reference product, relied upon by the generic applicant in showing that the protection period had expired, had been approved in accordance with Community provisions. The provisions in question were those current at the date of original approval and the authority was entitled to rely upon the fact of registration ten years before, provided Directive 65/65 applied at that time and the authorisation had been renewed thereafter for ten years.[26] The Court did not accept that any interpretation of the Directive allowed the protection of the Monsanto data.

'Essential similarity'

It is clear that the protection attaches to approved products rather than compounds but the Directive did not seek to define the critical phrase 'essentially similar product'. Clearly, a number of medicinal products may have the same active constituent, but the data required under Directive 75/318/EEC to obtain a marketing authorisation will turn on the way in which the compound is presented in the market, including the amount (dose) of the active ingredient that it is recommended the patient should take, the dosage form (sometimes called pharmaceutical form), the route of administration and the proposed indication. A medicinal product is no more than the sum total of its characteristics. These characteristics are reflected in the provisions of Article 4a of Directive 65/65/EEC, inserted by Directive 83/570,[27] which notes that a Summary of Product Characteristics must be developed for all products and will include indications.

However, when the provisions of Article 4.8(a) of the Directive were being drafted, it is not clear whether the Commission attached any weight to the fact that between the time when a product containing a particular active ingredient is first marketed and the expiry of the protection period of six/ten years, that product may undergo consider-

---

[26] The case did lead the MCA to emphasise the need for continuous authorisation for the protection period: see MAIL 96 of July/August 1996.

[27] Council Directive 83/570 amending Directives 65/65/EEC, 75/318/EEC and 75/319/EEC on the approximation of provisions laid down by law, regulation or administrative action relating to proprietary medicinal products [1983] OJ L332/1.

able further development. New pharmaceutical forms are developed that may carry significant therapeutic advantages, e.g. modified release formulations. New dosage regimes may be researched, particularly for paediatric use. Importantly, products may be researched for new indications. Such incremental research carried out by pharmaceutical companies will rarely involve a substantial amount of pre-clinical work, as the existing toxicological profile of the compound, as established in animal tests for the first presentation of the product, will often provide adequate information for new dosage forms, doses and indications. However, new clinical work may be as extensive (if not more extensive) than that required to support the original indication. Indeed, the commercial and public health pressures encouraging early launch of new products mean that products are increasingly authorised with narrow indications which are thereafter extended when new clinical data become available.

The proposition that 'essential similarity' must involve consideration of the indications for the product is supported by the overall framework of the Directive. As, *prima facie*, complete compliance with the criteria for 'essential similarity' creates an exemption under both Article 4.8(a)(i) and (iii) from the need to supply additional data, it would seem to follow that an applicant seeking a different indication to that of the innovator, either where the innovator consents to his data being accessed or where data protection has expired, would have met the conditions of the exemption and would be entitled to an authorisation, even without its having presented data demonstrating the efficacy and safety of the proposed new indication.

Whilst it is clear that the requirement for 'essential similarity' is not synonymous with a requirement for identicalness, the characteristics that are taken into account in determining whether a product is 'essentially similar' are critical to the operation and implications of the provisions of Article 4.8(a)(iii). If 'essential similarity' is interpreted in a way that focuses only upon the active constituent(s) and physical presentation of a product, as opposed to all the characteristics of it that trigger new research requirements under Directive 75/318/EEC,[28] the authorisation of the first presentation of a product in the EU may start the clock ticking on a single data protection period. Thus, new data added subsequently, either to support variations or new applications for different products based upon the same compound, will enjoy pro-

---

[28] Council Directive 75/318/EEC on the approximation of the laws of Member States relating to analytical, pharmaco-toxicological and clinical standards and protocols in respect of the testing of proprietary medicinal products [1975] OJ L147/1.

tection only for such portion of the single protection period as remains unexpired at the date of such variation or new application.

Alternatively, if the first presentation of the product and the product referred to in the second application are to be treated as 'essentially similar' only where the data requirements for a presentation having the characteristics of that sought in the second application are met by the data lodged for the first product, then any significant variation of the product in the interim will carry with it protection of the underlying new data (not the older data) for a further period of six/ten years. Whether the authorisation to market a product with the changed characteristics is obtained through variation of an existing authorisation or by grant of an entirely new authorisation, the product with those characteristics will be treated as sufficiently different to be a reference product in its own right, rendering the exemption inapplicable, at least as to the data underlying the change. The second applicant would then be able to compete with the more advanced product in all its presentations and for all its indications only if he obtains the consent of the innovator to cross-refer to the incremental research data or develops his own data to bridge the gap between the data that is no longer protected and the data that remains protected.

Whilst the preparatory materials for Directive 87/21/EEC do not suggest that the change in the abridged procedures was motivated by the desire of the Commission to encourage the marketing of generics, over time there have been many ready to argue the public health benefits of improving generic competition. In *R* v. *Licensing Authority, ex parte SmithKline & French Laboratories Ltd*, the Court of Appeal stated[29] that the effective protection of public health 'demanded that medicinal preparations should be sold at reasonable prices'. Against this it should be noted that the pricing of products is dealt with by all Member States under separate legislation and it has never been an overt aim of the regulatory system to exert pressure on pricing of products. On the contrary, when assessing whether products should be authorised, Directive 65/65/EEC and Regulation 2309/93 (creating the centralised system of approval in the EU) expressly state that quality, safety and efficacy are the only relevant criteria and economic issues are to be left out of account.

In any event, the research-based industry argues that the burden upon the generic manufacturer to repeat any of the tests already carried out by the innovator will vary with the degree of difference in the authorisation sought, as compared with the characteristics of the six/ten-year-old

---

[29] [1990] 1 AC 64 at 77G.

authorisation. Where the innovator has spent a considerable sum on new research to establish a new indication, the burden on the generic manufacturer may be significant. Where, however, the innovator has merely been able to obtain authorisation for a different dosage by the submission of a modest amount of information, the burden on the generic manufacturer will be correspondingly small. It may be said, therefore, that the extent of the burden on the second applicant is directly proportionate to the investment made by the innovator.

Guidance of the CPMP on the concept of essential similarity

The absence of a definition of 'essential similarity' was despite the fact that, when considering the proposal for a Directive in 1986, a Council of Ministers Working Party had developed a working definition of essential similarity that was reflected in the Minutes of the Council. This focused upon the physical form of the product, stating that a product is 'essentially similar' to another if: '(i) . . . it has the same qualitative and quantitative composition in terms of active principles; and (ii) the pharmaceutical form is the same; and (iii) where necessary, appropriate bio-availability studies have been carried out'. This was, in practice, the working definition used by Member States but soon there was recognition of its shortcomings.

Further discussion gave rise to CPMP guidance that was published in 1992 and subsequently incorporated in a revised edition of the Notice to Applicants of 1993. The Annex to Directive 75/318 requires the Notice to Applicants to be used in the interpretation of the relevant Community requirements.[30]

The 1993 edition of the Notice to Applicants (which was current at the time Generics UK applied for the authorisations that led to the landmark decision on 'essential similarity' of the European Court of Justice (ECJ) in 1998, discussed below) defined (in paragraph 3.2.3) an essentially similar product as one: 'made by more than one manufacturer *for the same therapeutic use*, interchangeable with, and with compar-

---

[30] See introduction to the Annex to Directive 75/318 on the approximation of the laws of Member States relating to analytical, pharmaco-toxicological and clinical standards and protocols in respect of the testing of medicinal products, as amended by Commission Directive 91/507/EEC [1991] OJ L270/32:

The particulars and documents accompanying an application for marketing authorisation pursuant to Article 4 of Council Directive 65/65/EEC shall be presented in four parts, in accordance with the requirements set out in this Annex and taking account of the guidance published by the Commission in the Rules governing medicinal products in the European Community Volume II: Notice to Applicants for marketing authorisations for medicinal products for human use in the Member States of the European Community.

able bioavailability to, a medicinal product which has been authorised in the Community for 6/10 years and which is marketed in the Member State concerned' (emphasis added).

The idea that indications must form some part of the analysis of 'essential similarity' was also supported by the Advocate-General in his Opinion delivered in the *Smith and Nephew* case[31] concerning the grant of parallel import licences. The Advocate-General, at paragraph 19, stated:

According to its ordinary meaning 'similar' refers to things that are comparable to one another, that is to say, that they may be regarded as being alike. I would therefore say that medicinal products are similar if their characteristics and methods of manufacture do not display any significant differences. Article 4a of Directive 65/65 lists the characteristics of a medicinal product.

The English courts have not had cause to define the concept in detail. In *R* v. *Licensing Authority, ex parte SmithKline & French Laboratories Ltd*[32] the Court of Appeal defined the concept in the following manner: '. . . the very word "similarity" implies comparison, and "essential" that there is no difference which is of material importance'.

The concept of essential similarity was also considered by the Italian courts in 1992 in a case brought by Sandoz against the Ministry of Health regarding a product called Tonacalcin. The short report of the case merely notes that the Court found that a spray presentation of a product could not be essentially similar to an injectable one and that in consequence an abridged procedure was inapplicable. Whilst this may well be correct, the decision lacks any detailed reasoning.[33]

In the context of the protection of research data, it could be argued that a difference will be material where it gives rise to an additional data requirement, but the concept was not germane to the central issue in the *SmithKline & French* case because it was common ground that the ten-year period had expired. The issue was not whether the copy product was essentially similar to the SmithKline product, but whether the saving provision appearing at the beginning of Article 4.8 (that the exemption for providing the relevant test and trial data was 'without prejudice to the law relating to the protection of industrial and commer-

---

[31] Case C-201/94 *R* v. *The Medicines Control Agency, ex parte Smith and Nephew Pharmaceuticals Ltd and Primecrown* v. *The MCA* [1996] ECR I-5819, per Advocate-General Léger.

[32] *R* v. *the Licensing Authority, ex parte SmithKline & French Laboratories Ltd* [1990] 1 AC 64 at 86G–H per Staughton LJ.

[33] *Sandoz* v. *The Ministry of Health and Schiapparelli Searle*; TAR Lazio, Section 1, 218, 22 February 1992; *Sandoz* v. *Ministry of Health* (*Il Repertorio del Foro Italiano*, 1992, 506–10). An identical decision was issued on the same day in the related case of *Menarini* v. *Ministry of Health and Pulitzer Italiana* regarding a product called Rulicalcin.

cial property') created a further potential hurdle at national level to the utilisation by the competent authority of the data submitted by Smith-Kline in assessing the application of the generic company. The innovator was successful at first instance, but not in the Court of Appeal, which understandably noted that such an interpretation would undermine the whole rationale for a ten-year protection period under Directive 87/21. The House of Lords reached the same conclusion as the Court of Appeal but by a different route.[34]

In summary, therefore, there are conflicting implications of the decision as to what characteristics are to be taken into account in defining 'essential similarity'. On the one hand, if companies marketing generics are entitled to access at no cost valuable research data recently lodged with the competent authorities, the incentive for research-based companies to incur the costs inherent in developing new and improved products based upon the same active ingredient is reduced or extinguished (which would be contrary to a main aim of the Directive). When, in 1987, the Commission issued a note on the consequences of Directive 87/21/EEC[35] it stressed that 'the fundamental aim of the Directive is to improve the protection of innovation'. As very often patents will protect the innovation during the first ten years from its launch, data protection becomes commercially meaningless unless it encourages and protects incremental research carried out on known substances.

On the other hand, granting protection to all new incremental research data might mean that generic companies would need to repeat a significant amount of research if they wished to compete head on with the most advanced form of the product before the expiry of the protection period. This, it is said, would undermine another principle underlying Directive 87/21 which is that there must come a point at which the avoidance of repetitive animal and human testing takes precedence over the interests of the innovator in keeping its data confidential. In practice, generic companies argue that enabling them to compete effectively with the innovator's most recent product presentations brings down prices and that this in turn benefits public health by releasing funds for investment in other health initiatives.

Ultimately, therefore, the issue becomes a political one – the precise balance to be struck between encouraging innovation and, through it, improvements in public health, as against avoiding repetitive testing,

---

[34] *R* v. *Licensing Authority, ex parte SmithKline & French Laboratories Ltd* [1990] 1 AC 64.
[35] Note from the Services of the Commission on the Consequences of the Entry into Force of Directive 87/21/EEC, 111/8/6 29.07.1987 Rev. 3 at para. 2.

promoting competition through increased generic penetration of the market and with it a reduction in prices.

The Generics UK litigation

Background

In many ways it is surprising that the lack of clarity in this provision did not lead to substantial litigation earlier than was the case. Some say that this was because in practice the competent authorities in many Member States continued to protect new indication data lodged by innovators and data underlying other significant changes in presentation.[36] Others note that, despite the cost of developing clinical data to support new indications, prescriptions do not specify the condition prompting the prescription and, therefore, if prescriptions are written generically, data protection for new indications is illusory anyway. Whilst this may have reduced the interest of some companies to seek to litigate the issue, for companies researching new indications for compounds already marketed independently by others and out of patent, the importance of data protection had always been acute. Moreover, the overall increase in, and importance of, incremental research in the 1990s undoubtedly increased the sensitivity of all research-based companies. The introduction of compulsory patient package leaflets through Directives 89/318 and 92/27[37] also increased the significance of the specific indications approved for particular products. As the leaflets had to reflect the licensed indications and the prescribing information relevant to such indications, doctors realised that patients might be confused if information relating to the condition for which they were being treated did not appear in the leaflet they received because they had received a product that had not been authorised for all the indications of the innovator. As with the published literature exemption, it was the English court that was first called upon to consider the difficult issues.

Generics (UK) Limited ('Generics') is a major manufacturer of generic products in Europe and it was its applications for copy authorisations in respect of three major products due to go out of patent that prompted a reference to the European Court on the critical issue of how

---

[36] See, for instance, protection of new indications discussed in A. C. Cartwright and B. R. Matthews, *Pharmaceutical Product Licensing, Requirements for Europe* (New York: Ellis Horwood, 1991) at para. 6.6.4, and D. B. Jeffreys, 'Medicinal Issues in the Assessment of Abridged Applications' (1989) 8(3) (supplement) *British Institute of Regulatory Affairs Journal* at 10.

[37] Council Directive 92/27/EEC of 31 March 1992 on the labelling of medicinal products for human use and on package leaflets [1992] OJ L113/8.

'essential similarity' should be defined. Between 1993 and 1995 it made applications for copies of Capoten® (captopril) manufactured by Bristol-Myers Squibb and for Zantac® (ranitidine) and Zovirax® (aciclovir) manufactured by Glaxo Wellcome. Capoten® had been the subject of intensive further research by BMS for new indications. Several variations had been granted in the last years of patent protection. The same applied to Glaxo Wellcome's products but, unlike the BMS product, these products had also been the subject of some changes in the available strengths of the products and in the recommended dosage schedule. The common feature, however, was the new indications and, as the case developed, the attention focused on the status of the data underlying new indications as illustrative of the principle in issue.

Generics made applications well before the expiry of the patent in order that it would be in a position to launch the products immediately the patent expired. By the time the applications were made, the changes in the environment mentioned above, coupled with the renewed interest in data protection that the *Scotia* case had prompted, had led research-based companies and competent authorities to revisit their interpretation of the relevant legislation. With some force, the Medicines Control Agency has noted that if it interpreted the meaning of 'essential similarity' narrowly it was likely to be sued by the research-based company seeking to protect the investment in its data, and if it interpreted the provisions of the Directive broadly it was likely to be sued by the generic company, which might see little point in seeking to compete with the innovator with a presentation of the product that was less sophisticated than that which the innovator was currently promoting.

Initially, the MCA decided to grant authorisations only for indications in respect of which ten years had elapsed since first authorisation within the EU. Generics then threatened to challenge that approach and the MCA reviewed its position once more and developed a policy that focused upon whether or not a change in a product represented a major change. In deciding whether a change was major, the MCA had regard to whether administratively a new application would be required (as opposed to a variation) under Annex II to Commission Regulation (EC) 541/95.[38] It took the view that it was difficult to defend as fair a position where data underlying fundamental changes in a product, such as the research of a major new indication, would gain no protection. Accordingly, in the absence of any other dividing line apparent in the legislation, it considered that, on a pragmatic basis, the Variation Regulation

---

[38] Commission Regulation 541/95/EC concerning the examination of variations to the terms of a marketing authorisation granted by a competent authority of a Member State [1995] OJ L55/7, hereafter referred to as the Variation Regulation.

could be applied to determine whether the fruits of new research could benefit from their own protection period.[39]

The MCA developed its national policy only after it became clear that there was no consensus within the Member States, as reflected in the lack of agreement within the Pharmaceutical Committee (a committee of representatives of Member States and the Commission established to consider the workings of the regulatory system and new legislative proposals). The practice of other Member States varied enormously: countries such as Denmark granted no additional protection for any new presentations of a product, while countries such as Germany *de facto* protected the data underlying major changes and in particular new indications. German law had been amended prior to Directive 87/21 by a change to the German Drug Law in 1986. This effectively protected all new data included in an application that, when granted, would concern a product subject to prescription-only status. Any product that represented a material change to what had gone before automatically gained prescription-only status, reflecting the lack of experience with the product.

Others adopted a half-way house; Sweden adopted the UK approach pending the resolution of the *Generics* litigation.[40] The European Commission's position was that new data reflecting major therapeutic innovation 'should legitimately enjoy the same protection as any new medicinal product'. However, it seemed to find it as difficult to define what constituted 'major therapeutic innovation' as it was to define what constituted an 'essentially similar' product. It said, without elaboration, that such innovation was likely to arise 'chiefly' in the area of new indications,[41] a stance which was reflected in the draft 1998 revision to the Notice to Applicants. This suggested that the competent authorities should approach products 'on a case-by-case basis' considering first, whether the level of innovation was such that the change would have been sufficient to justify an application under the centralised procedures[42] and second, whether the innovation had been patented.

Under Directive 87/22/EEC, biotech products, although authorised nationally, could only be so authorised after centralised assessment and the issue of an opinion by the CPMP (the 'concertation procedure'). As noted earlier, products subject to this procedure gained ten years' data protection across the whole Community. This concertation procedure

---

[39] The policy was notified in MAIL 92 of November/December 1995.
[40] Medical Products Agency 581: 1491/96 Circular 011 of 12 March 1996.
[41] Pharm 113 of 1996 entitled 'Interpretation of Article 4.8(a)(iii) of Dir. 65/65'.
[42] For further details of the European marketing authorisation procedures, see chapter 6 below.

was also allowed for other products that were sufficiently high tech that the CPMP was prepared to entertain concertation under Part B of the Annex to the Directive. The innovative element was viewed as creating a Community interest that justified a level of centralised assessment. Directive 87/22/EEC has now been overtaken by Regulation 2309/93 which has converted the principle of concertation into a fully centralised authorisation. Products of biotechnology and related processes contained in Part A of the Annex to the Regulation have to be authorised through the centralised procedures, and an extended list of criteria for high-tech products is contained in Part B. For these Part B products, on the application of the innovator, the CPMP will determine whether the Community interest justifies a centralised authorisation. In such a case, the innovator will gain ten years of protection for the data, in the same way as for a product of biotechnology.

The Commission's approach ignored the fact that one of the reasons for Directive 87/21 was that patents were an inadequate protection of innovation in this field. Clearly, the MCA did not find the Commission's approach to be easier to defend and apply than the criteria set out in the Variation Regulation, which at least had the benefit of representing criteria rooted in legislation, albeit not legislation expressly concerned with the application of Article 4 of Directive 65/65.[43]

Applying the Variation Regulation, the MCA decided that Generics should be granted an authorisation that reflected some but not all of the current indications for Capoten and all of the indications attaching to, and the changes illustrated by, the most recent presentations of the two Glaxo Wellcome products. Generics rejected the MCA's approach and commenced judicial review proceedings against the MCA in relation to its refusal to grant all Capoten indications. As it was directly affected by this judicial review, BMS intervened. Glaxo Wellcome commenced its own proceedings against the MCA's decision not to protect any of its underlying data and Generics intervened in those proceedings. All relevant proceedings were consolidated. There was no substantive hearing before the English court. The parties agreed that, as the litigation could not be resolved without clarification of the law by the ECJ, there should be an immediate reference to the ECJ. The English High Court agreed that such a reference was appropriate and its reference set out a series of questions relating to the protection of data for new indications and changes in dosage forms, doses and dosage

---

[43] Annex II is expressly stated to be without prejudice to the provisions of Article 4 of Directive 65/65, and a Commission Regulation cannot be applied in a way that effectively renders it an amendment to a Council Directive.

schedules. The starting point, however, was a request that the ECJ define an 'essentially similar' product.

The submissions of the parties

In its written submissions Generics, not surprisingly, focused upon the definition of 'essential similarity' contained in the minutes of the Council of Ministers. It argued that indications were irrelevant to a definition which looked at the physical composition and characteristics of the product. It also submitted that a central aim of Directive 87/21 was to facilitate the approval of generic copies and to avoid repetitive testing and that innovation was adequately protected by patents and Supplementary Protection Certificates. In contrast, the research-based companies argued that the preparatory materials that explained the Commission's rationale for Directive 87/21 conceded that patent protection was inadequate to protect research underlying new indications developed for known compounds. Accordingly, it was said that the concept of 'essential similarity' should bear a purposive meaning and that, when comparing the generic applicant's product with a product authorised for six/ten years in the Community, the therapeutic use approved should be taken into account, consistent with the references to 'therapeutic use' in the Notice to Applicants of 1993.

Both the UK and the Commission espoused the middle ground, with the UK arguing that the definition of the Council of Ministers that focused upon the physical characteristics of the product was 'a necessary, but not sufficient, criterion' and that the data underlying significant changes to a product ought to be protected in order that innovation was not stifled. The UK continued to suggest that the Variation Regulation provided some 'inspiration' in this regard but it had now begun to recognise that the manner in which the Regulation distinguished between minor and major changes in indication was unsatisfactory. The Regulation refers to the Anatomical, Therapeutic and Chemical (ATC) classification which was developed by the WHO to categorise drug usage by therapeutic area and has no real regard to the significance of changes or the data requirements to obtain approval. The Commission did not accept that the Variation Regulation was a useful tool in interpreting Article 4.8, but did accept the need to provide a further protection period for some innovation.

Neither the UK nor the Commission pretended that the language of the Directive itself supported the middle ground and the research-based companies pointed out that subjective decisions on what was, and what was not, sufficiently innovative to qualify for additional protection presented many difficulties. Not only would such an approach lead to different decisions among Member States which could give rise to problems in mutual recognition, but in addition it was wholly unsatisfactory for companies to pursue a research initiative not knowing whether the resulting products would later be judged to be sufficiently innovative to justify data protection. There was also a question mark as to when such an assessment should take place, as there were many examples where it had taken many years before the full implication for public health of new products had been demonstrated. Despite the importance of the issues, of the Member States only France, Denmark and Sweden made any written submissions. Norway, as a member of the EEA, also made submissions.

The oral hearing and Advocate-General's Opinion

At the oral hearing on 11 December 1997, the parties reiterated their positions and the President of the Court made it clear that the tribunal found the case a very difficult one. The Advocate-General, Mr Ruiz-Jarabo Colomer, delivered his Opinion very soon afterwards on 27 January 1998. He conceded that the Directive provided 'no direct and clear answer' to the questions that were the subject of the reference.[44] He noted that conflicting objectives were pursued by the Directive and sought to distinguish between the definition of 'essential similarity' (where he found the minutes of the Council of Ministers persuasive) from the overall interpretation that would create 'the best possible balance' between the competing objectives. On this basis, he found it 'advisable to apply the six or ten year protection period to all new indications of considerable importance, authorised for an original medicinal product essentially similar to a generic medicine or product'.[45] In deciding whether a new indication was of 'considerable importance', he encouraged the Court to follow the Commission's proposed criteria, to which he added a further requirement that account should be taken of the scope of the tests and trials required of the innovator to discover and gain approval for the indication.[46] He dismissed the Variation Regulation as non-contributory, as it did not distinguish adequately between major variations of considerable therapeutic importance and those that were less important. As the Regulation was expressly stated to be

---

[44] Case C-368/96 *R* v. *The Licensing Authority established by the Medicines Act 1968 (acting by the Medicines Control Agency), ex parte Generics (UK) Ltd*; *R* v. *Same, ex parte Wellcome Foundation Ltd*; *R* v. *Same, ex parte Glaxo Operations UK Ltd and Others (E. R. Squibb & Sons Ltd, Generics (UK) Ltd, intervening)* [1999] ECR I-7967; [1999] 2 CMLR 181, A.-G. Opinion at §42.

[45] *Ibid.* at §54.   [46] *Ibid.* at §60.

without prejudice to Article 4 of Directive 65/65, he thought that the MCA's reliance upon it was misconceived.[47]

The Advocate-General dismissed, in rather cursory fashion, the suggestion that research underlying new dosage forms/routes of administration, doses and dosage schedules could attract its own period of protection. He suggested that such changes did not 'require significant research deserving of special protection, because the innovation involved in those modifications is of little significance'.[48] As the focus of the written and oral submissions had been upon new indications, the research-based companies were sufficiently concerned by the unqualified dismissal of research in these other areas to ask that the hearing be re-opened. The Court did not re-open the hearing, but its treatment of non-indication changes may have been more tentative as a result of this intervention.

Decision of the European Court

Essential similarity

The Court's decision was delivered in December 1998 and was relatively short. It did not address the arguments and counter-arguments in any depth and there was virtually no discussion of the specific rationale for Directive 87/21. The Commission's memorandum of 1984, which had prompted the Directive, was not mentioned. The Court clearly felt that the language of the Directive did not really assist in defining 'essential similarity'. In interpreting the concept, the Court emphasised the fact that the definition must be one which optimises the protection of public health and it reiterated its statement in the *Scotia* case that the abridged procedure could not be interpreted as a relaxation of the normal requirements concerning demonstration of safety and efficacy.[49] Accordingly, the definition must be one that points to identicalness or differences that are sufficiently minor that the products concerned would not have a significantly different safety or efficacy profile.[50] Whilst noting that the minutes of the Council were not legally binding, on this occasion, it suggested that they should be treated as persuasive, particularly as the draft Notice to Applicants of 1998 now referred to the same definition.[51]

In its formal answers on the reference, the Court declared that two products, when compared, will only be 'essentially similar' if they satisfy

---

[47] *Ibid.* at §62. [48] *Ibid.* at §60. [49] *Ibid.* at §22. [50] *Ibid.* at §24.

[51] *Ibid.* at §§26–8. Curiously, the draft 1998 version of the Notice to Applicants put before the Court now omitted the statement in the 1993 version that the products had to be interchangeable to the extent of being marketed for the same therapeutic use.

three central criteria, namely that they have the same qualitative and quantitative composition in terms of active principles; have the same pharmaceutical form; and are bio-equivalent.[52] The Court added one rider to this definition, having noted that the CPMP had accepted that other changes in a product (e.g. in excipient) could affect safety or efficacy. The Court found that satisfying the three main criteria was not sufficient if 'it is apparent in the light of scientific knowledge that [the medicinal product satisfying those criteria] differs significantly from the original product as regards safety or efficacy'.[53] The Court added that the competent authorities have no margin of discretion in determining the criteria to be applied.[54]

New indications

The Court refused to entertain any foray into judicial lawmaking that adoption of the middle ground put forward by the MCA and the Commission (and supported by the Advocate-General) would have involved. The Court recognised that the answer to the question of how one defines 'essential similarity' automatically determined whether data, added to a file after first authorisation in the EU, are protected or not. As the definition put forward by the Council of Ministers and adopted by the Court took no account of indications, there could be no protection of the data underlying new indications.[55] The possibility of granting further protection for 'major therapeutic innovation' was found to be unsupported by the language of Article 4.8(a)[56] and the Court noted that such an imprecise test would 'tend to undermine the principle of legal certainty'.[57] It is interesting to note that, in July 1998, Mr Justice Collins heard another case of judicial review in the English High Court that concerned Article 4.8(a)(iii).[58] He also suggested that further data protection should arise if a varied product had a different 'therapeutic value' from the original product. This reasoning for the decision (which also involves subjective judgements) is now questionable in the light of the ECJ's decision, although it implicitly recognises

---

[52] *Ibid.* at §36. The investigation of bioavailability and bioequivalence is discussed in guidance from the CPMP (III/54/89 – EN final December 1991) and new guidance was circulated for comment to the EMEA in December 1998 (CPMP/EWP/QWP/1401/98 draft) but has not yet been finalised.

[53] Case C-368/96 *R* v. *The Licensing Authority established by the Medicines Act 1968 (acting by the Medicines Control Agency), ex parte Generics (UK) Ltd; R* v. *Same, ex parte Wellcome Foundation Ltd; R* v. *Same, ex parte Glaxo Operations UK Ltd and Others (E. R. Squibb & Sons Ltd, Generics (UK) Ltd, intervening)* [1999] ECR I-7967; [1999] 2 CMLR 181 at §36.

[54] *Ibid.* at §37.   [55] *Ibid.* at §§42–4.   [56] *Ibid.* at §47.   [57] *Ibid.* at §48.

[58] *R* v. *MCA, ex parte Rhône-Poulenc Rorer Ltd and Others*, QBD 10 July 1998, unreported.

the need to strike a fairer balance between the interests of the innovator and those of the copier.

Perhaps a clue to the rather limited examination of the issue by the European Court is to be found in paragraph 52 of the judgment, where the Court pointedly notes that, if it is thought appropriate to reinforce protection of innovation, this can only be properly achieved in a harmonised fashion throughout the EU by the legislature.[59] Some commentators have suggested that the Court was clearly frustrated by the limited assistance given to it by the text of the Directive and baulked at the extensive rewriting that would be required in order to strike a better balance between competing interests. Rather than embark upon such lawmaking, by adopting the definition of the Council of Ministers, the Court was pointedly handing back the issue to the legislature for resolution.

New dosage forms and doses

It has been noted that the parties used the issue of new indications added to an authorisation within the six/ten-year period to illustrate the issues, and that changes in other characteristics of the product were not explored in any real depth. The Court made no attempt to define these other characteristics of a product, but determined that, where the generic application concerned a medicinal product, which on the Court's definition was 'essentially similar' to a product authorised for six/ten years, the applicant could be granted all dosage forms, doses and dosage schedules already authorised for the originator product.[60] However, this raises the question of whether differences in dosage form or dose between the applicant's product and the product authorised for six/ten years will exclude a finding of 'essential similarity' in the first place. This is recognised by the Court: 'Assuming that the terms dosage form, dose and dosage schedule as used by the national court do not preclude essential similarity between the medicinal products in accordance with the definition adopted in paragraph 36 of this judgment, the third question is identical, *mutatis mutandis*, to the second question [concerning new indications].'[61] The fact that the questions set out in the reference were agreed between the parties in the absence of a hearing on the basis of the types of changes to products described in the Notice to Applicants, meant that the Court had not sought to define the

---

[59] Case C-368/96 *R v. The Licensing Authority established by the Medicines Act 1968 (acting by the Medicines Control Agency), ex parte Generics (UK) Ltd; R v. Same, ex parte Wellcome Foundation Ltd; R v. Same, ex parte Glaxo Operations UK Ltd and Others (E. R. Squibb & Sons Ltd, Generics (UK) Ltd, intervening)* [1999] ECR I-7967; [1999] 2 CMLR 181 at §52.

[60] *Ibid.* at §56.   [61] *Ibid.* at §55.

terms used in the reference. However, the quantitative composition in terms of the active principles is defined by Directive 75/318/EEC as a reference to dose/strength of the active ingredient.

Pharmaceutical/dosage form is not defined in the Directive, but the Notice to Applicants explains the need to follow the Standard Terms document of 1996 (amended in 1998) issued by the Council of Europe.[62] This lists many variants of pharmaceutical form, with a view to ensuring that the description properly reflects the characteristics of a particular presentation. It describes the pharmaceutical form of a product as a combination of the form in which a product is presented by the manufacturer (form of presentation) and the form in which it is administered, including the physical form (form of administration). The standard terms are regularly updated on application by competent authorities to reflect the development of more sophisticated pharmaceutical forms. Where a product has special characteristics relevant to its use, these are to be included in the term and it is noted that the Summary of Product Characteristics may require a more detailed expression of the form than does the label. The definitions in the 'Standard Terms' document have become part of the European Pharmacopoeia. The application of this guideline would seemingly render a modified release presentation, for instance, a new reference product, such that any new clinical data required to register it would be protected. A judicial review pending in the UK may help to elucidate the implications of developing different pharmaceutical forms.[63]

It follows that the Court's definition of essential similarity may have the effect of denying protection for the data underlying new indications, but granting it in respect of changes in pharmaceutical form and dose, which might involve less costly research. However, the 1986 definition from the minutes of the Council of Ministers reflects the domination of the working party by pharmacists who had focused upon the physical characteristics of the product, rather than upon the clinical applications which might in due course be researched for that product. There would appear, however, to be a disagreement on the Pharmaceutical Committee as to how the decision of the Court should be interpreted and further guidance from the Commission is being developed.[64] In the meantime, the Mutual Recognition Facilitation Group (MRFG) (a non-statutory body) has issued guidance stating that, in operating

---

[62] 'Standard Terms – Pharmaceutical Dosage Forms: Routes of Administration: Containers' (Strasbourg, October 1996).

[63] *R* v. *Licensing Authority, ex parte Novartis Pharmaceuticals Ltd and SangStat UK Ltd (intervening)*, QBD 5 November 1999.

[64] See Minutes of the meeting of the Committee of 15/16 April 1999 and 27/28 September 1999.

mutual recognition, it recommends that the innovator's 'line extensions' to different pharmaceutical forms or doses are not granted any protection.[65]

Clearly, there is a danger in assuming that any failure to meet the definition of 'essential similarity' will be fatal to the application made by the generic company. However, in relation to some changes in dose or pharmaceutical form proposed by an innovator, a competent authority may feel able to extrapolate from existing unprotected data relating to his first product presentation. Accordingly, there may be no new data requirement to meet and, therefore, no data to protect. Where, however, material new data is developed to support a change in the physical characteristics of the product, the changed product may seemingly be treated as a reference product and be protected accordingly. The Court's approach may, nevertheless, produce some strange results; for instance, if a higher dose is developed in order to treat a new condition, the underlying data may be protected because the quantitative element of the active principle has changed from that of the original product, but if research establishes that the condition can be treated with the same dose, there will be no protection for the underlying clinical data. This raises further question marks about how rational are the provisions as they stand and have hitherto been interpreted.

Infringement of general principles of EC law

The research-based companies also argued before the European Court that to adopt the narrow definition of 'essential similarity' would render Article 4.8(a)(iii) invalid through being contrary to established principles of European law relating to respect for property, protection of innovation and non-discrimination.[66] However, the principle of non-discrimination was said not to have been infringed because the original applicant and the generic applicant are required by the legislation to meet different tests.[67] Arguments of proportionality were also raised.[68] The Court noted that the relevant provisions need to strike a balance between competing objectives.[69] The balance struck by the provision was not treated as infringing the principle of proportionality,[70] but the decision lacks any intellectual underpinning as there is no discussion in

---

[65] MRFG, September 1999.
[66] Case C-368/96 *R* v. *The Licensing Authority established by the Medicines Act 1968 (acting by the Medicines Control Agency), ex parte Generics (UK) Ltd*; *R* v. *Same, ex parte Wellcome Foundation Ltd*; *R* v. *Same, ex parte Glaxo Operations UK Ltd and Others (E. R. Squibb & Sons Ltd, Generics (UK) Ltd, intervening)* [1999] ECR I-7967; [1999] 2 CMLR 181 at §§62, 68, 77 and 80.
[67] *Ibid.* at §63.   [68] *Ibid.* at §68.   [69] *Ibid.* at §§71–4.   [70] *Ibid.* at §75.

the judgment as to the matters to be taken into account in judging proportionality.

In relation to potentially the most important general principle – the right to property and protection of innovation – the Court noted that these rights were not absolute and could be restricted to meet objectives 'of general interest pursued by the Community', provided that the 'very substance of the right guaranteed' is not impaired.[71] Again, rather baldly the Court found that the right to property had not been fundamentally impaired, because the provisions did not seemingly render it 'practically impossible for innovatory firms to carry on their business of producing and developing medicinal products'.[72] This is arguably an over-confident suggestion – whilst innovatory firms will continue to research and develop new products, the implications of the judgment may have a profound effect upon incremental research.

The proviso to Article 4.8(a)

There is a proviso added to Article 4.8(a) which appears tacked on to sub-paragraph (iii) but may originally have been intended to have equal application to circumstances where an application is made by reference to the provisions of Article 4.8(a)(i), where the consent of the existing authorisation holder to cross-reference is obtained. This proviso reads:

However, where the medicinal product is intended for a different therapeutic use from that of the other medicinal products marketed or as to be administered by different routes or in different doses, the results of appropriate pharmacological and toxicological tests and/or of appropriate clinical trials must be provided.[73]

The interpretation of this proviso is obscure. It could be viewed as an indication that the concept of 'essential similarity' is not met and, therefore, the exemption is not applicable where the indication, route of administration or dose sought for the copy is different from that of the original product whose protection period has expired. But if this was the

---

[71] *Ibid.* at §79.   [72] *Ibid.* at §85.

[73] When the proposal for Directive 87/21 was presented to the Council of Ministers, the text was tabled in such a way that the proviso clearly applied to the whole of Article 4.8(a): proposal for a Council Directive amending Directive 65/65: COM(84) 437 final; submitted to the Council on 3 October 1984 (84/C293/05: [1984] OJ C293/43, 5 November 1984). When published following adoption, the proviso was indented so that it was aligned with the text of Article 4.8(a)(iii), albeit with a gap between the two. This appears to have led to confusion, but it is noteworthy that the proviso was treated as applicable to all heads of exemption when the UK implemented the provisions under the Medicines Act 1993: see Regulation 4(3) and Schedule 2, paragraphs 1–2, of the Medicines (Applications for Grant of Product Licences – Products for Human Use) Regulations 1992.

intention of the draftsman, why single out these characteristics and not the nature of the active or dosage form? Alternatively, the proviso might be viewed as merely stating the obvious, namely that where the generic company seeks an authorisation that is different in any of these characteristics to that of the originator's product and in any of the presentations currently marketed (regardless of for how long they have been marketed), the generic company must generate the appropriate data to establish safety and efficacy for the different product. However, the question again arises why only certain characteristics are mentioned and it is hardly necessary to clarify that no exemption arises where the competent authority has received no relevant data from anyone.

The proviso has, in fact, more generally been interpreted as showing that part-abridgement is possible and 'essential similarity' is not an 'all or nothing' passport to exemption. It would arguably be inconsistent with the rationale of protecting innovation and avoiding repetitive testing if, where the second applicant fails to meet any component of the test of 'essential similarity', he loses the benefit of any exemption in respect of any of the 'old' data. However limited the shortfall, from 'essential similarity', the second applicant would then be required to supply all the toxicity and clinical trial data afresh, which would be a disproportionate result. It would be more logical that, while the proviso still requires a comparison to be made with the characteristics of a reference product that has lost its protection, any difference between the products being compared that is covered by the definition of 'essential similarity' can be met by appropriate study data generated in accordance with Directive 75/318.

If this were correct, where the innovator has changed the product such that it can no longer be said to be 'essentially similar' to the product authorised for more than six/ten years, the proviso would allow the generic company to access the original tests to the extent that it seeks a product with the same characteristics as the product authorised for six/ten years, while allowing supplementation of the second application with appropriate research data to demonstrate the safety and efficacy of a product with the new characteristics not exhibited by any product authorised for six/ten years. This interpretation is supported by the Notice to Applicants, which introduces the concept of a 'hybrid' application and provides some guidance on the data that are likely to be appropriate where there are material differences between the products being compared:

After 6 or 10 years' knowledge and experience with a medicinal product, it would be inappropriate for ethical and scientific reasons to require a second applicant to repeat all tests, studies and trials, which are already known to the authorities. For a medicinal product which does not fall within the strict requirements of essential similarity, and therefore does not benefit from the exemption from providing results of pharmacological, toxicological and clinical trials, the second paragraph of Article 4.8(a)(iii) requires results of appropriate pharmacological and toxicological tests and/or appropriate clinical trials.

One would still expect the proviso to refer comprehensively to the other characteristics that it is generally accepted must be met before the test of 'essential similarity' is met. However, it does not. Whilst the reference to 'different doses' may be viewed as covering the 'quantitative' element of the active ingredient (but the French language version translates 'doses' as covering total daily dose rather than merely the strength of the individual dosage form), the requirement for the pharmaceutical form to be the same is not met by the reference merely to a different route of administration. All relevant guidance makes clear that dosage/pharmaceutical form and route of administration are different concepts. For instance, there are very many types of pharmaceutical forms for presenting the same active ingredient that have a different therapeutic profile but are administered orally.

In the *Scotia* case in Ireland, Scotia argued that Norgine's product was not 'essentially similar' to the comparator because the comparator relied upon by the competent authority was authorised only for multiple sclerosis. On this basis Scotia argued that Article 4.8(a)(iii) could not be relied upon at all. The Irish court took the view that the proviso would be unnecessary if the concept of 'essential similarity' included consideration of the indications. No reference was made by the Court to the alternative view that such a provision would be necessary to ensure that the obligation imposed on the generic company was proportionate to the extent of the shortfall from 'essential similarity' found in the comparison of the two products.

In the *Generics* case, all concerned found some difficulty in fitting the proviso within the framework of the Directive in any meaningful way. The Commission went so far as to advise the Court at the oral hearing that the proviso would not aid the Court in defining the concept of 'essential similarity' and was best ignored. The judgment of the Court indeed makes no reference to the proviso.[74]

[74] The implications of the proviso will be considered by the English court in the case of *R v. Licensing Authority, ex parte Novartis Pharmaceuticals Ltd*, 1999. In this case, Novartis marketed an immunosuppressant called Sandimmun used principally in transplant surgery to avoid rejection of the grafts. It later developed a second product (Neoral) that relied in part upon data it had already filed but also upon new clinical data. Novartis considered the new data protected because it viewed the second product as having a different pharmaceutical form and being bio-inequivalent to the first product. A second applicant (SangStat UK Ltd) made a hybrid application, after expiry of the Sandimmun protection period, for an authorisation for a product bioequivalent to

Conclusion

The text of Article 4.8(a) of Directive 65/65 is unsatisfactory in many respects and the ECJ's strong suggestion that the legislature should be invited to consider revisions is unanswerable. The changes made in relation to the published literature exemption have solved most of the issues surrounding use of published literature. However, there is a powerful case that can be made that Article 4.8(a)(iii), as interpreted by the ECJ, does not represent a fair balance between the competing interests involved. It discourages innovation in important areas where patent protection will not be available. Currently, it is problematic to rely upon data protection to provide any protection for the fruits of incremental research using known compounds, however innovative, costly and valuable to the promotion of public health such research may be. Despite the many statements of the Commission that the European regulatory environment must be sympathetic to innovation if European industry is to remain competitive on the world stage, the EU environment is now less favourable than that of the United States or Japan.

Incremental research is protected in the United States for five or three years according to the type of change involved and provided the changes to existing products could not have been approved without the submission of the data in respect of which protection is sought.[75] The Food and Drug Administration Modernisation Act 1997 also provides an additional six-month protection where clinical studies have been conducted in paediatric patient populations. In Japan pre-clinical and clinical data are also protected for a period.[76]

There is good evidence that the scale of research costs can be a major disincentive to the development of new treatments where the ability to recover those costs is compromised. The recent decision of the Community to grant a monopoly period of data protection (where a second application will not be entertained for ten years even with the same

Neoral, saying that it could supplement its application under Article 4.8(a)(iii) with clinical data pursuant to the proviso to cover the difference between its product and Sandimmun. In the event, the MCA also cross-referenced to the Neoral data, arguing that Neoral and Sandimmun were 'essentially similar' and, therefore, Neoral's data was not protected beyond the expiry of the Sandimmun protection period. Novartis was granted permission to bring judicial review proceedings against the MCA in October 1999.

[75] See Title 1 to the Drug Price Competition and Patent Term Restoration Act 1984, amending the Food, Drug and Cosmetic Act at Section 505(c)(3)(D)(ii)–(iv) and (j)(4)(D)(ii)–(iv); see also 21 CFR Section 314 108(b)(2) and (4).

[76] See Article 14–4 of the Pharmaceutical Affairs Law (No. 145 of 10 August 1960) and Article 21–4 of the Ministerial Regulation for Enforcement of that law (Order No. 1 of 1 February 1961).

data) in respect of so-called orphan drugs (where the patient population is small but the condition to be treated is serious) is further recognition of the economic context in which regulatory requirements must be met.[77] In related fields where the protection of innovation has been strengthened more recently, greater protection periods have been granted. For instance, the Database Directive allows protection for fifteen years for the original data and material additions to it.[78]

It remains significant that approval of new indications and other innovative changes may be viewed as of sufficient interest by the CPMP that a centralised assessment will be allowed under Part B of Regulation 2309/93. The decision of the ECJ does not of itself remove the ten-year protection afforded to the data supporting such applications. However, it must surely be an arbitrary and unintended result that the route of approval changes significantly the protection granted to the same product. Trade associations representing the research-based industry have called for a change in the law and harmonisation of the protection periods throughout the EU.

In reality, changes are likely to take several years to negotiate and in the meantime there is no doubt that many clinical research projects will be suspended (and in some cases terminated) in view of the implications of the law as it is presently interpreted. Some may argue that the financial and other research resources are, in any event, better directed at developing entirely new products rather than modifications to existing products. However, this approach ignores the telling fact that of the WHO's Essential Drug List in the year Directive 87/21/EEC came into force, 50 per cent of the 195 drugs recommended are not the innovator drugs of their respective class and 25 per cent are included for uses approved subsequent to the first approved indication, indicating that research aimed at improving the efficacy or safety profile of established products, and finding new uses, is of significant importance to the promotion of public health.[79] The debate concerning data protection, therefore, has some way to run.

[77] Regulation 141/2000/EC [2000] OJ L18/1.
[78] Directive 96/9/EC on the Legal Protection of Databases [1996] OJ L77/20.
[79] L. J. Wastila *et al.*, 'The World Health Organisation's Essential Drug List. The Significance of Me-too and Follow-on Research' [1989] 3(2) *Journal of Clinical Research and Drug Development* 105–15 (Center for the Study of Drug Development, Tufts University, Boston, Mass.).

6   The role of the European Medicines Evaluation Agency in the harmonisation of pharmaceutical regulation

Antoine Cuvillier

Introduction

The creation of the European Agency for the Evaluation of Medicinal Products (EMEA) in 1995[1] was the result of a long process of co-operation and harmonisation between European Union[2] (EU) Member States initiated by the European Commission. Developments can be seen in a number of defined stages and often ran parallel to the successive increases in the number of Member States.

Initially the impact was felt only in the EU and its neighbours, but it became more visible in the early 1990s with a significant influence on the international harmonisation process. It was also well documented with the publication of EU legislation and adopted guidelines in the series *The Rules Governing Medicinal Products in the European Union*. This is available both in paper form and also on the Internet,[3] and is regularly updated.

A solid EU marketing authorisation system is in place, with the EMEA as the focal point. The focus of attention has now turned back to the European region as a whole. In the current political context, this in particular means the central and eastern European countries, Norway and Iceland, and possibly even Russia and the newly independent States.

At a more global level, the EU–Japan–US trilateral working relation-

---

The opinions expressed in this chapter do not necessarily represent those of the EMEA or European Union institutions.

[1] Council Regulation 2309/93/EEC [1993] OJ L214/1.

[2] The term 'European Union' is used throughout the chapter for the sake of ease and should be read to include European Economic Community and European Community as appropriate.

[3] All EU legislation referred to in this chapter can be found in *The Rules Governing Medicinal Products in the European Union*. There are nine volumes in total and further information can be found on the Internet at: http://dg3.eudra.org/eudralex/index.html.

ship is well established within the International Conference for Harmonisation (ICH) process, which also has a duty to promote international harmonisation through the World Health Organisation (WHO), in particular at fora such as the International Conference of Drug Regulatory Authorities (ICDRA). Over 100 countries were represented at the ICDRA meeting in Berlin in April 1999 where ICH activities were reviewed.

To aid understanding of the European marketing authorisation system as it currently stands, an outline of the thirty-five-year history of harmonisation in the pharmaceutical sector will be provided. The key features of the current system will then be reviewed, including a brief description of the procedures for placing a new medicine on to the market, the networking of European expertise that the system relies on, together with existing guarantees of independence and resource efficiency, which are of primary importance in ensuring the credibility of the system. The role of the EMEA in providing technical and scientific support for European Union health policies will then be discussed together with its increasing role in international activities, both in preparation for the extension of the European Union and towards worldwide harmonisation of pharmaceutical regulation.

The step-by-step harmonisation process in the European Union

1965–84: laying down the building blocks

Beginning in the 1960s, the emphasis of the six founding Member States of the European Economic Community was the implementation of the concept of pre-marketing approval of medicines before they were made available to patients. The first piece of Community legislation was enacted in 1965[4] and still provides the foundation of the regulatory framework today, namely the assessment of medicines on the basis of quality, safety and efficacy.

Building on this, further legislation was introduced in 1975,[5] setting

---

[4] Council Directive 65/65/EEC of 26 January 1965 on the approximation of provisions laid down by law, regulation or administrative action relating to proprietary medicinal products [1965] OJ L369/65; OJ spec. edn 1965–6, 20.

[5] Council Directive 75/318/EEC of 20 May 1975 on the approximation of the laws of Member States relating to analytical, pharmaco-toxicological and clinical standards and protocols in respect of the testing of proprietary medicinal products [1975] OJ L147/1 and Second Council Directive 75/319/EEC of 20 May 1975 on the approximation of provisions laid down by law, regulation or administrative action relating to proprietary medicinal products [1975] OJ L147/13.

out the basic requirements for the evaluation of medicines. The legislation turned its focus from the products themselves to the evaluation and marketing authorisation process. Rules on chemical and pharmaceutical testing, pharmacological and toxicological testing (generally in animals) and clinical trials (in healthy volunteers and patients) were harmonised. Common criteria for the evaluation of medicines by Member States' competent authorities were laid down.

A committee was created in 1977 through which Member States could work together with the European Commission in their efforts to harmonise evaluation criteria and co-ordinate the authorisation of medicines. The formation of this committee – the former Committee for Proprietary Medicinal Products (CPMP) – was an important milestone. It provided the first EU-level forum for Member State representatives, from which grew networks of contacts as the committee gained more experience working together. The experience was extended to the veterinary medicines sector in 1981, with the creation of the former Committee for Veterinary Medicinal Products (CVMP) which had similar regulatory requirements.[6]

The supervisory responsibilities of the Member States were also addressed, particularly with regard to inspections and pharmacovigilance. The principle of manufacturing authorisations was established whereby each national competent authority is required to check that a qualified person in each company is made responsible for batch release, thereby introducing the practice of 'self-certification'. The competent authorities are also required to conduct regular inspections to verify compliance with good manufacturing practices.

When these measures were adopted they had to be in the form of Directives adopted unanimously by the Council of Ministers, which were then transposed into national legislation by the Member States. Through the scientific committees' work, a body of supplementary 'soft law' also emerged in the form of detailed scientific guidelines on drug testing. While non-legally binding, they were the result of consultation between the regulators and the regulated. They had the advantage of offering a transparent regulatory environment for all parties, permitting continuous interpretation in the light of scientific and technological advances without the need to seek frequent amendments to legislation.

---

[6] Council Directive 81/851/EEC of 28 September 1981 on the approximation of the laws of the Member States relating to veterinary medicinal products [1981] OJ L317/1 and Council Directive 81/852/EEC of 28 September 1981 on the approximation of the laws of the Member States relating to analytical, pharmaco-toxicological and clinical standards and protocols in respect of the testing of veterinary medicinal products [1981] OJ L317/16.

1985–94: Completion of the internal market in the pharmaceutical sector

In the mid-1980s, a major shift in legislative policy was taking place in Brussels. The traditional approach of harmonising Member States' rules was being supplemented by mutual recognition of national rules and standards provided that they met certain essential requirements laid down in EU legislation.

The principal factor behind this change was the realisation that harmonisation alone was too slow and cumbersome a legislative tool to achieve the fundamental objective of the EU of creating a single internal market. This was spelt out in particular in the European Commission's 1985 white paper on completion of the single market[7] launched by the then Commission president, Jacques Delors.

Unlike in many other sectors, the completion of the single market in pharmaceuticals was complicated by the fact that pharmaceuticals are not ordinary commodities bought and sold in a free market. Consumers rarely choose their medicines themselves and social security systems generally pay wholly or partly for medicines consumed. In addition, even if all the rules were fully harmonised, the final decision based on marketing authorisations would always have to be made on a case-by-case risk/benefit assessment. Decisions would therefore often differ in the absence of a unified decision-taking procedure.

The white paper contained in excess of 300 legislative initiatives covering almost all sectors across Europe, of which a dozen were in the pharmaceutical sector. This proportionately large number of proposals reflected the need for special pharmaceutical measures. Their adoption was made easier by the move from unanimity to qualified majority voting in the Council introduced by the Single European Act. The Council was also increasingly willing to delegate power to the Commission for the adaptation of pharmaceutical requirements through so-called 'regulatory committees'. This was due in part to the enormous legislative burden brought on by the single market white paper, but also to the confidence and trust built up in the sector over the previous years.

Other measures introduced ranged from the authorisation procedures themselves, to issues of transparency in national pricing,[8] to promoting

---

[7] Commission of the European Communities, *Completing the Internal Market. White Paper from the Commission to the European Council* (Luxembourg: Office for Official Publication of the European Communities, 1985).

[8] Council Directive 89/105/EEC of 21 December 1988 relating to the transparency of measures regulating the prices of medicinal products for human use and their inclusion in the scope of national health insurance systems [1989] OJ L40/8.

the rational use of medicines.[9] All industrially produced medicines were covered, including vaccines,[10] radiopharmaceuticals,[11] blood and plasma products,[12] veterinary immunological products[13] and homeopathic remedies.[14]

One important step towards co-ordination of decision-taking between Member States was the introduction of legislation concerning biotechnology and other high-technology medicinal products in 1987.[15] Member States had the obligation to deal with these medicinal products in a concerted manner within the so-called 'concertation procedure'. Products nationally authorised through the concertation procedure were given a ten-year protection against a second applicant. This was particularly important at that time given the lack of harmonisation of patent protection across the Community.

The so-called 'rational use package' introduced a new dimension beyond marketing authorisation requirements. The Summary of Product Characteristics (SPC) had already been established as the reference information for each medicine for health professionals. The innovation was to use the SPC as the basis from which all other

---

[9] Council Directive 92/25/EEC of 31 March 1992 on the wholesale distribution of medicinal products for human use [1992] OJ L113/1; Council Directive 92/26/EEC of 31 March 1992 concerning the classification for the supply of medicinal products for human use [1992] OJ L113/5; Council Directive 92/27/EEC of 31 March 1992 on the labelling of medicinal products for human use and on package leaflets [1992] OJ L113/8 and Council Directive 92/28/EEC of 31 March 1992 on the advertising of medicinal products for human use [1992] OJ L113/13.

[10] Council Directive 89/342/EEC of 3 May 1989 extending the scope of Directives 65/65/EEC and 75/319/EEC and laying down additional provisions for immunological medicinal products consisting of vaccines, toxins or serums and allergens [1989] OJ L142/14.

[11] Council Directive 89/343/EEC of 3 May 1989 extending the scope of Directives 65/65/EEC and 75/319/EEC and laying down additional provisions for radiopharmaceuticals [1989] OJ L142/16.

[12] Council Directive 89/381/EEC of 14 June 1989 extending the scope of Directives 65/65/EEC and 75/319/EEC on the approximation of provisions laid down by law, regulation or administrative action relating to proprietary medicinal products and laying down special provisions for medicinal products derived from human blood or human plasma [1989] OJ L181/44.

[13] Council Directive 90/677/EEC of 13 December 1990 extending the scope of Directive 81/851/EEC on the approximation of the laws of the Member States relating to veterinary medicinal products and laying down additional provisions for immunological veterinary medicinal products [1990] OJ L373/26.

[14] Council Directive 92/73/EEC of 22 September 1992 widening the scope of Directives 65/65/EEC and 75/319/EEC on the approximation of provisions laid down by law, regulation or administrative action relating to medicinal products and laying down additional provisions on homeopathic medicinal products [1992] OJ L297/8.

[15] Council Directive 87/22/EEC on the approximation of national measures relating to the placing on the market of high-technology medicinal products, particularly those derived from biotechnology [1987] OJ L15/38.

information for patients and for advertising was to be derived, to encourage a more rational use of medicines. Information for patients was introduced in some Member States and harmonised for all. In a region where there was increasing cross-border television advertising, national rules were converged, in particular with regard to advertising for self-medication or so-called 'over-the-counter' medicines.

1995: creation of the European marketing authorisation system and the EMEA

A level playing field had therefore been established – a significant achievement – but the opinions of the PMP and the CVMP were still not binding. Since the people around the table were Member State representatives, national considerations sometimes came into play. There are sensitive public interests in this sector and Member States have traditionally shown great reluctance in letting go of their national sovereignty in the area of public health. Nevertheless, through their co-operation and mutual trust Member States had enough confidence to face the next phase – the move from harmonisation of rules to harmonisation of decision-taking.

The European integration process was coming under attack in the early 1990s more than at any other time in its history. Tension between the need to complete the single market and political resistance to further centralisation in some Member States led to wide discussion of the concept of subsidiarity, i.e. doing something at EU level only when it cannot be sufficiently achieved by the Member States acting alone, therefore reinforcing the idea of the 'added value' of Community actions.

In addition, protection of public health had been used since the creation of the European Economic Community as a basis to obtain exceptions to rules and obligations. It is only with the entry into force of the Amsterdam amendments to the EC Treaty[16] that it has now become an EC policy.

The creation of the European marketing authorisation system, with the EMEA as its focal point, was an example of the EU's response to this challenge. In agreeing to create the EMEA, Member States pooled rather than gave away their sovereignty for the authorisation of medicines. Safeguard measures were built into the system to allow Member States to raise objections. Member States retained their traditional role

---

[16] See Article 152 (ex 129) EC. For further details on the role of the EC in public health matters, see chapter 3 above.

of territorial enforcement (e.g. inspections) which they now performed on behalf of the EU. After five years of operation, EMEA scientific opinions have always been widely accepted and recognized.

While it meets the same objectives as the US Food and Drug Administration (FDA), the EMEA represents a different manner of organising resources, in particular in its use of outsourcing for its scientific expertise.

Role, functioning and key features of the EMEA

The EMEA was inaugurated in January 1995 and at the same time two new marketing authorisation procedures were introduced: the centralised and the mutual recognition procedures.[17]

European marketing authorisation procedures

Centralised procedure
This procedure is compulsory for all medicinal products derived from biotechnology and is optional for other innovative new medicines.[18] Applications are made directly to the EMEA and are evaluated by one of the scientific committees. The EMEA has 210 days to perform the evaluation, but this period may be interrupted where the committee requires further information from an applicant. On the basis of the Agency's opinion, the European Commission takes its decision on the granting of a marketing authorisation, usually within three months.

A Community marketing authorisation is valid throughout the whole of the EU. The EMEA, using the network of national authorities, carefully monitors all centrally authorised products once they are in use ('pharmacovigilance').

Mutual recognition procedure
This procedure is based on the principle of mutual recognition of national authorisations between Member States and applies to the majority of other medicines. Under the procedure a marketing authorisation granted by one Member State is extended to one or more other Member States selected by the applicant. If a Member State cannot recognize the original marketing authorisation, the points in dispute are

---

[17] A third route exists for purely national marketing authorisations, where the product will be marketed in one Member State only.
[18] See Annex to Council Regulation 2309/93/EEC [1993] OJ L214/1.

referred to the EMEA for arbitration. The opinion of the EMEA is then enforced by a decision of the European Commission.

Scientific committees

New scientific committees were created within the EMEA. While they have the same names as the former committees, the EMEA scientific committees now participate directly in the preparation of decision-taking. Their mandate and functioning are consequently fundamentally different and in particular their composition has been changed to increase the range of scientific expertise available.

The scientific committees – better known by their abbreviations CPMP and CVMP – are now made up of individuals nominated by reason of their scientific competence. The committees meet monthly at the EMEA in London. Each committee has thirty members and an

---

Optional any time before submission
Scientific advice

Up to 4 months before submission
Pre-submission assistance

15 days before submission
Submission and validation

Day 0
Evaluation starts

Day 70
Initial assessment considered

Day 120
List of questions and first orientations
Clock stopped for answers by applicant

Day 180
Decision to hold hearing
Clock stopped for hearing

Day 210
Opinion adopted

Day 240
Opinion (in eleven EU languages) and assessment sent to Commission

Day 300
Commission decision after consultation with regulatory committee

---

Simplified centralised decision-taking process

elected chairperson.[19] Members of the scientific committees act in the name of the EMEA and their nominating authority may not give them instructions in this respect. Scientific opinions adopted by the committees are transformed into legally binding decisions by the European Commission.

The Management Board, which generally meets four times a year, has two representatives from each Member State, two from the European Commission and two from the European Parliament.[20] The Board, which is the governing body of the EMEA, principally oversees budgetary and policy matters and appoints the Executive Director. It is also a forum for discussion of key policy issues and future orientations of the European system. The results since 1995 (see tables) show an effective European system for the evaluation of medicinal products.

Medicines for human use	
Total applications	245
CPMP opinions	134
Community marketing authorisations granted	118
Variations	759
Scientific advice given	142
Medicines for veterinary use	
Total applications	40
CVMP opinions	25
Community marketing authorisations granted	16
Variations	21
Maximum residue limits established for 'old' substances	562
Maximum residue limits established for 'new' substances	74
Scientific advice given	15

Results of the centralised procedure (February 1995 to January 2000)

Finalised procedures	650
Arbitrations on applications for marketing authorisation	6
Variations	1952
Arbitrations on variations	8

Results of mutual recognition procedure (since 1995)

[19] The chairmen of the CPMP and CVMP at the beginning of 2000 were Prof. Jean-Michel Alexandre from France and Prof. Reinhard Kroker from Germany respectively.

[20] The Management Board Chairman at the beginning of 2000 was Mr Strachan Heppell from the United Kingdom.

Partnership and a networking agency

The European system is based on the partnership with some twenty-five different national agencies, the European Commission and all other interested parties (institutional and public). The structure of national authorities is different in each Member State; some are independent self-financing agencies, others are departments of ministries of health; some deal only with human or veterinary medicines, some with both, and others with other types of health-related products, e.g. medical devices. However, full participation of national competent authorities and consultation with other interested parties is important for the acceptability and credibility of the system.

The Agency has been primarily designed to co-ordinate the existing scientific resources of national competent authorities instead of creating additional new resources. It is not a Food and Drug Administration for Europe, but rather it is a 'virtual agency', interfacing with its partners without dismantling their structures.

The small number of staff at the EMEA illustrates this. It is expected to have 210 staff members by the end of 2000 and 220 by the end of 2001. While this is considerably smaller than some other regulatory authorities, the EMEA staff work with a network of about 2,300 European experts made available by the national competent authorities in all areas, including initial evaluation, post-marketing activities and inspections.[21]

These experts cover all disciplines necessary for the evaluation of medicines in both the human and veterinary fields. Along with members of the scientific committees and EMEA staff, they must make public declarations of interests.[22] The primary function of these European experts is to assist CPMP and CVMP members in evaluating medicines, but they also participate in working parties and other groups. Altogether they will convene at the EMEA for a total of over 380 meetings in 2000. This reinforces a central theme of the system, constant peer review between high-level scientists at European level.

This interface with partners is supported by a high-speed Intranet link to allow for exchange of information (e.g. exchange of safety alerts) – the European Union drug regulatory authorities' network (EudraNet). The EudraNet supports a range of services, some of which are available to the general public. This includes access to relevant EU legislation (http://dg3.eudra.org/eudralex/index.htm) and the EMEA website

---

[21] See in particular Council Regulation 2309/93/EEC [1993] OJ L214/1 Article 53.3.
[22] *Ibid.* Article 54.2. By decision of the Executive Director, this obligation has been extended to EMEA staff.

(http://www.eudra.org/emea.html). This information technology link has existed since the beginning of the EMEA and is operated through a special office of the European Commission Joint Research Centre. The link has gradually been expanded to enable greater communication between the national competent authorities and to assist the decision-taking process.

The EudraNet also facilitates communication with the public and general scientific community through the increasingly popular EMEA website – some 4 million visits to the site were recorded during the first quarter of 1999 alone.

Resource efficiency

The rationale behind both procedures of the European marketing authorisation system is resource optimisation. In the centralised procedure, scientific evaluation is carried out at EU level by two teams of independent rapporteurs and subjected to peer review in the scientific committees, instead of repetition of the same activity in each Member State. Similarly, in the mutual recognition procedure, the first Member State carries out the bulk of the scientific evaluation work only once and other Member States verify this on the basis of the initial assessment report.

The EMEA itself is a resource-effective interface and many of its working methods are novel within European regulatory circles, in particular the concept of outsourcing for scientific services. This is similar to the way multinational pharmaceutical companies conduct some of their research and development programmes.

Fees paid to the EMEA were reformed at the end of 1998.[23] As part of this reform, both the European Parliament and the Council have requested that the EMEA and the national competent authorities produce an analysis of their costs to justify both the level of fees and their use.[24] Scientific evaluation and inspection work is contracted out by the EMEA to the national competent authorities on the basis of contracts for services.[25] These contracts set out quality requirements, performance indicators and other conditions, in return for which the EMEA pays part of the fee it receives from applicants or marketing authorisation holders, currently one-third of total EMEA expenditure.

---

[23] Council Regulation 297/95/EEC as amended by Regulation 2743/98/EC [1998] OJ L345/3.
[24] *Ibid.* Article 12.
[25] Council Regulation 2309/93/EEC [1993] OJ L214/1 Article 53.3

Independent scientific opinions

It is not easy to explain scientific issues to the general public or indeed the concept of benefit/risk, especially in societies that are showing themselves increasingly averse to any risk at all. This is the challenge faced by all drug regulatory authorities worldwide. Putting in place a reliable and independent source of scientific opinion and information is an important means of ensuring public credibility. One aspect of this is creating a robust legislative framework, but there must also be confidence in the professionalism and competence of the regulatory body managing the system.

Public opinion surveys have traditionally shown high levels of support and confidence in the work of the FDA. One of the reasons for this is the FDA's long-standing record of scientific excellence and perceived independence of its scientific opinion. This model of scientific agencies, independent from their political authority, is one that is increasingly being applied in Europe, particularly in the pharmaceutical sector, where an increasing number of countries have created independent agencies built around scientific and technical committees. This was the model used when creating the EMEA.

EMEA scientific opinions are adopted on the basis of best science, without national or political interference. The EMEA carries out the scientific risk assessment and, where the science is clear, points to the decision to be taken by the responsible authority (in principle the European Commission). Where there are alternatives for risk management then these are identified. The responsible authority can then take an informed decision based on independent scientific evidence. In the majority of cases there is no need for political judgements; where exceptionally there is, they can be clearly and publicly justified by public order, ethical or other legitimate considerations.

In addition to its core tasks, the EMEA is increasingly called on to provide a scientific forum for EU institutions, national competent authorities and economic operators. The Agency has provided scientific and technical guidance to EU institutions in a number of cases, including scientific opinions on bovine spongiform encephalopathy, and supports the Commission in the technical aspects of international relations (e.g. implementation of mutual recognition agreements with third countries). Other examples include the question of antimicrobial resistance, orphan drugs for rare diseases and the continued availability of veterinary medicines. Scientific advice can also be provided to individual economic operators during the research and development phase of a new medicine many years before any application is made, thus reducing uncertainties and costs.

Transparency and benchmarking in the regulatory system

The key to public and political confidence is transparency; both in the way a regulator operates and in the results it produces. This has been an important and sometimes difficult objective of the EMEA since its inception.

Wide support for EMEA initiatives was given at a workshop held in October 1997, which was attended by representatives of various EU political institutions, of Member States, and also of patients, consumers and industry associations. A representative of FDA freedom of information staff reminded the meeting of their experience that only 5 per cent of requests for information actually come from members of the public, with the rest coming mainly from commercial organisations.

As an independent drug regulatory authority, the EMEA must be open to public and political scrutiny to ensure that procedures are correctly followed, that resources are correctly spent and that independence is ensured. The Agency has concentrated on making available all documents it produces, unless there is a legitimate reason to keep them confidential.

One of the most important tools at the Agency's disposal is the European Public Assessment Report (EPAR). This is published for every authorised medicinal product as soon as the Commission decision granting the marketing authorisation is taken.[26] These documents rapidly became the most popular category of documents produced by the Agency. They describe in detail the scientific evaluation, with the deletion of any commercially confidential information. In addition they include the product labelling, information to health professionals (Summary of Product Characteristics) and information for patients, available in all eleven EU official languages.

EPARs are intended to give confidence to patients, health professionals and the general scientific community that decisions behind the authorisation of medicines are made on the basis of best science. Information contained in EPARs is constantly updated in line with evolution of the products. Their format and content is also kept under review as the Agency seeks to improve the information made available, in particular through dialogue with patient and health professional

---

[26] *Ibid.* Articles 12(4) and 34(4).

organisations. Despite initial resistance, the EPAR is now well established as part of the regulatory landscape in Europe.

A recent initiative further increased transparency of the EMEA procedure with the publication of the scientific opinions of the CPMP and CVMP after the adoption of the final opinion. This is an important initiative to allow all parties to judge the basis on which the European Commission will take the decision whether or not to grant marketing authorisations.

Furthermore, a catalogue of documents is made available on the Internet, the principle being that there is public access to all documents unless the EMEA can show that it is covered by predefined confidentiality exceptions. These rules, introduced in 1998, are in line with the transparency requirements of the Amsterdam Treaty that came into force on 1 May 1999. In parallel to developments at the European Commission, EMEA codes of conduct for members of its scientific committees, European experts and staff are currently being reviewed. The Agency is also exploring ways of further improving transparency through early communication of scientific opinions, in consultation with all interest groups representing patients, consumers, health professionals and the industry.

2001 review

An important milestone in the evolution of the system will be the review of the European marketing authorisation system in 2001, to be initiated under Article 71 of Council Regulation 2309/93/EEC. By the end of 2000, the European Commission will publish a general report on the operation of the procedures. The objective of this report will be to assess whether the principal objectives of the system have been achieved and to evaluate to what extent additional efforts are to be made to meet these objectives. In this context, the key issues to be looked at are: (1) reinforcement of EU harmonisation; (2) better and safer medicines made available to patients; (3) cost-effectiveness of the system; and (4) transparency and openness. Subject to the findings, the review process may well lead to legislative amendments which the European Commission may wish to propose.

International co-operation and harmonisation

The EMEA and harmonisation

The evaluation of medicines, post-marketing surveillance and scientific advice are major parts of the Agency's work. However, the EMEA also invests considerable resources in harmonisation activities, particularly the development of testing guidelines. These guidelines are adopted following six months of consultation with all interested parties both within the EU and internationally (especially with Japan and the United States in the context of the international harmonisation initiatives, the International Conference on Harmonisation (ICH) and the Veterinary International Conference on Harmonisation (VICH)). Once adopted they are published and widely disseminated. International harmonisation work is therefore not a separate activity but is part of the core business of the EMEA.

Guidelines address specific issues relating to the assessment of quality, safety and efficacy of medicines. They are not binding, but offer guidance to applicants in the conduct of clinical trials. In this the CPMP and CVMP are each assisted by a number of permanent working groups and ad hoc working parties and experts' groups.

This work supports both the centralised and the mutual recognition procedures to ensure that the same rigorous scientific criteria are used to evaluate all medicines available to patients in the EU. For economic operators, this also means that the same interpretation prevails in all Member States.

One important aim of this harmonisation work is to support the mutual recognition procedure and in particular to minimise the risk of disagreement between Member States which gives rise to arbitration. To date, only a small number of arbitrations have been referred to the EMEA.

The EMEA is also about to start playing a key role in the implementation of the European Union policy on orphan medicines.[27] Key tasks will include designation of orphan status within the Committee for Orphan Medicinal Products (COMP), the provision of protocol assistance to sponsors and ensuring co-ordination and communication of all measures relating to orphan medicines, including research grants and other incentives.

Towards international harmonisation

The EU's harmonisation activities operate in three concentric circles: between Member States, in its wider European context and internationally. Behind each of these lies not only the acknowledgement that pharmaceutical markets and companies are increasingly global, but also that the EU – or rather the wider European Economic Area (EEA) –

---

[27] Regulation 141/2000/EC of the European Parliament and of the Council of 16 December 1999 on orphan medicinal products [2000] OJ L18/1.

constitutes the world's most integrated regional market with over 380 million consumers.[28]

The harmonisation work has been undertaken in co-operation or in consultation with the EU's neighbours. This not only benefits EU pharmaceutical companies, but is also an important mechanism to prepare for future accessions to the EU.

In recent months, the EMEA has collaborated with central and eastern European countries in preparation for future membership of the EU and as part of the pre-adhesion strategy. One concrete outcome was the introduction at the beginning of 1999 of a simplified procedure for the recognition of EMEA scientific assessments and the subsequent marketing authorisations by the eleven countries of the Collaboration Agreement of Drug Regulatory Authorities in European Union Associated Countries (CADREAC).[29] As part of the pre-adhesion strategy, the EMEA also has an instrumental role in furthering the dialogue with central and eastern European countries within the Pan-European Regulatory Forum (PERF). Financed by the PHARE programme,[30] PERF is ultimately directed at helping EU-associated countries meet the requirements of the White Paper for Technical Regulations. Priority areas include practical arrangements for implementing the *acquis communautaire*; dossier assessment; pharmacovigilance; and good manufacturing practices.[31]

The European Pharmacopoeia, begun in 1975, brings together about thirty member countries of the Strasbourg-based Council of Europe. It continues to be an important mechanism for harmonisation of quality standards for pharmaceutical control methods. It also provides the EU with a network of official medicines control laboratories. The European Pharmacopoeia participates with the Japanese and US Pharmacopoeia in the ICH process.

---

[28] The EEA Agreement includes all EU pharmaceutical legislation. See Decision 74/1999 of the Joint Committee of the EEA, 28 May 1999. The Decision provides for the formal participation of Iceland and Norway in the work of the EMEA.

[29] These are Bulgaria, Cyprus, the Czech Republic, Estonia, Hungary, Latvia, Lithuania, Poland, Romania, the Slovak Republic and Slovenia.

[30] 'PHARE originally stood for Poland Hungary Aid for the Reconstruction of the Economy. It is the European Union's (EU) financial instrument designed to assist the Central European countries (CECs) in their transition from an economically and politically centralised system to a decentralised market economy and democratic society based on individual rights, and to support the reintegration of their economies and societies with the rest of the world and especially with the European Union': An Evaluation of Phare Public Administration Reform Programmes Final Report (March 1999): http://europa.eu.int/comm/scr/evaluation/reports/phare/951465.pdf.

[31] Further information is available at the following website: http://perf.eudra.org.

International Conference of Harmonisation

Rather than engage in complex and detailed bilateral negotiations with its two major partners, Japan and the United States, the EU suggested the creation of a trilateral technical forum bringing together the regulatory authorities and pharmaceutical industries of the three regions. The European Commission, Japan's Kosheisho (national regulatory authority for medicines) and the US FDA launched the ICH initiative in 1990, with the support of the research-based industry of the three regions.

The ICH process had three major objectives:

1. To establish a constructive scientific dialogue on the differences in registration requirements;
2. To identify areas of mutual acceptance of research results without jeopardising safety; and
3. To recommend practical ways to achieve greater harmonisation of registration requirements.

An important aim in this context was to reduce the unethical repetition of tests in animals and humans.

Ten years later the international harmonisation process has proved a success. Thanks to the practical approach taken, almost fifty trilateral guidelines will have been adopted by the last major conference process, ICH 5, which is to be held in San Diego in November 2000.

Like much of the EU harmonisation activity, the impact of the ICH process spreads further than just the participating countries and includes observers from Canada, Switzerland and the WHO. All participants, in particular the WHO, have a role in disseminating the results of the ICH to other countries, regionally and worldwide.

The ICH goals have now almost been achieved, but its success will now open a new chapter in international co-operation between regulatory authorities on good regulatory practice and benchmarking.

Conclusion

After five years of operation, the European marketing authorisation system appears to have given satisfaction to its stakeholders. The confidence of EU institutions and interest groups representing consumers, patients and the health professions has been clearly demonstrated. In particular, European patients are now able to have speedier access to new medicines, usually within one year.

The new system also helps reinforce the safety of medicines for humans and animals, particularly through a pharmacovigilance network and the establishment of safe limits for residues in food-producing animals. The type of organisation chosen has proven efficient and cost effective. This model is being considered as a possible system for other fields of regulation activities at European Union level.[32]

[32] See Commission *White Paper on Food Safety*, 12 January 2000, COM(199) 719 final.

Part III

Biotechnology

7 The morality clauses of the Directive on the Legal Protection of Biotechnological Inventions: conflict, compromise and the patent community

Deryck Beyleveld, Roger Brownsword and
Margaret Llewelyn

Introduction

After a decade of intensive lobbying, legislation and litigation, the regulatory framework in Europe for the legal protection of biotechnological inventions is now taking shape. The fundamental issue within this framework is whether, in principle, the products and processes associated with modern biotechnology (in humans, animals and plants) are to be treated as patentable.

In the European Union (where the chequered history of the recently agreed Directive on the Legal Protection of Biotechnological Inventions[1] stretches back to 1988), as at the European Patent Office (operating under the European Patent Convention), the concept of patentability has been the focal point for debates reflecting, on the one side, the interests of the biotechnology industry (aided by the generally scientific and technical approach of the patent community) and, on the other side, the interests of various constituencies concerned about such matters as human dignity and the commercialisation of life, animal welfare and environmental harm.[2]

The emerging regulatory framework responds to these competing interests in two ways. First, in general, biotechnology is to be treated no differently from any other inventive science that comes forward with patent claims. Thus, provided that the particular claim relates to an invention (with a declared industrial application) rather than to a mere

[1] Directive 98/44/EC on the legal protection of biotechnological inventions [1998] OJ L213/13.
[2] For discussion of these issues under the European Patent Convention, see Deryck Beyleveld and Roger Brownsword, *Mice, Morality, and Patents* (London: Common Law Institute of Intellectual Property, 1993). Generally, see Sigrid Sterckx (ed.), *Biotechnology, Patents and Morality* (Aldershot: Ashgate, 1997).

157

discovery, genetically engineered products – even those incorporating human gene sequences – will satisfy the technical criteria of patentability. Similarly, there are to be no new *general* tests of exclusion for biotechnological inventions: the standard exclusions from patentability, concerning in particular morality, public policy, essentially biological processes for the production of plants or animals, and plant and animal varieties, will apply. To this extent, a level playing field is maintained for biotechnology. Secondly, however, the concerns of those who have opposed the opening of the patent system to modern biotechnology are reflected in a number of specific exclusions. Thus, under the rubric of the general exclusion for *ordre public* or morality, Article 6(2) of the Directive identifies the following as unpatentable: processes for cloning human beings or for modifying the germ line of humans; uses of human embryos for industrial or commercial purposes; and (following the lead given at the European Patent Office in the Harvard Onco-mouse case),[3] transgenic animals and the associated processes for modifying the genetic identity of animals where suffering is caused without any substantial medical benefit to man or animal.

Against this background of conflict and compromise, this chapter evaluates the adequacy of the morality provisions of the new Directive.[4] Our central thesis is not that the Directive is incapable of being given a good faith interpretation that brings its various moral elements to bear on the question of patentability in a coherent and defensible fashion. Rather, we suggest that, because the Directive rests on a fragile consensus, any weaknesses in its drafting are liable to present hostages to fortune for those seeking a particular sectional interpretation. Above all, the patent community's orientation towards technical argument, free of moral consideration or ethical constraint,[5] is liable to put pressure on those parts of the Directive where opportunities can be found to limit the scope of the morality exclusions.

---

[3] [1990] 1 EPOR 4 (original examination); [1990] 7 EPOR 501 (Board of Appeal): OJ EPO 10/1992, 590 (re-examination).

[4] Indeed, the conflict associated with the passage of the Directive has hardly abated. Almost immediately, the Dutch Government launched a challenge against the Directive in the European Court of Justice (ECJ) on the grounds (1) that the Commission wrongly presented the Directive as a trade measure under what is now Article 95 (ex 100A) EC (thereby requiring only a majority vote in the European Parliament) and (2) that the Directive does not clearly distinguish between patentable and unpatentable material. See Case C-377/98 *Kingdom of the Netherlands* v. *European Parliament and Council of the European Union*: [1998] OJ C378/13.

[5] See Geertrui Van Overwalle, 'Biotechnology Patents in Europe: From Law to Ethics' in Sterckx, *Biotechnology, Patents and Morality*, p. 139 at p. 147: 'The confrontation of ethics and patent law is difficult, to say the least, and usually ethics are seen in this context as a disturbance, as "die grosse Störung".'

The morality clauses

One of the most controversial questions addressed by the Directive is whether – and, if so, on which terms – patents should be excluded on moral grounds. In line with Article 53(a) of the European Patent Convention[6] as well as the permissive regime of Article 27(2) of TRIPs,[7] the Directive provides for a morality exclusion in Article 6; and, in Article 7, it is declared that the Commission's European Group on Ethics in Science and New Technologies is to evaluate, *inter alia*, the ethical aspects of patents on biotechnology.

The morality exclusion in Article 6 is in two parts. First, Article 6(1) provides:

Inventions shall be considered unpatentable where their commercial exploitation would be contrary to *ordre public* or morality; however, exploitation shall not be deemed to be so contrary merely because it is prohibited by law or regulation.

Secondly, Article 6(2) provides:

On the basis of paragraph 1 [i.e. Article 6(1)], the following, in particular, shall be considered unpatentable:
(a) processes for cloning human beings;
(b) processes for modifying the germ line genetic identity of human beings;
(c) uses of human embryos for industrial or commercial purposes;
(d) processes for modifying the genetic identity of animals which are likely to cause them suffering without any substantial medical benefit to man or animal, and also animals resulting from such processes.

Article 6 builds on a number of Recitals. Most obviously, Article 6(1) draws on Recital 37 (in conjunction with Recital 39);[8] and Article 6(2) draws on Recital 38 (in conjunction with Recitals 40, 41, 42 and 45).[9] However, other Recitals are clearly relevant to the interpretation of Article 6, particularly, we suggest, Recitals 16, 26 and 43.[10] We will

---

[6] Article 53(a) provides that patents shall not be granted for 'inventions the publication or exploitation of which would be contrary to "ordre public" or morality, provided that the exploitation shall not be deemed to be so contrary merely because it is prohibited by law or regulation in some or all of the Contracting States'. For analysis of Article 53(a), see Beyleveld and Brownsword, *Mice, Morality, and Patents*, ch. 3.

[7] See p. 12, n. 3. The exclusion permitted by Article 27(2) also runs in terms of protecting public order or morality, but it includes protecting 'human, animal or plant life or [the avoidance of] serious prejudice to the environment'.

[8] The first part of Article 6(1) copies in Recital 37. Recital 39 is drafted in obscure terms but, whatever else it might mean, it certainly signals that it is important to attend to moral considerations in the field of biotechnological inventions.

[9] For the text of Recital 38, and discussion of its relationship to Article 6(2), see below at pp. 167–9. Recitals 40, 41, 42 and 45 relate to each of the four specific exclusions listed in Article 6(2).

[10] For discussion of Recitals 16 and 26, see below at pp. 171–8. Recital 43 rehearses the EU's commitment 'to respect fundamental rights, as guaranteed by the European

return to Article 6 and the accompanying Recitals, particularly Recitals 16 and 38 (at pp. 168 and 172–3 below) and Recital 26 (at pp. 174–8 below).

Alongside Article 6, the Directive provides in Article 7:

The Commission's European Group on Ethics in Science and New Technologies evaluates [*sic*] all ethical aspects of biotechnology.

To this, Recital 44 merely adds that the 'Group may be consulted only where biotechnology is to be evaluated at the level of basic ethical principles, including where it is consulted on patent law.'

So much for the bare provisions of the Directive. Although such provisions eventually sufficed to secure the safe passage of the Directive through the European Parliament, the controversy continues. On the one side, critics of the Directive (especially critics in the patent community) argue that Articles 6 and 7 concede too much to morality; on the other side, opponents of the Directive contend that the morality clauses simply do not go far enough.[11]

We present our comments on the morality clauses of the Directive in four parts. First, we take issue with the view that morality exclusions have no place in patent law and that a provision such as Article 6 simply should not figure at all in the Directive. Secondly, we suggest that the drafting of Articles 6 and 7 (and their associated Recitals) leaves something to be desired. Given the fragile consensus on which the Directive was built, it is hardly surprising that the morality provisions bear the marks of political compromise. What this has yielded is not so much a Directive that cannot be given a sound interpretation as a legal instrument that leaves too much room for unsound interpretation – particularly for interpretations that are designed to marginalise the morality exclusions. Thirdly, we give two specific illustrations of our general claim that the Directive is prey to competing cultures and conventions of interpretation. In the first illustration, we consider the key provisions (namely Articles 5 and 6 and Recitals 16 and 38) that apparently bear on the question of whether a patent on a copy of a human gene sequence would be open to challenge as contrary to morality. In the second illustration, we focus on the informed consent requirement of Recital 26

Convention for the Protection of Human Rights and Fundamental Freedoms . . . and as they result from the constitutional traditions common to the Member States, as general principles of Community law'.

[11] For the view that, if anything, the Directive concedes too much to morality, see, e.g., Robin Nott, '"You Did It". The European Patent Directive at Last' [1998] *EIPR* 347; and Nick Scott-Ram, 'Biotechnology Patenting in Europe: The Directive on the Legal Protection of Biotechnological Inventions – Is This the Beginning or the End?' [1998] 2 *Bio-Science Law Review* 43. For the opposite view, see Sterckx, *Biotechnology, Patents and Morality.*

and its relationship to Article 6. Fourthly, we outline how we think the morality clauses should have been drafted.

Morality exclusions in patent law in general

Article 6 of the Directive, like Article 53(a) of the European Patent Convention (EPC), provides for the exclusion of patents on the grounds of immorality. Considerable controversy surrounds clauses of this kind. In Europe, opposition to such exclusions has been based on two principal grounds, one local, the other more general. The local objection is that such exclusions place Europe at a competitive disadvantage with the United States and Japan;[12] the general objection is that morality as such has no business being considered within the patent system. The reasons that are most commonly cited for this latter (general) objection are that

1. moral standards are difficult to judge;
2. patent authorities lack moral expertise or authority;
3. moral ideas change quite rapidly as compared with patent lifetimes (up to twenty years in Europe);
4. moral ideas differ across the territory covered by the EPC and the Directive; and
5. technical procedures that are abhorrent should be forbidden by law and not merely denied patent protection.

In outline, we would respond to the first (local) objection in the following way:

(a) Whether or not Europe is placed at a competitive disadvantage against the United States and Japan will depend on what criteria of morality are employed.

(b) Being placed at a competitive disadvantage against the United States/Japan could, in certain cases, have morally bad consequences which could override the *prima facie* immorality involved in granting a patent. Thus, considerations of morality could even argue for permitting particular patents.

(c) It is by no means axiomatic that patents (as against some other kinds of incentives) are necessary to encourage the investment required to protect European economic interests in biotechnology.

(d) If, all things considered, it would be immoral (according to the appropriate or even required criteria) to grant a particular patent, then the patent must be denied; the fact that this would place Europe at a competitive disadvantage is no overriding objection.

[12] See Ulrich Schatz, 'Patents and Morality' in Sterckx, *Biotechnology, Patents and Morality*, p. 159, esp. at p. 170.

As for the second objection, those who make this claim might be maintaining *either* that, as a matter of principle, morality has no bearing on patentability *or* that, for pragmatic reasons, it is not sensible to incorporate morality exclusions within the patent regime. Starting with the latter, to those who put their objection on more pragmatic grounds (such as objections (1) to (5) above), we would respond along the following lines.

1. Moral standards are only difficult to judge if no standards are laid down for examiners or judges to employ. Such standards are laid down in constitutions and human rights conventions, and judges have competence to deal with these.

2. If patent examiners lack moral expertise, they should be replaced by persons who have it; and it is nonsense to say that they have no authority. The morality exclusions in both the EPC and the Directive grant authority to patent examiners working under those legal regimes.

3. While it is true that *some* moral standards change reasonably rapidly (as compared with patent lifetimes), others (indeed, the most important) are very much more stable (such as those that inform human rights conventions).

4. While it is true that *some* standards vary across Europe, this is not true of all standards such as those, again, enshrined in the European Convention on Human Rights and the international human rights conventions of the United Nations.

5. Although it may be true that technical procedures that are morally abhorrent should be forbidden by law and not merely denied patent protection, it does not follow that technical inventions that are morally abhorrent cannot *also* be denied patent protection.

To those who put their objection as a matter of principle, there is a compelling answer. Unless those who so object deny that action is subject to categorically binding moral standards, then it must be admitted that the granting of a patent (like any other action) is, in principle, subject to moral evaluation (as morally required, permitted or prohibited). In other words, not even patent practitioners (unless they assume amoralism) can believe that it is impossible for it ever to be immoral to grant a patent. Given the common ground that there are at least some inventions the patenting of which would be immoral, then while it is debatable what forums (in particular situations and settings) are the most appropriate for making decisions about whether or not to exclude a patent on the ground of immorality, this is not something that a patent system cannot deal with, as a matter of principle. Indeed, since the central issue concerning the morality of granting a patent concerns the morality of granting a monopoly right to control the invention, then it is difficult to see where the decision could be more appropriately made.

In sum, our view is that it is perfectly proper for patent law to incorporate morality exclusions – not, in the final analysis, because there are only poor arguments against such provisions but because acceptance of morality points quite naturally to the incorporation of moral constraints on patentability. It follows that, in principle, we support the inclusion of morality exclusions in the Directive. Whether or not the particular way in which the Directive has incorporated its morality provisions is satisfactory, is our next question.

The adequacy of Articles 6 and 7: competing cultures

It is trite that legal interventions, of any description, do not take place in a cultural vacuum. Any particular field within which the law attempts to function will have its own cultural features, its own standards, its own economic imperatives, and so on.[13] The particular field in which the morality clauses of the Directive are to function, it scarcely needs pointing out, is one riven with conflicting views about the merits and demerits of biotechnology. Two particular features of this regulatory field, however, are worth highlighting. First, the relationship between morality and patentability is deeply contested. Crucially, those to whom the Directive principally applies, namely, patent practitioners (and their clients), tend to take a technical view of their activities. According to this view, morality is seen as having either no relevance to, or only a marginal bearing upon, the patentability of inventions. The patent system, as patent practitioners are fond of saying, is predominantly designed for the granting of patents.[14] Secondly, because the Directive is a *European* legal instrument, it is located in a community in which there are different cultures of legal interpretation – indeed, even within the English legal system, there are competing cultures of interpretation.[15] Putting these two features together, we can expect the patent community to argue for interpretations of the morality clauses that confine their impingement on patent-

---

[13] See, e.g., Gunther Teubner, 'Substantive and Reflexive Elements in Modern Law' (1983) 17 *Law and Society Review* 239; Ulrich Beck, *Risk Society* (trans. Mark Ritter) (London: Sage Publications, 1992); and Julia Black, 'Regulation as Facilitation: Negotiating the Genetic Revolution' (1998) 61 *Modern Law Review* 621.

[14] See Edward Armitage and Ivor Davis, *Patents and Morality in Perspective* (London: Common Law Institute of Intellectual Property, 1994).

[15] See, e.g., John N. Adams and Roger Brownsword, *Understanding Law* (2nd edn, London: Sweet and Maxwell, 1999) ch. 4.

ability to a minimum.[16] In brief, the nature of our general reservation about the drafting of the morality clauses of the Directive is that they invite the patent community to pay lip service to moral considerations while, for the most part, continuing to operate as though morality has little relevance to patent practice.

In the next section, we will give two specific illustrations of the way that this weakness might manifest itself; but, in the present section, we will make some general remarks about the drafting of Articles 6 and 7.

Article 6(1)

Following the general pattern (if not precisely the same wording) of Article 53(a) EPC, Article 6(1) comprises two parts, the first part setting out the general exclusion based on reasons of *ordre public* or morality, the second part (the proviso) distancing the general exclusion from law or regulation. In our view, both the drafting of the general exclusion and the inclusion of the proviso are open to criticism.

Starting with the general exclusion, we need to remind ourselves of the significance of the grant of a patent. In fact, Recital 14 puts the matter accurately, saying that the grant of a patent for an invention 'does not authorise the holder to implement that invention, but merely entitles him to prohibit third parties from exploiting it for industrial and commercial purposes'. In other words, whilst the grant of a patent does not, as it were, confer a 'positive right' to exploit the invention, it puts the patent holder in a monopoly position where commercial exploitation is possible. Accordingly, the focal question for a morality exclusion is whether putting the applicant in a monopoly position in relation to the commercial exploitation of a particular invention gives rise to any moral difficulty.

On this analysis, Article 6(1) does not quite get the question in focus. Rather than directly targeting the morality of granting *monopoly control* to the applicant, Article 6(1) focuses instead on whether *commercial exploitation* of the invention would be immoral. Now, while it is not improper as such to hold that the grant of monopoly control would be immoral if commercial exploitation would be immoral, it does not follow that if commercial exploitation would *not* be immoral, then neither would the grant of a patent be immoral – in other words, it does

---

[16] As demonstrated by the Technical Board of Appeal of the EPO in the *Plant Genetic Systems* case (T356/93) [1995] EPOR 357 at 367: '[T]he exceptions to patentability have been narrowly construed, in particular in respect of plant and animal varieties . . . In the Board's view, this approach applies equally in respect of the provisions of Article 53(a) EPC.'

not follow that there can be no moral objection to the grant of a patent if commercial exploitation of the invention would not be immoral. On the contrary, one of the paradigms of immorality would be the case where private monopoly control impeded access to a public good (distributed via commercial exploitation of the invention).[17] In other words, there is commercial exploitation of more than one kind: we should not equate commercial exploitation by a patent-protected monopolist (and its licensees) with the very different case of commercial exploitation in a market free of a patent-holding monopolist. If morality dictates that commercial exploitation of the latter kind is required, then far from the grant of a patent being morally unobjectionable, this is precisely the situation where the required nature of the commercial exploitation renders the grant of a patent morally impermissible.[18]

So long as we focus on the question of whether it would be immoral to put the applicant in a monopoly position in relation to the particular claimed invention, we can (and quite properly should) take account of any moral argument militating against giving the applicant such a private advantage. The focus on commercial exploitation in Article 6(1), however, could misdirect examiners by narrowing the range of material considerations to forward-looking questions concerning the morality of commercial exploitation. The point is that there are many other reasons why it might be immoral to grant the patent.

Consider the case of an invention the research and development of which has involved some arguable violation of morality – for example, if samples have been taken from patients without their informed consent or have been smuggled out of a country without due authorisation.[19] How would an objection of this kind fit with the terms of Article 6(1)? Immediately, we can anticipate two opposed interpretations of this Article. According to one (correctly focused) interpretation, the objection falls within the ambit of Article 6(1) because the moral test, although framed in terms of commercial exploitation, must be read as looking backwards as well as forwards. On this view, Article 6(1) does not draw a line under any (past) immorality associated with the research

---

[17] See Recital 35, according to which the Directive is 'without prejudice to the provisions of national patent law whereby processes for treatment of the human or animal body by surgery or therapy and diagnostic methods practised on the human or animal body are excluded from patentability'. Similarly, see Article 52(4) of the European Patent Convention.

[18] Although patent law makes provision for compulsory licensing, such powers only become available after three years of non-use (which, of course, is a long time in modern genetics).

[19] See Jeremy Rifkin, *The Biotech Century* (London: Victor Gollancz, 1998) at p. 59 (concerning the illegal taking of DNA and blood samples from patients at private eye hospitals in India).

and development of the particular invention for which a patent is sought. On the contrary, it is implicit that the commercial exploitation of an invention can be judged to be immoral, because the immoral manner of its development is deemed to taint any future exploitation – no inventor, in other words, should be permitted to profit from his wrong by being put in a monopoly position. Against this interpretation, however, it may be argued that the focus on commercial exploitation in Article 6(1) signals that the manner in which the invention was researched and developed is irrelevant; what matters is simply whether future commercial exploitation (disregarding the past) would be immoral. Such an interpretation would involve a distortion of a morality exclusion however drafted – but the danger is that the drafting of Article 6(1) leaves room for such a distorted reading.

Much the same could be said about considerations pertaining to the immorality of publishing the invention. As we have said, Article 6(1) runs in very similar terms to the morality exclusion in Article 53(a) of the European Patent Convention. However, whereas the latter is drafted in terms of the immorality of 'publication or exploitation' of the invention, the former, to repeat, focuses only on the immorality of commercial exploitation. The omission of 'publication' from the clause would not be a problem if Article 6(1) were drafted in a way that invited a full consideration of the morality question – nor, for that matter, would the omission be a problem if it were understood that Article 6(1) must be read in a way that harmonised with Article 53(a) of the European Patent Convention.[20] Drafted as it is, though – and with some uncertainty about the long-term prospects of Article 53(a) – Article 6(1) has the potential to deflect attention from the full set of relevant considerations.

Turning to the proviso in the second part of Article 6(1), there is – as there is in the proviso in Article 53(a) EPC – a certain lack of clarity.[21] As far as it goes, the proviso indicates that commercial exploitation is not to be deemed to be contrary to *ordre public* or morality 'merely' because it is prohibited by law or regulation. Where it suits, the patent community might argue that this means that prohibition by law or regulation is irrelevant. However, the force of 'merely' is that prohibition of this kind would not of itself constitute a *sufficient* reason for exclusion

---

[20] At any rate, this would be so if Article 53(a) remained a part of the EPC, and if the reference to 'publication' stood. However, given the disenchantment of the patent community with Article 53(a), and given continuing talk about the possible revision of the Article (including its possible abrogation), it would be unwise to rely on the EPC to undergird the morality clauses of the Directive. (Although see the developments referred to in n. 42 below).

[21] For analysis of the proviso to Article 53(a), see Beyleveld and Brownsword, *Mice, Morality, and Patents* at pp. 74–82.

under Article 6(1). In other words, the morality exclusion in Article 6(1) does not operate entirely independently of law and regulation. Yet, if this is so, the question arises of precisely how much weight prohibition by law or regulation carries. If the particular law or regulation is at the level of an EU constitutional commitment – and it should be borne in mind that Recital 43 underlines the EU's commitment to 'fundamental rights' as guaranteed by the European Convention on Human Rights – then this must carry considerable weight; indeed, one might be tempted to argue that law or regulation at this level would amount to a sufficient reason. If, however, the particular law or regulation is at national level only, then although (other things being equal) this might weigh quite heavily with the relevant national examiners making a local moral judgement, it is less plausible that it should have anything like such weight if a judgement is being formed by national examiners in another jurisdiction or with a view to EU-wide exclusion.

In sum, relative to our general claim about competing cultures of interpretation, the weakness in the drafting of the first part of Article 6(1) is that it invites the patent community to argue for a narrow reading of the exclusionary test, a reading that focuses only on commercial exploitation, only on the future, and only on commercial exploitation without reference to the context in which exploitation is to be permitted. The weakness of the proviso is that it could be used to marginalise the morality exclusion by detaching it altogether from the evolving framework of European law as well as detracting from the most fundamental constitutional and moral commitments of that legal order.

Article 6(2)

According to Recital 38 (to which we will return shortly), the purpose of Article 6(2) is 'to provide national courts and patent offices with a general guide to interpreting the reference to *ordre public* and morality [in Article 6(1)]'. Such guidance is given in the form of four processes/ uses/products that are to be considered unpatentable (as violating *ordre public* or morality or both). Different people, no doubt, will have different ideas about the appropriateness of these specific exclusions. In the case of cloning, germ-line modification and embryos, for example, some might think that the exclusions are both premature and inflexible, the Directive reacting before a considered moral judgement has had the opportunity to form and allowing no room for moral judgements to change over time. By contrast, the exclusion for unwarranted modification of animals can hardly be accused of being premature; and, whether or not by intent, the requirement of 'substantial' medical benefit builds some flexibility into the provision. On the other hand, critics of the Directive may think that this exclusion is altogether too weak, requiring a substantial medical benefit but without explicitly incorporating a proportionality test – and, of course, some will believe that Article 6 should simply exclude patents on genetically modified animals or the associated processes for modification.[22]

In structural terms, however, the more significant aspect of this part of the Directive is, first, the way that Article 6(2) relates to Recital 38 and, secondly, the way that these provisions relate to Article 5. We can deal with the first of these questions here; the second will be addressed in the next section.

How does Article 6(2) relate to Recital 38? This Recital states:

Whereas the operative part of this Directive should also include an illustrative list of inventions excluded from patentability so as to provide national courts and patent offices with a general guide to interpreting the reference to *ordre public* and morality; whereas this list obviously cannot presume to be exhaustive; whereas processes, the use of which offend against human dignity, such as processes to produce chimeras from germ cells or totipotent cells of humans and animals, are obviously also excluded from patentability.

As we have said, this Recital presents the examples given in Article 6(2) as 'an illustrative list of inventions excluded from patentability' under the morality test of Article 6(1). One might detect a hint of a tension between the drafting of Article 6(2), according to which the examples given are to be understood as categorically unpatentable, and the idea advanced in Recital 38 that the list is illustrative only, this perhaps suggesting a grey-list rather than a black-list. For our purposes, however, the more important point is that Recital 38 goes on to emphasise that the list is not exhaustive. Given that the patent community might want to argue that the limits of Article 6 are set by the four exclusions identified in Article 6(2) – this notwithstanding that, in the Article itself, the four cases are prefaced by the words 'in particular' – Recital 38 potentially has a role to play in barring such an interpretation. Of course, one could try to talk down the effect of Recital 38 by marginalising it as being a mere Recital provision – but such a style of interpretation would be to disregard the accepted European conventions for the interpretation of Directives.[23]

---

[22] See Deryck Beyleveld and Roger Brownsword, 'Patentability of Genetically Engineered Animals: The Emerging European View' (1995) 8 *Asia Business Law Review* 19.

[23] Although commentaries on the precise relationship between the Recitals and the Articles of a Directive are not readily found, it is trite (and taken as read amongst EC lawyers) that the Recitals are relevant to the interpretation of the spirit and purpose of the particular Directive (see, further, below). That the spirit and purpose of a Directive is to be taken into account by *national* courts in the interpretation of *national* law is

The fact that the list in Article 6(2) is not intended to be exhaustive is further underlined in Recital 38 by the final sub-clause, according to which processes offending against human dignity (such as processes to produce chimeras) are also excluded. Nevertheless, the inclusion of the example of 'processes to produce chimeras from germ cells or totipotent cells of humans and animals' in Recital 38 is puzzling. Why, one might ask, was it felt necessary to give any example at all in the Recitals, when three stock examples of dignity-violating processes/uses (relating to cloning, germ line modification and embryos) are given in Article 6(2) itself? If it was felt necessary to give an example, why use the chimera, rather than one of the other examples, in the Recital?

In a similar vein, and altogether more significantly, we might wonder why the general principle of respect for human dignity is written into the Recitals rather than the Articles. However, this thought leads into matters that we will deal with in the next section. The most that we can say at this stage is that the drafting of Article 6(2) is a little puzzling but that, provided Recital 38 is taken into account, the force of the morality exclusion is not spent by the four cases cited in the Article. As we shall see shortly, though, a much deeper question is hidden away in these provisions.

Article 7

Article 7 is something of a mystery. It is drafted in a curious way, apparently declaring (when read alongside Recital 44) that the Commission's European Group on Ethics in Science and New Technologies is to act in a consultative capacity – and, what is more, that the Group is to be consulted only 'at the level of basic ethical principles'. These bare provisions leave more questions than answers. For instance, what counts as a 'basic' ethical principle? Where the Group is consulted, is its opinion merely advisory or does it have binding effect? Who is able to refer questions to the group, and how? And, what precisely is the relationship between the Group and patent examiners authorised to apply the morality test under Article 6?

Taking up this last question, in principle, the Group could: (a) operate alongside the examiners as an adjunct to the mainstream patent system, addressing the ethical issues to which patent applications give rise; (b) operate at some distance from the day-to-day working of the

evident from the jurisprudence of the ECJ in the indirect effect case law: see, e.g., such leading cases as Case 14/83 *Von Colson and Kamann* v. *Land Nordrhein-Westfalen* [1984] ECR 1891, and Case C-106/89 *Marleasing SA* v. *La Comercial Internacional de Alimentacion SA* [1990] ECR I-4135.

patent system, occasionally offering opinions on difficult ethical issues; or (c) operate somewhere between these two positions. The problems with (a) are obvious. The Group simply could not handle the volume of applications filed in all Member States; and, even if the Group comprised superhumans for whom the opening of the floodgates held no fear, the question remains why the patent examiners in national offices should not take on the moral assessment themselves. The drafting of Recital 44 suggests that (b) is closer to the intended mark. Yet, if this is so, why the work of the Group needed picking up in an Article (even such an oddly drafted clause as Article 7) is unclear: would it not be taken as read anyway that the advisory opinions of such a Group would be weighed by patent examiners? The other possibility is (c). However, (c) covers a broad spectrum of intermediate positions and, if the Group's role lies at any of those intermediate positions, the Directive needs to tell us which one it is.

Given such a lack of clarity about the function of the Group, and in a culture of hostility towards morality exclusions, there is a dual danger: on the one hand, the work of the Group could be entirely marginalised; on the other hand, the existence of the Group could be used as an excuse to divert (and lose) complex moral issues from the mainstream patent system.

Two specific illustrations

In the *Relaxin* case,[24] the leading case at the European Patent Office (EPO) concerning the morality of patenting human gene sequences (or copies thereof, or associated processes), the opponents of the patent argued (unsuccessfully) that the grant of the patent was immoral as evincing a lack of respect for human dignity. They also argued (and, with this, the EPO agreed) that the patent would be immoral if the human tissue on which the inventors worked had been obtained without the consent of the donors.

To highlight the weakness of the Directive, we consider how the points (above) taken by the opponents in the *Relaxin* case would be pleaded (and counter-pleaded). We look, first, at the general dignity-based moral objection to patents on human gene sequences; and then we discuss the informed consent requirement set by Recital 26.

---

[24] [1995] OJ EPO 388.

Articles 5 and 6; Recitals 16 and 38: the patentability of human gene sequences

No part of the Directive was more deeply contested than the position to be taken on the patentability of human gene sequences. Article 5 represents the compromise eventually struck on this most controversial of questions. Conceding something to the opponents of patents on human gene sequences, Article 5(1) provides:

The human body, at the various stages of its formation and development, and the simple discovery of one of its elements, including the sequence or partial sequence of a gene, cannot constitute patentable inventions.

Claiming ground for the patent community, however, Article 5(2) states:

An element isolated from the human body or otherwise produced by means of a technical process, including the sequence or partial sequence of a gene, may constitute a patentable invention, even if the structure of that element is identical to that of a natural element.

To this, Article 5(3) adds that it is a condition of patentability that the 'industrial application of a sequence or a partial sequence of a gene [is] disclosed in the patent application'. If we assume a distinction between unisolated human gene sequences (in a person's body) and isolated copies of human gene sequences (in a laboratory), the effect of these provisions is to treat the former as unpatentable (under Article 5(1)) and the latter as patentable provided that the copy is produced by means of a technical process (Article 5(2)) and provided that the industrial application of the sequence is disclosed (Article 5(3)).

Now, suppose that we put the following two questions in relation to the Directive. First, is the patenting of unisolated human gene sequences excluded as immoral? Secondly, is the patenting of copies of human gene sequences excluded as immoral? To the first question, we might expect a short answer, namely that Article 5(1) unequivocally excludes such patents; that it does so on the technical ground that the subject matter of such a patent claim constitutes a mere discovery; and, thus, that the moral question simply does not arise. Academic though the moral question might be, the answer is worth pursuing; for no one should doubt that there must be room to object to the idea that the *only* reason for excluding a patent on the gene sequences in some person's body is of a purely technical kind. Lack of invention might be a good reason for exclusion; but the re-invention of slavery is an even better reason.[25]

---

[25] Recital 16 gives both moral and technical reasons. It opens by saying that 'patent law must be applied so as to respect the fundamental principles safeguarding the dignity

When we turn to the second question, the position is less clear. And the reason why this is so is that the strategy underlying the compromise in Article 5 is to rely on the technical distinction between mere discovery and invention in order to draw the line between that which is patentable and that which is not. The effect of this exercise is that copies of human gene sequences fall on the patentable side of the line; but this is prior to any kind of moral question yet having been asked. If opponents of patents on copies of human gene sequences now wish to argue that such patents should be excluded as immoral, does the Directive allow for this moral challenge to be presented?

Those seeking to minimise the opportunity for moral objection (and potential exclusion) might argue along the following lines:

1. On the particular question of the patentability of copies of human gene sequences, Article 5 settles the issue, Article 5 taking priority over Article 6; this, it could be said, follows from the patent community's favourite canon of construction, namely that exclusions in patent law are to be construed narrowly.

2. Failing this, if it is conceded that Article 6 is relevant, it does not exclude patents on copies of human gene sequences because, if the drafters of the Directive had had any moral reservations about the patentability of such matter, they surely would have so indicated *explicitly* somewhere in Article 6.

3. The claim that the drafters did not intend Article 6 to apply to copies of human gene sequences is further supported by the absence of such matter from the list of examples given in Article 6(2). Granted, Recital 38 indicates that the list is not exhaustive; even so, an exclusion for copies of human gene sequences could not be read into Article 6(2) without wholly eradicating the saving for such material so carefully crafted in Article 5(2) and (3).

4. Finally, the Recitals themselves do not clearly point to a dignity-based exclusion of patents on copies of human gene sequences. Recital 38 is inconclusive (because it gives the example of chimeras rather than human gene sequences); and the same applies to Recital 16 where there is a striking equivocation between applying patent law 'so as to respect the fundamental principles safeguarding the dignity and integrity of the person' and respecting the principle that 'the simple discovery of one of [the human body's] elements or one of its products, including the sequence or partial sequence of a human gene, cannot be patented'.

---

and integrity of the person', but it then goes on to say that mere discoveries relating to elements or products of the human body cannot be patented.

Against this reading of the Directive, opponents of patents on copies of human gene sequences might respond in the following terms: that Article 5 must be read as subject to the morality test in Article 6; that it is in the nature of morality clauses that they set overriding standards for patentability; that every patent, therefore, must satisfy such tests; and, thus, that Article 5 could foreclose the question only if it provided explicitly (which it does not) that patents on copies of human gene sequences are to be treated as satisfying the morality test in Article 6.

Having established that the Directive allows for such a challenge under Article 6, the way would then be cleared for a dignity-based opposition of the kind advanced in the *Relaxin* case. Whether or not such a challenge would, or should, succeed is another matter. It is eminently arguable that respect for human dignity is one of the corner-stone principles of the Directive (this can be derived from Recital 38 in conjunction with the first three examples given in Article 6(2) as well as from Recital 16 and the provisions of Recital 43, integrating the Directive with the fundamental rights guaranteed by the European Convention on Human Rights). However, the concept of human dignity is open to many competing interpretations and, in our view, it is far from clear that respect for human dignity militates against granting patents on copies of human gene sequences.[26] Yet, for present purposes, the question of whether the opponents would win this particular argument is not the central point. Rather, the point is that the drafting of the Directive is unsatisfactory if it does not at least ensure that there is the right to argue the case under Article 6.

The weakness of the Directive, then, is not that it gives the opponents no chance of winning the moral argument but that it invites the patent community to plead that, on this particular issue, the moral question is no longer open to argument. If Article 6 is to operate as a morality exclusion, it must be understood to be overriding. And if the Directive is to function as an evolving 'living law', facilitating the formulation of morally defensible positions on patentability, it is counter-productive to

---

[26] See Deryck Beyleveld and Roger Brownsword, 'Human Dignity, Human Rights, and Human Genetics' (1998) 61 *Modern Law Review* 661, esp. at 674–6; and 'Patenting Human Genes: Legality, Morality, and Human Rights' in J. W. Harris (ed.), *Property Problems – From Genes to Pension Funds* (London: Kluwer Law International, 1997) p. 9, esp. at pp. 19–22. And compare Alain Pottage, 'The Inscription of Life in Law: Genes, Patents, and Bio-politics' (1998) 61 *Modern Law Review* 740.

Interestingly, in the Dutch challenge to the Directive (see above, n. 4), point 2, fifth indent states: 'Breach of fundamental rights: Violation of human dignity: The human body is the bearer of human dignity. Under Directive 98/44/EC, it will be possible to make isolated parts of the human body patentable. Such treatment of living human material as an object is unacceptable in the context of human dignity.'

allow interpretive arguments that are designed to close off the doors to moral debate.

Recital 26 and Article 6: informed consent

Recital 26, which appears at the end of a cluster dealing with the matters provided for in Article 5, states:

Whereas if an invention is based on biological material of human origin or if it uses such material, where a patent application is filed, the person from whose body the material is taken must have had an opportunity of expressing free and informed consent thereto, in accordance with national law.

On the face of it, this is an extremely important provision, linking directly to Article 6(1), because the requirement to obtain informed consent to the taking of human material (at least from the living) is a basic ethical (and legal) requirement in the EC.[27] Yet, the obtaining of consent is not always convenient (or possible) and there may well be pressure to interpret the Directive in such a way that allowance is made in the patent system for the inconvenience (or impossibility) of obtaining informed consent. To simplify our discussion, let us assume that Recital 26 gives some margin of appreciation to national law to adopt a surrogate test (best interests or substituted judgement or the like) where a person is not able to give free and informed consent. The question then is whether the Directive offers any openings for an interpretation that gives ground to the inconvenience of obtaining proper consents.

If Recital 26 was not legally binding, or could simply be ignored, then researchers would not be at all inconvenienced. However, while the ECJ has, on occasion, said that Recitals have no legally binding force,[28] extreme caution should be exercised in interpreting such remarks. There is considerable ECJ case law that indicates that Recitals *must* be taken into account by national authorities in interpreting national law under the Directive.[29] Thus, it is certainly wrong to infer that prescriptive Recitals, like Recital 26 appears to be,[30] are mere suggestions that

---

[27] See, too, Article 22 of the Council of Europe Convention on Human Rights and Biomedicine, 1996, and the UNESCO Universal Declaration on the Human Genome and Human Rights, 1997.

[28] See, e.g., Case C-62/97 *Gunnar Nilsson, Per Olav Hagelgren, Solweig Arrborn, Agriculture* [1998] ECR I-7477 §54 of the judgment.

[29] See above, n. 23.

[30] Some of the Recitals are only indirectly and generally prescriptive, outlining the context of the Directive and the background thinking of its proposers (e.g., those Recitals rehearsing the need for harmonisation and clarification of the law). Other Recitals, however, are much more directly and specifically prescriptive. It is quite clear, for example, that Recital 38 excludes 'processes to produce chimeras from germ cells or totipotent cells of humans and animals', as it is that Recital 42 permits patents on

Member States *may* either take into account or ignore entirely at their own discretion. Indeed, there are numerous instances in which the ECJ has ruled that Member States are in breach of a Directive because one or more of its Recitals requires a reading of an Article that does not permit the actions taken by the Member State.[31] Investigation of how the ECJ actually uses Recitals in its rulings reveals that Recitals can be *decisive* in determining legal obligations under a Directive. Logic dictates that it is quite impossible for them to function in this way if they are *in no way* legally binding themselves! Thus, the most that can safely be inferred from the 'doctrine' that Recitals have no legally binding force is that, if they have any effect in determining obligations, this must be in their interpretive role. Correlative to this, Recitals (unlike Articles) do not have legally binding force *in their own right* or *regardless of* other considerations (e.g., the other Recitals, Articles of clear meaning and scope, other EC law, and even non-EC law that is valid under EC law) that Member States must take into account alongside them. On this basis,[32] the essential difference between a prescriptive Recital (as such) and a prescriptive Article is that prescriptive Articles must be given effect to *regardless of* any other considerations, whereas prescriptive Recitals must be given effect to (via their interpretation of one or more Articles) only *if other relevant considerations do not override them*. In other words, prescriptive Recitals are only legally binding *all things being equal* and are, thus, only legally binding *prima facie* – because the presumption must be that, not being Articles, all things *may* very well not be equal. However, if this is correct, then what Recital 26 prescribes will be legally binding on any Member State, *unless* that Member State can find legitimate derogating considerations that override the considerations that indicate that the Recital 26 requirement should be imposed. We suggest that, because of the importance of informed consent in EC law and European morality, no such derogations are available to Member States.

Thus, it should be assumed that it is a legally binding obligation of the EC's Nation States to ensure that patent applications are refused unless the persons from whose bodies source material was taken were given an opportunity to express free and informed consent, in accordance with national law.[33]

'inventions for therapeutic or diagnostic purposes which are applied to the human embryo and are useful to it'.

[31] See, to cite just one recent example, Case C-112/97 *Commission of the European Communities* v. *Italian Republic* [1999] ECR I-1821.

[32] See Deryck Beyleveld, 'Why Recital 26 of the EC Directive on the Legal Protection of Biotechnological Inventions should be Implemented in National Law' (2000) 4 *Intellectual Property Quarterly* 1.

[33] In ostensibly prohibiting the filing of a patent when the material from which the

Unfortunately, the way in which the closing clause 'in accordance with national law' appears in Recital 26 renders the Recital, from a purely grammatical point of view, ambiguous. Recital 26 can be read as saying either:

1. Nation States must ensure that patent applications are refused when the opportunity for expressing free and informed consent was not given; but that the precise procedures for ensuring this are (at least to some extent) at the discretion of national legislative authority; or

2. The requirement to ensure that patent applications are refused when the opportunity for expressing free and informed consent was not given is contingent upon the legislative position in each country – in the sense that if (a) there is no law (or, quaere, official procedure?) in a country requiring there to be an opportunity for expressing free and informed consent to the taking of human tissue; or (b) national law does not require patents to be refused if evidence shows that the opportunity for free and informed consent was not given, then that country can still be said to have fulfilled its obligations under Recital 26 if it does not now regulate accordingly.

It should, however, be apparent that (2) is not a permissible reading. If it is, then Recital 26 becomes completely redundant; for it then says that Nation States may go on doing whatever they were doing (prior to the Directive) about providing opportunities for expressing free and informed consent, in which case there is hardly need for specific attention to be drawn to the requirement. If, to this, it is objected that the point is precisely to clarify that Nation States may, if they wish, regulate for such a requirement, but need not, then it can be countered that it is odd in the extreme to explain that Nation States need not so regulate (but may if they wish) by actually saying that they *must* refuse patents subject to a condition that they only *may* impose. Indeed, we suggest that this is so ridiculous that if it really is what Recital 26 is intended to say then Recital 26 is worse than redundant, for it can then only be construed as serving to deceive the European Parliament (who wanted it in an Article under reading (1) above).[34]

---

invention was developed was obtained without providing 'an opportunity of expressing free and informed consent', Recital 26, furthermore, indicates that *immorality in the way in which the invention is developed* is to be taken as a reason for considering it to be immoral to grant a patent (and, because of the wording of Article 6(1), as a reason for considering it to be immoral to exploit the invention commercially). See our comments above at pp. 165–6.

[34] To this, it might be said that it has to be (and generally is) understood that the function of the Directive is to harmonise national *patent* practice, not to stipulate (and thus harmonise) national practice regarding the obtaining of consent in research settings. See Dominique Vandergheynst, 'The New Proposal on the Legal Protection of Biotechnological Inventions' in Sterckx, *Biotechnology, Patents and Morality*, p. 173 at

Even if we discount reading (2), there still remain a number of difficulties in reading (1). For example:

(a) Is it enough merely to give the *opportunity* for expressing free and informed consent, or must such consent *actually be given*? At one level, consent must actually be given, for it is, at the very least, misleading about one's intent to offer a person the opportunity to consent and then not to act on the consent or refusal when given. However, it is possible that the wording gives scope to the idea that non-objection as well as explicit consent will satisfy the requirement (and that this is a choice open to national discretion).

(b) Assuming our answer to (a), then is the required consent (i) to the taking of the material as such or (ii) specifically to the taking out of a patent (or the attempt to develop the material for the purpose of producing a patentable invention)? On the grounds that consent needs to be free and informed, we take the view that the consent must be to both the taking and the patenting.[35]

(c) Assuming our answers to (a) and (b), Recital 26 does not tell us anything about the precise procedures that need to be followed to satisfy its requirement. For example, it does not say anything about the form in which consent is to be evidenced for the purpose of filing a patent. This is not surprising, as patents can be developed from tissue taken from a single person (as happened with John Moore)[36] or on information gained from many samples, as would happen in developing test kits for genetic polymorphisms. Whereas

p. 174: '[S]ince the patent law system comes into play at the interface between research and product marketing, it cannot possibly provide the means of resolving ethical problems that arise at earlier and later stages of the process.'

[35] But note the distinction between treatment and non-treatment situations as drawn by the Nuffield Council on Bioethics in its Report, *Human Tissue: Ethical and Legal Issues* (London, 1995). There, the Council has a different recommendation when the material is removed for the purpose of treatment – in which case, specific consent to particular uses is *not* required – from when the material is removed for purposes other than treatment – in which case, specific consent is required. This should be contrasted with the position taken by the Health Council of the Netherlands, in *Proper Use of Human Tissue* (Publication No. 1994/01E) (The Hague, 1994), which requires specific consent in both cases. However, though we agree with the Health Council of the Netherlands, we should note that Article 22 of the Convention on Human Rights and Biomedicine states merely that the taking of human tissue must be subject to the 'appropriate consents being given', leaving judgement about this to national discretion. Generally, see Deryck Beyleveld and Roger Brownsword, 'Articles 21 and 22 of the Convention on Human Rights and Biomedicine: Property and Consent, Commerce and Dignity' in Peter Kemp (ed.), *Research Projects on Basic Ethical Principles in Bioethics and Biolaw* (Copenhagen: Centre for Ethics and Law, 1998) p. 33.

[36] *Moore v. Regents of the University of California* (1990) 793 P 2d 479; on which see, e.g., James Boyle, *Shamans, Software, and Spleens* (Cambridge, Mass.: Harvard University Press, 1996) esp. at pp. 21–4 and 99–107.

in the first case it would seem appropriate to show an actual signed consent, in the second case this would not be practicable and it might be sufficient to show that the research had Research Ethics Committee (REC) approval, coupled with a copy of the information/consent form that was given to the subjects who agreed to provide tissue. Again, these matters can be said to be at national discretion.

However, there are surely limits to the discretion to be allowed to Nation States on procedural matters. In the UK, the taking of human tissue within the NHS for research purposes is regulated by a system of RECs operating under guidance issued by the Department of Health (though at least some of the system's activities may soon be covered by an EC Directive on Good Clinical Practice). It might be tempting for the UK to claim that it is unnecessary for it to legislate procedures for checking on consent within the patent system, because RECs deal with appropriate consents for research studies and are responsible for ensuring that research studies that have inadequate consent procedures do not take place.

There are, however, at least two reasons why this will not suffice. First, the REC system only applies to NHS research, and tissue is and can be taken in other contexts. Secondly, whatever Recital 26 is about, it is plainly about what must be done to have a patent filed. As such, Recital 26 must be seen as an instruction to Nation States about the activities of the national patent offices, not as an instruction to RECs (which have no direct control over patenting). Granted, it is possible in effect to comply with Recital 26 through RECs. But for this to be the case, RECs need to be informed about Recital 26 and advised that it is necessary to obtain the appropriate consents to patenting as a condition of permitting research to go ahead. In effect, this would give RECs a role in the patent system as such.

Gathering together these strands, we see again that the Directive gives unnecessary opportunities for the important ethical requirement of informed consent to be talked down or diluted. Of course, if the interpretation of Recital 26, in conjunction with Article 6, were to be put to the test before the ECJ, the Court might put an end to any uncertainty about the import of the Directive. In the meantime, though, the culture of opposition to the Directive can be expressed not by open non-compliance but through several nice questions of interpretation.

How the morality clauses should be drafted

Starting afresh, how should a morality exclusion clause be drafted?[37] To answer this question, we need to distinguish two interpretive contexts, one in which it is understood that the Directive is to be read as subject to an overriding critical cultural morality centred on respect for human rights,[38] and the other in which there is resistance to the entry of moral criteria into the patent system as well as a tendency to treat that system as detached from other legal–moral instruments in Europe. In the former context, drafting a morality exclusion would present little challenge. It would suffice to provide, quite simply, that patents should not be granted where it would be immoral to do so – indeed, strictly speaking, it would not even be necessary to do this, for the interpretive community would already know that this was the case. To adopt such a minimalist approach in the latter context, however, would be a recipe for disaster: apart from engendering uncertainty, such an approach would give the morality exclusion no secure foothold in the patent system – it would be too easy to say that patents should be excluded only in the most exceptional of cases, where the grant would be morally inconceivable, or where gross immorality was involved, or where an overwhelming moral consensus opposed the patent, or something of that sort.[39] In such a context, the Directive should be drafted in such a way that opportunities for marginalising the morality exclusion and detaching the patent regime from European critical cultural morality are minimised. Since the context in which the Directive is to be implemented and applied is more like the latter than the former, a defensive approach is indicated. How, then, should Article 6 have been drafted?

First, the morality exclusion should have the right focus. As we have suggested, the focal question for any such exclusion is whether putting the applicant in a monopoly position in relation to the possible commercial exploitation of a particular invention gives rise to any moral difficulty. It follows that Article 6 should provide that inventions are to be considered unpatentable where it would be contrary to *ordre public*[40] or morality to place the applicant in a monopoly position in relation to such an invention and with a view to its commercial exploitation.

[37] See D. Beyleveld, R. Brownsword, J. Kinderlerer and M. Llewelyn, *Opinion on the European Commission's Proposal for a Directive on the Legal Protection of Biotechnological Inventions* (Sheffield Institute of Biotechnological Law and Ethics, 1996).

[38] See the analysis in Beyleveld and Brownsword, *Mice, Morality, and Patents.*

[39] See the line of argument in Armitage and Davis, *Patents and Morality in Perspective.*

[40] The concept of *ordre public* is notoriously difficult and there is a case for omitting it. For analysis of the relationship between *ordre public* and morality in the context of Article 53(a) EPC, see Beyleveld and Brownsword, *Mice, Morality, and Patents.*

Secondly, even with the proper focus, Article 6 might be argued to leave open questions about the range of relevant considerations. To avoid any doubt about the matter, therefore, it might be as well to provide explicitly that the morality of the research and development, publication and exploitation of the invention are relevant. In some contexts, such guidance might best be written into the Recitals but, in a defensive regime, it probably needs to go into the Articles. Of course, this still leaves plenty to argue about in relation to particular applications; but at least the argument should take account of all the material considerations and it should be properly focused.

Thirdly, the proviso to Article 6(1) should be redrafted to give national patent offices clear guidance that, in applying the morality test, they are applying the standard of critical cultural European legal-morality. There should be no possibility of thinking that the morality exclusion of the patent system is free-standing. Rather, patent examiners should be directed to give due consideration to such instruments as the European Convention on Human Rights, the Convention on Human Rights and Biomedicine, the opinions of the Group, and so on.

Fourthly, we would concede that there is room for argument about whether a list of specific exclusions should be included in the Directive. On the one hand, the attraction of such a list is that it at least ensures that the morality clause has some bite by definitely excluding some inventions – although it should be added that a defensive approach would advocate putting all the prohibited cases in the Articles (rather than splitting them, as in the Directive, between Article 6(2) and Recital 38). On the other hand, the argument against such a list (apart from it potentially entrenching errors of moral judgement) is that it makes no allowance for the contested nature of morality and the shifts that can take place in a community's critical moral judgements. If such counter-considerations were to be acted upon, a better drafting technique might be to employ an indicative list of questionable types of patent application.[41]

To be sure, it would be naive to suppose that a more defensive drafting of Article 6 would make all the difference, radically transforming the culture of the patent community. Equally, though, we would have to be extremely sceptical about the impact of the law to think that it would make no difference. The drafting of Article 6, we suggest, does matter. However, the test of the adequacy of its drafting is not that it has the power to overcome all forms of resistance but that it is at least drafted in

---

[41] Directive 93/13/EC on unfair terms in consumer contracts is a model for such an approach: [1993] OJ L95/29.

a way that makes no unnecessary concessions to a culture of reluctant compliance.

Conclusion

It is hardly surprising that Directive 98/44/EC should bear the marks of its troubled and tortuous passage. After all, this is a Directive that began its life as a response to developments in plant and animal genetics but then had to address developments in human genetics; that was apparently lost but then was reincarnated; that struggled every inch of the way to find a formula that would secure its acceptance by its various opponents in the European Parliament; and that had to do all this within the context of eliminating any trade barriers resulting from national differences in patent practice without compromising existing patent law obligations created by membership of the European Patent Convention. The problems with the Directive, however, are not over. For, it now finds itself sitting alongside the patent regime administered under the European Patent Convention, a regime that for more than a decade has been developing its own biotechnology jurisprudence while the EU has debated its position.[42] Quite clearly, the EU had good intentions in addressing the framework of European patent law, as it did in seeking to give guidance to national patent offices. Whether or not these good intentions will translate into good practice depends largely upon the willingness of the patent community to act upon both the moral spirit and the letter of the Directive. In a climate of conflicting cultures, our view is that there must be real doubts about whether the Directive will succeed in ensuring that biotechnological inventions are subjected to serious moral scrutiny in the national patent systems of Europe.

[42] This jurisprudence, of course, remaining untouched by decisions relating to the Directive. However, in the light of the decision of the Administrative Council of the European Patent Office to implement the Directive for the purposes of supplementary interpretation via Part II of the Implementing Rules ([1999] OJ EPO 437, [1999] OJ EPO 573 – these came into force on 1 September 1999) and the subsequent decision of the Enlarged Board of Appeal in *Novartis* (decision of 20 December 1999, Case G 0001/98; [2000] EPOR 303), which followed the principles laid down in the Directive, it would appear that the aim is to ensure greater symmetry between the two.

Part IV

Product liability and transnational health care litigation

8   The development risk defence and the European Court of Justice; increased injury costs and the Supplementary Protection Certificate

Richard Goldberg

Introduction

This chapter attempts to address and to link two major issues of European law in respect of medicinal products, one in the product liability arena and the other in the intellectual property arena. First, the role of the development risk defence of the UK Consumer Protection Act 1987, Part I, which implemented the EC Product Liability Directive, is discussed.[1] Examination is made of the implications of the decision of the Court of Justice of the European Communities (ECJ) concerning the UK's alleged failure to implement the Directive, in particular in respect of the development risk defence. Secondly, the chapter discusses the potential role of intellectual property rights in addressing the difficulty of increased injury costs as a result of the Product Liability Directive. A review is made of the Regulation establishing the so-called 'Supplementary Protection Certificate' (SPC), which was designed to address the problem of patent life erosion caused by the increased testing and authorisation requirements of new medicinal products. The possibility is then discussed of increasing patent restoration or marketing exclusivity in order to redress the adverse impact of product liability litigation on drug innovation. It is hoped that the interlinking of both product liability and intellectual property issues in this way will promote a greater understanding of the role of intellec-

---

For further details on the development risk defence and the economic consequences of increased injury costs in medicinal product liability, readers are referred to chapters 7 and 8 of Richard Goldberg, *Causation and Risk in the Law of Torts: Scientific Evidence and Medicinal Product Liability* (Oxford, Oreg.: Hart Publishing, 1999).

[1] Directive 85/374/EEC on the approximation of the laws, regulations and administrative provisions of the Member States concerning liability for defective products [1985] OJ L210/29. Article 7(e) of the Directive establishes the development risk defence in European law.

tual property rights as a potential tool in addressing the problem of increased injury costs in product liability litigation.

The nature of the development risk defence

One of the most controversial elements of the Product Liability Directive (the Directive) and its implementing Statute in the UK, the Consumer Protection Act 1987 (the Act), has been the development risk defence (the defence). The inability to foresee with certainty the long-term effects of technologically innovative products raises the problem of development risks.[2] Medicinal products, more than any other type of product, exemplify this lack of certainty. As a result of the concern of several States about the impact of the Directive on innovative industries if no such defence were included, the European Commission was forced to concede the inclusion of the defence.[3] The UK's identification with the defence's inclusion was clear from the outset. Indeed, during the last period of negotiation of the final text of the Directive in 1985, the Thatcher Government demanded that producers' interests be properly represented by the inclusion of such a defence. It was only when the defence was included that the UK was willing to sign the Directive, which required unanimity under Article 100 (now 94) EC for its adoption.[4]

The development risk defence is defined in Section 4(1)(e) of the Act. It is a term preferable to 'state of the art defence', since 'development risk' refers to undiscoverable defects[5] whereas 'state of the art' is associated with the most up-to-date technology and safety standards in a particular industry, the latter term (state of the art) being relevant to ascertaining defective products.[6]

---

[2] Commission of the European Communities Green Paper: Liability for Defective Products, Brussels, COM(99) 396 final (28 July 1999); hereafter Commission Green Paper.

[3] G. Howells and M. Mildred, 'Is European Products Liability More Protective than the Restatement (Third) of Torts: Products Liability?' (1998) 65 *Tennessee Law Review* 985 at 998.

[4] J. Stapleton, 'Products Liability in the United Kingdom: The Myths of Reform' (1999) 34 *Texas International Law Journal* 45 at 56–7.

[5] 'Development risks' have been defined as 'risks present in production sectors in which an advance in technological and scientific knowledge may make a product appear defective *ex post*, whereas it was not regarded as such at the time when it was manufactured': Case C-300/95 *Commission of the European Communities v. United Kingdom of Great Britain and Northern Ireland* [1997] ECR I-2649, per Advocate-General Tesauro, §18. Cf. Professor Stapleton's view that the term 'development risk defence' is misleading since Section 4(1)(e) of the Act covers not only those risks present in newly developed innovative products but also risks in established goods which have been on the market for a considerable amount of time: Stapleton, 'Products Liability', 51 n. 50, 56 n. 3.

[6] A. Clark, *Product Liability* (London: Sweet & Maxwell, 1989) 151; C. Newdick, 'The

Section 4(1)(e) of the Act states that there will be a defence to the person proceeded against to show that the state of scientific and technical knowledge at the relevant time was not such that a producer of products of the same description as the product in question might be expected to have discovered the defect if it had existed in his products while they were under his control. Article 7(e) of the Directive states that the defence will arise if 'the state of scientific and technical knowledge at the time when [the producer] put the product into circulation was not such as to enable the existence of the defect to be discovered'. *Prima facie*, it would seem that these two versions of the defence are different and that the UK version is apparently broader in its interpretation and more amenable to the interests of innovative producers, particularly of pharmaceuticals. The alleged distinction between the two versions of the defence led to infringement proceedings being brought by the Commission against the UK under Article 169 (now 226) EC for failure to fulfil the obligation of implementing the Directive correctly in this respect. The UK made a formal reply to the Commission's formal notice regarding incorrect implementation of the Directive, saying that they considered that they had implemented it in the only way possible in the UK. A reasoned opinion for failure to implement the Directive on Product Liability was sent by the European Commission to the UK,[7] to which the UK replied. The Commission considered that the complaint relating to Section 4(1)(e) of the Consumer Protection Act was justified and brought an action for a declaration that the UK did not correctly implement Article 7(e).[8] An oral hearing took place on 7 November 1996.[9] The Commission argued that the UK had broadened the defence under Article 7(e) of the Directive and converted strict liability imposed by Article 1 of the Directive into mere negligence

Development Risk Defence of the Consumer Protection Act 1987' (1988) 47 *Camb. L.J.* 455. Indeed, Advocate-General Tesauro seemed aware of this distinction when he said that since Article 7(e) referred 'solely to the scientific and technical knowledge at the time when the product was marketed, it [was] not concerned with the practices and safety standards in use in the industrial sector in which the producer [was] operating': Case C-300/95 *Commission of the European Communities* v. *United Kingdom of Great Britain and Northern Ireland* [1997] ECR I-2649, per Advocate-General Tesauro, §20. This position was affirmed by the ECJ's judgment: Case C-300/95 *Commission of the European Communities* v. *United Kingdom of Great Britain and Northern Ireland* [1997] ECR I-2649, §26.

[7] J. Searles and U. Scott-Larson, 'European Update' [October 1990], 12 *Product Liability International* 155.

[8] Case C-300/95 *Commission of the European Communities* v. *United Kingdom of Great Britain and Northern Ireland* [1997] ECR I-2649, I-2664, §1.

[9] M. Mildred, 'Class Actions', in C. J. Miller, *Product Liability and Safety Encyclopaedia* (London: Butterworths, 1997), Division IIIA, §131.

liability.[10] They submitted that the Article 7(e) test was objective, referring 'to a state of knowledge and not to the capacity of the producer of the product in question . . . to discover the defect', whereas Section 4(1)(e) of the Act presupposed 'a subjective assessment based on the behaviour of a reasonable producer'.[11]

The UK Government, on the other hand, argued that both the test in the Act and the Directive were objective.[12] Article 7(e) laid down an objective test in the sense that the 'state of scientific and technical knowledge [did] not refer to what the producer in question actually [knew] or [did] not know, but to the state of knowledge which producers of the class of the producer in question, understood in a generic sense, may objectively be expected to have'.[13] The UK Government stated that the UK courts were required to interpret Section 4(1)(e) of the Act consistently with Article 7(e) of the Directive, in accordance with Section 1(1) of the Act.[14] It was the UK's view that the Commission could only succeed in arguing that Section 4(1)(e) had failed to implement Article 7(e) of the Directive if Section 4(1)(e) was 'completely incapable of bearing the same legal meaning as Article 7(e)'.[15] In view of Section 1(1) of the Act, and the absence of any national decision on the meaning of Section 4(1)(e), the UK submitted that the Commission was not in a position to state that Section 4(1)(e) was incompatible with Article 7(e).[16]

Advocate-General Tesauro delivered his Opinion on 23 January 1997 and proposed that the Court should dismiss the application and order the Commission to pay the costs.[17]

The Advocate-General's Opinion

The Advocate-General attempted to describe in his Opinion what the concept of the state of scientific knowledge actually was. He observed: '[T]he state of scientific knowledge cannot be identified with the views expressed by the majority of learned opinion, but with the most advanced level of research which has been carried out at a given time.'[18] *Prima facie*, this would appear to give clear guidance to researchers in the pharmaceutical industry. However, it is at this point that his observations appear to become unclear. He observes that 'one isolated

---

[10] Case C-300/95 *Commission of the European Communities* v. *United Kingdom of Great Britain and Northern Ireland* [1997] ECR I-2649, I-2667, §16.
[11] *Ibid.*, I-2668, §17.   [12] *Ibid.*, I-2668, §19.   [13] *Ibid.*, I-2668–9, §§ 20–1.
[14] *Ibid.*, I-2669, §21.   [15] *Ibid.*, I-2669, §22.   [16] *Ibid.*
[17] Case C-300/95 *Commission of the European Communities* v. *United Kingdom of Great Britain and Northern Ireland* [1997] ECR I-2649, per Advocate-General Tesauro, §31.
[18] *Ibid.*, per Advocate-General Tesauro, §21.

opinion' which might eventually become the generally accepted view as to the potentially defective nature of a product is outside the scope of liability.[19] It would seem, however, that the word 'isolated' could have two possible connotations, namely isolated in terms of the accessibility of scientific and technical knowledge and isolated in terms of general acceptance of such knowledge.[20] Although Advocate-General Tesauro closely links isolation with availability and accessibility of such knowledge,[21] his choice of the word 'isolated' creates an uncertainty as to whether there is a link between an isolated opinion and one which might be regarded as a maverick opinion and lacking general acceptance. If there is such a link, then it would have been useful for the Advocate-General to have made this clear in his Opinion.

The Advocate-General defined the state of knowledge as including 'all data in the information circuit of the scientific community as a whole, bearing in mind, however, on the basis of a reasonableness test, the actual opportunities for the information to circulate'.[22] There is obviously a need to take into account the instantaneous nature of modern scientific knowledge on CD Rom, the Internet and other data retrieval systems for scientific and medical research.[23] The Opinion lacks discussion of the impact of the information superhighway on scientific and technical knowledge, and this is to be regretted.

The Advocate-General considered that there was no 'irremediable conflict' between Article 7(e) and Section 4(1)(e) of the Act, although he conceded the potential ambiguity of Section 4(1)(e).[24] Three reasons were given for this conclusion. First, the producer was central not only to the rules of the Directive as a whole, but also to Article 7(e), which is aimed at the producer. Thus Section 4(1)(e) of the Act was merely expressing in a clear way a concept which was implied in the Directive.[25] Secondly, the reference to the producer's ability to discover the defect was insufficient to make the test which it laid down a subjective one. To exclude the producer's liability, it had to be proved, 'in the light of the

---

[19] *Ibid.*, §22.   [20] *Ibid.*   [21] *Ibid.*, §23.   [22] *Ibid.*, §24.

[23] It has been argued that powerful computerised databases are available without regard to the industrial sector within which a producer works and that there is therefore no reason to confine discoverability to accessibility to a particular sector: M. Mildred and G. Howells, 'Comment on "Development Risks: Unanswered Questions"' (1998) 61 *Modern Law Review* 570 at 572. However, since the knowledge content of databases is great, it is arguably impossible and unjust for a producer to be aware of all knowledge in respect of a defect in *every* sector.

[24] Case C-300/95 *Commission of the European Communities* v. *United Kingdom of Great Britain and Northern Ireland* [1997] ECR I-2649, per Advocate-General Tesauro, §25.

[25] *Ibid.*, §26. Cf. the criticism by Howells and Mildred that this is tantamount to arguing that since the producer is the defendant, he should be judged by the standard of the producer, despite Article 7(e)'s language and purpose: Howells and Mildred, 'Is European Products Liability More Protective?' 1008.

most advanced scientific and technical knowledge objectively and reasonably obtainable', that the product was defective.[26] Thirdly, the system of liability was not one based on negligence, since under Section 4(1)(e) the burden of proof to rely on the defence was on the manufacturer.[27] However, it has been rightly pointed out that there is a distinction between substantive rules of liability, e.g. rules of negligence or strict liability, and those relating to the burden of proof.[28]

The Advocate-General reaffirmed the settled legal position of the ECJ that the scope of national laws, regulations or administrative provisions had to be assessed in the light of their interpretation by national courts[29] and that the failure of the Commission to wait until the Act was applied by the national courts before bringing an action against the UK for incorrectly implementing the Directive was 'overhasty'.[30]

In the light of these observations, the Advocate-General opined that the Commission had failed to show that Section 4(1)(e) of the Consumer Protection Act had not correctly implemented Article 7(e) of the Directive.[31]

The Judgment of the European Court of Justice

The ECJ, in its Judgment of 29 May 1997, followed the Opinion of the Advocate-General in dismissing the application and ordering the Commission to pay the costs on five grounds.[32]

First, Section 4(1)(e) placed the burden of proof on the producer, as required by Article 7. Nevertheless, it would seem that the defence itself has been constructed in a manner which reflects the requirements of negligence in that it stresses the conduct of producers and whether they might be expected to discover the defect. There is thus a marked failure of the Court, as there was with Advocate-General Tesauro,[33] to appreciate the distinction between substantive liability rules and those which concern the burden of proof.

Secondly, the Court held that Section 4(1)(e) placed no restriction on

[26] Case C-300/95 *Commission of the European Communities* v. *United Kingdom of Great Britain and Northern Ireland* [1997] ECR I-2649, per Advocate-General Tesauro, §26.
[27] *Ibid.*, §27.
[28] Howells and Mildred, 'Is European Products Liability More Protective?' 1008.
[29] Case C-382/92 *Commission* v. *United Kingdom* [1994] ECR I-2435, §36; Joined Cases C-732/91, C-138/91 and C-139/91 *Katsikas and Others* [1992] ECR I-6577, §39.
[30] Case C-300/95 *Commission of the European Communities* v. *United Kingdom of Great Britain and Northern Ireland* [1997] ECR I-2649, per Advocate-General Tesauro, §29.
[31] *Ibid.*
[32] Case C-300/95 *Commission of the European Communities* v. *United Kingdom of Great Britain and Northern Ireland* [1997] ECR I-2649, §§34–40.
[33] Cf. Howells and Mildred, 'Is European Products Liability More Protective?' 1008.

the state and degree of scientific and technical knowledge at the material time which was to be taken into account. The Court held that Article 7(e) was unreservedly directed at 'the most advanced level of such knowledge, at the time when the product in question was put into circulation'.[34] Arguably, however, the discoverability and accessibility of such knowledge is more restrictive than the ECJ held. Indeed, the Court stressed that it was implicit in Article 7(e)'s wording 'that the relevant scientific and technical knowledge must have been *accessible* at the time when the product in question was put into circulation'.[35] Moreover, Advocate-General Tesauro had already stated that although Article 7(e) was not concerned with the practices and safety standards in use in the industrial sector in which the producer was operating, it was concerned with assessing the producer's conduct by the 'yardstick' of the 'knowledge of an expert in the sector'.[36] In addition, the state of knowledge 'included all data in the information circuit of the scientific community as a whole, *bearing in mind, however, on the basis of a reasonableness test the actual opportunities for the information to circulate'*.[37] There is clearly therefore *some* restriction on the discoverability and accessibility of scientific and technical knowledge. Professor Stapleton has confirmed this view by explaining that although the Court did not consider that accessibility was relevant to the issue of whether information was part of the state of scientific and technical knowledge, it did rule 'that accessibility was relevant to the discoverability of information within that state of knowledge'.[38]

Thirdly, the Court held that the wording of Section 4(1)(e) did not suggest that the defence's availability depended on the subjective knowledge of a producer taking reasonable care in the light of the standard precautions of the relevant industrial sector. The producer's ability to discover the defect was formulated as an objective test by Advocate-

---

[34] Case C-300/95 *Commission of the European Communities* v. *United Kingdom of Great Britain and Northern Ireland* [1997] ECR I-2649, §26.

[35] *Ibid.*, §28, emphasis added. See also *ibid.*, §29, where the Court emphasised that 'for the relevant scientific and technical knowledge to be successfully pleaded as against the producer, that knowledge must have been accessible at the time the product in question was put into circulation'.

[36] Case C-300/95 *Commission of the European Communities* v. *United Kingdom of Great Britain and Northern Ireland* [1997] ECR I-2649, per Advocate-General Tesauro, §20.

[37] *Ibid.*, §24, emphasis added.

[38] Stapleton, 'Products Liability' 59–60. Cf. C. J. S. Hodges, Note, 'Development Risks: Unanswered Questions' (1998) 61 *Modern Law Review* 560, pp. 565, 567, who considers that the ECJ's approach of requiring the most advanced level of scientific and technical knowledge does not accord with the *reality* of scientific and technical knowledge, and is so high a standard that it could arguably never succeed in practice. However, the reality of such knowledge is the issue of its discoverability, which is delimited by the ECJ's judgment.

General Tesauro[39] on the basis that reference to the producer's ability is an 'objectively verifiable assessable parameter, which is in no way influenced by consideration of the actual subjective knowledge of the producer or by his organizational and economic requirements'.[40] But even if one was to concede that the test was objective, there would seem to be a subjective element in the sense that the judge is left to decide in the circumstances of the particular case whether a reasonable producer might have been expected to discover the defect. This is in line with Lord MacMillan's description of the standard of foresight of the reasonable man in negligence, when assessing whether a breach of duty of care has occurred, in *Glasgow Corporation* v. *Muir*.[41] He observed:

The standard of foresight of the reasonable man is in one sense an impersonal test. It eliminates the personal equation and is independent of the idiosyncrasies of the particular person whose conduct is in question . . . The reasonable man is presumed to be free both from over-apprehension and from over-confidence, but there is a sense in which the standard of care of the reasonable man involves in its application a *subjective* element. It is still left to the judge to decide what, in the circumstances of the particular case, the reasonable man would have had in contemplation and what, accordingly, the party sought to be made liable ought to have foreseen.[42]

Fourthly, having reaffirmed the rule that national laws, regulations or administrative provisions must be assessed in the light of the interpretation given to them by national courts,[43] the European Court held that the Commission had failed to refer to any national judicial decision which interpreted Section 4(1)(e) (the national law) as inconsistent with Article 7(e) (the Directive Provision). However, to give the Commission its due, there was always a legitimate fear that this issue would only be triable in a case involving the discoverability of unforeseeable or undiscoverable defects, often of medicinal products, which would take several years to come to trial in the UK. If such a case was to be decided on this issue, the development risk defence in its Section 4(1)(e) form might operate to deny liability in circumstances where the Article 7(e) definition might accept liability.

Fifthly, the European Court held that nothing in the material submitted to the Court suggested that the UK courts, if called upon to interpret Section 4(1)(e), would not do so in the light of the wording

---

[39] Case C-300/95 *Commission of the European Communities* v. *United Kingdom of Great Britain and Northern Ireland* [1997] ECR I-2649, per Advocate-General Tesauro, §26.

[40] *Ibid.* However, the pharmaceutical industry has consistently argued that discoverability should be linked to economic feasibility. See Goldberg, *Causation and Risk in the Law of Torts*, p. 230.

[41] [1943] AC 448.

[42] *Ibid.* at 457, emphasis added.

[43] See Case C-382/192 *Commission* v. *United Kingdom* [1994] ECR I-2435, §36.

and purpose of the Directive, as required by Article 189 (now 249) EC. Moreover, Section 1(1) of the Consumer Protection Act 1987 imposed such an obligation on the national courts.[44]

Professor Stapleton argues that the ambiguous nature of Article 7(e) 'allowed the possibility that the UK implementation [had] captured the, as yet, undetermined meaning of the article'.[45] She opines that since Article 7(e) is ambiguous, specifically in respect of the degree of accessibility of knowledge required to render a defect discoverable and thus overturning the defence, the ECJ was unable to rule that the 'covert, paraphrased "reasonableness" standard of [Section 4(1)(e) of] the Act had clearly not achieved' the Directive's intended result.[46] However, it is arguable that the UK draftsmen were also ambiguous in the way they in fact drafted Section 4(1)(e). Surely such a 'covert, paraphrased "reasonableness" standard'[47] is potentially misleading in its impact. It must have gone through the UK draftsmen's minds that the one clear situation in which the need for regard to the Directive is apparent is where the *UK legislation* is ambiguous. Since the legislation in Section 4(1)(e) *is* arguably ambiguous in *its* drafting,[48] regard should be had to the Directive. However, the UK remains protected from an allegation of failure to implement under Article 226 EC since the Directive will assist in the interpretation of Section 4(1)(e). To put it another way, only if Section 4(1)(e) had been *unambiguous* would there have been a strong argument that the legislation should have clearly enforced the Directive. The UK therefore seems to have benefited from the ambiguous way in which Section 4(1)(e) has been drafted.[49]

It is apparent from the Directive that Member States are at liberty to choose whether to adopt or to derogate from the development risk defence.[50] All Member States, including now France,[51] have adopted

---

[44] Case C-300/95 *Commission of the European Communities* v. *United Kingdom of Great Britain and Northern Ireland* [1997] ECR I-2649, §§34–40.

[45] Stapleton, 'Products Liability', 60.

[46] *Ibid.*   [47] *Ibid.*

[48] Cf. the view of Professor Stapleton that it is the *Directive* which is ambiguous, and that the producer-friendly construction of the Act is unambiguous: *ibid.* 57–8.

[49] Cf. the view of A.-G. Tesauro that the ambiguity of Section 4(1)(e) was irrelevant. What was at issue was the 'irremediable inconsistency with the Community provision which it purports to implement': Case C-300/95 *Commission of the European Communities* v. *United Kingdom of Great Britain and Northern Ireland* [1997] ECR I-2649, per A.-G. Tesauro at §14. However, it is submitted that the ambiguous nature of Section 4(1)(e) reduced the possibility of any such 'irremediable inconsistency' with Article 7(e) of the Directive.

[50] Article 15 of Directive 85/374/EEC [1985] OJ L210/29.

[51] France had been censured by the ECJ in 1993 for failing to transpose the Directive within the time limit of three years from the date of its notification (see Article 19 of the

national legislation implementing the Directive. All Member States except Luxembourg and Finland are adopting the development risk defence. Germany has adopted the defence, except with regard to pharmaceuticals; Spain has adopted the defence, except in respect of medicines, food or food products intended for human consumption,[52] and France has adopted the defence, except in respect of products derived from the human body.[53] The reason for Germany not adopting the defence in respect of pharmaceuticals is that Germany has its own separate strict liability regime for drugs under the German Pharmaceuticals Act of 1976. Section 84 of the Act imposes strict liability on a manufacturer or producer of pharmaceuticals in respect of harmful side-effects of his products. There is liability for development risks under the Act. Thus a manufacturer or producer of a medicinal product is legally responsible for adverse effects of the drug which were not apparent at the time when the medicinal product was first marketed.[54] Spain and France's reasons for excluding the defence in respect of pharmaceuticals are not precisely known, particularly where medicinal products and food products are those for which the defence would be most likely to be utilised.[55] However, Spain's exclusion of drugs, food or food products can be explained by a toxic syndrome in the early 1980s, which was caused by poor-quality cooking oil, and several drug disaster cases, which all had their effect in Spain, viz. MER 29 (a cholesterol-reducing drug which caused serious damage to the eyesight of at least 5,000 people), Aralen (an arthritis drug which caused blindness), quadrigen (a child vaccine which caused serious brain inflammation) and, of course, thalidomide. The cooking oil disaster resulted in the Spanish Consumer Protection Act of 1984, which introduced strict liability for high-risk products.[56] Perhaps Spain's position may have been prejudiced by its having a predominantly generic drug industry. France's reason for adopting the defence, except in respect of products derived from the

---

Directive): Case C-293/91 *Commission* v. *France* [1993] ECR I-1. In the absence of any transposition, the Commission decided in March 1998 to refer the daily fine of ECU 158,250 to be imposed in accordance with Article 171 (now 228) EC. As a consequence of the Commission's decision, France adopted Law No. 98–389 on 19 May 1998 to comply with its obligations: Commission Green Paper, p. 19.

[52] Commission of the European Communities, First Report on the Application of Council Directive on the Approximation of Laws, Regulations and Administrative Provisions of the Member States Concerning Liability for Defective Products (85/374/EEC) Brussels, COM(95) 617 final, p. 4. (13 December 1995).

[53] Commission Green Paper, pp. 24, 34.

[54] J. Finch and P. Ranson, *Product Liability in Europe: What the New EEC Directive Will Mean for Pharmaceutical Companies* (Richmond: PJB Publications, 1986) pp. 95–6.

[55] Howells and Mildred,'Is European Products Liability More Protective?' 1016.

[56] M. I. A. Vega, 'The Defence of Development Risks in Spanish Law' [1997] *Consum. LJ* 144 at 148–9.

human body, was confirmation of the decision of the Cour de Cassation on the 'contaminated blood' affair.[57]

It has long been argued that the Directive focuses upon a state of knowledge enabling discovery of a defect, while the UK Act stresses the conduct of producers.[58] However, it has been convincingly reasoned that the UK Government's interpretation, which manifested itself in the form of Section 4(1)(e) of the Act, is correct.[59] First, when an assessment of the relevant state of scientific and technical knowledge takes place, it will not require the defendant to prove 'a worldwide absence of knowledge of the defect'. In practice, the defence will operate when the defendant shows that there is no prior knowledge of the defect in the field with which he is expected to be familiar. Secondly, the plaintiff could expose information which revealed the defect but which could not reasonably be expected to be known to the producer. If such unrelated knowledge denied the defence's operation, the search for evidence would be 'haphazard and wasteful'.[60]

The Section 4(1)(e) definition is satisfactory for the Association of the British Pharmaceutical Industry (ABPI) in their capacity of representing the interests of the pharmaceutical industry.[61] Nevertheless, it is submitted that the words 'a producer of products of the same description as the product in question' cloud the definition with inherent complications. For example, does 'a producer of products of the same description as the product in question' refer to all producers of drugs of the same therapeutic class (the author's submitted view) or does the definition embrace a more comprehensive group of drugs? Perhaps courts will return to the Directive, in accordance with Section 1(1) of the Act, and to case law for an answer to these problems.

In considering the European Commission's comparatively uncontroversial proposal to extend the EC Product Liability Directive to cover primary unprocessed agricultural products and game,[62] the European

---

[57] Cass.1ere civ., *Cts X . . . C. GAN Incendie accidents et autres* [order No. 1395 P], as cited in Commission Green Paper, pp. 23, n. 45, 24.

[58] Clark, *Product Liability*, p. 153.

[59] Newdick, 'The Development Risk Defence' 459, 460.

[60] *Ibid.*, 465. Indeed, any narrower reading of the defence would fail to achieve the seventh recital of the Directive's goal of 'a fair apportionment of risk between the injured person and the producer [, which] implies that the producer should be able to free himself from liability if he furnishes proof as to the existence of certain exonerating circumstances': Directive 85/374/EEC, [1985] OJ L210/29 seventh recital; Stapleton, 'Products Liability', 60.

[61] See *ABPI Briefing on the Consumer Protection Bill*, 6 March 1987.

[62] Proposal for a European Parliament and Council Directive amending Council Directive 85/374/EEC on the approximation of the laws, regulations and administrative provisions of the Member States concerning liability for defective products COM(97) 478 final – COD 97/0244 [1997] OJ C337/54, Article 2. See now Directive 99/34/EC

Parliament's Committee on the Environment, Public Health and Consumer Protection sparked some controversy by proposing several significant changes to the Directive, including abolition of the development risk defence. The Committee stated that producers which enjoy the profits of putting a successful innovative product on the market should bear its risks.[63] However, the proposed changes to the Directive were rejected by the Council.[64] Nevertheless, before contemplating their second report on the Product Liability Directive in 2000, the European Commission have published a Green Paper on Liability for Defective Products, which has reopened a discussion of some of the most controversial elements of the Directive, including abolition of the development risk defence.[65] Indeed, when the relevant elements of the Green Paper are viewed, it seems that in one sense the Commission is actually putting the pharmaceutical industry on the defensive, to provide accurate information on the application of the defence in order to assess whether the defence's removal would discourage producers from innovation or would result in the uninsurability of such development risks. Since the obtaining of this information has always been patchy at best, this could prove to be difficult.

In the light of these discussions on the development risk defence, we can perceive the economic consequences of a medicinal product satisfying the requirements of the Consumer Protection Act 1987. If a medicinal product satisfies the requirements of defectiveness,[66] causation[67] and the development risk defence[68] in favour of the claimant in terms of the Consumer Protection Act 1987, liability of the producer

of the European Parliament and of the Council of 10 May 1999 amending Council Directive 85/374/EEC on the approximation of the laws, regulations and administrative provisions of the Member States concerning liability for defective products [1999] OJ L141/20. Since in all the major areas of health concern, particularly meat, the consumer is only exposed through eating the *processed* form of a product, the extension of the Directive to cover *unprocessed* agricultural products and game should produce no significant improvement, either doctrinal or practical, in consumers' rights: Stapleton, 'Product Liability', 68. On the other hand, the problem of salmonella infection in unprocessed poultry could be a practical issue.

[63] Report of the European Parliament Committee on the Environment, Public Health and Consumer Protection, on the proposal for a European Parliament and Council Directive amending Council Directive 85/374/EEC of 25 July 1985 on the approximation of the laws, regulations and administrative provisions of the Member States concerning liability for defective products (COM(97) 478 C4–0503/97–97/0244(COD)), doc. A4–0326/98 (28 September 1998).

[64] COD/1997/0244 on the European Parliament's website: http://wwwdb.europarl.eu.int/.

[65] Commission Green Paper, pp. 22–5.

[66] Sections 2(1), 3.

[67] Section 2(1).

[68] Section 4(1)(e).

would be established. Only then would an award of compensation result in injury costs.[69]

This essay now concludes with a proposed analysis of how such costs would be sustained by a pharmaceutical company, while at the same time protecting its ability to innovate, particularly in areas involving the manufacture of medicinal products with a high risk of adverse effects. The Supplementary Protection Certificate could be such a mechanism, by which there could be an increase in the effective monopoly of certain patented medicinal products.

Possible solutions to the problem of increased injury costs: the role of intellectual property rights

In circumstances where the hurdles of causation, defectiveness and the development risk defence have been overcome in favour of the claimant, pharmaceutical companies need to utilise insurance and self-insurance mechanisms in order to cover any overwhelming liability costs ensuing from a drug disaster. It is arguable, nevertheless, that insurance premiums cannot be expected to resolve the problem of untoward injury costs in high-risk and innovative areas involving medicinal products. It could be submitted that in order to protect innovation in such areas, an increase in effective patent life[70] of such drugs might be justifiable.

In January 1993, the European Community introduced a Regulation establishing the so-called Supplementary Protection Certificate to address the problem of patent life erosion caused by the testing and authorisation requirements of new medicinal products.[71] Any product

---

[69] Costs are an economic issue of considerable importance in the pharmaceutical industry, particularly in the context of product liability. The best way to conceptualise costs is in the form of a mathematical equation. It is clearly established that:

Economic performance   = social benefits minus social costs
(industry's contribution   (desirable   (undesirable
to living standards, i.e.   consequences)   consequences)
economic efficiency)

Social costs are defined as either resource costs (labour, buildings, machines and materials) or injury costs (the suffering of injuries from medicinal products and devices): see S. Garber, *Product Liability and the Economics of Pharmaceuticals and Medical Devices* (Santa Monica: RAND, 1993) pp. xxii–xxiii.

[70] Effective patent life is the period from the date of market introduction to that of patent expiry: H. Redwood, *Pharmaceutical Patent Term Restoration for the 1990s* (Felixstowe, Suffolk: Oldwicks Press, 1990) p. 18.

[71] Regulation 1768/92 concerning the creation of a supplementary protection certificate for medicinal products [1992] OJ L182/1. A resulting series of statutory instruments has helped establish the administrative procedures necessary for the SPC in the UK. These are: Patents (Supplementary Protection Certificate for Medicinal Products) Regulations 1992 SI 3091/1992; and Patents (Supplementary Protection Certificate for Medicinal Products) Rules 1997 SI 64/1997). A similar regulation has extended the

protected by a patent in a Member State and the subject of a marketing authorisation procedure can be the subject of a certificate.[72]

The Regulation for medicinal products establishes a five-year maximum period for the SPC's duration, with fifteen years' maximum effective monopoly.[73] The duration of the SPC is calculated by taking the time which has elapsed from filing the application for a basic patent to the date of first marketing authorisation and subtracting five years, subject to a maximum of five years total duration.[74] So if the period between patent filing and first marketing authorisation is less than or equal to five years, no SPC will be granted. If the period between filing and first marketing authorisation is between five years and ten years, an SPC will be granted. If the period between patent filing and first marketing authorisation is greater than or equal to ten years, the maximum duration of the SPC of five years will be granted.

It had previously been proposed by the European Commission that the maximum period of the SPC's duration be ten years, with sixteen years' maximum effective monopoly,[75] but political compromise and hostility from both patient groups and generic drug companies led to this period being reduced to five years duration and fifteen years' maximum effective monopoly.[76] The original proposal was described by the Common Law Institute of Intellectual Property as 'less than generous', and it stated that 'an effective life of sixteen years or less [was] not tolerable',[77] so it would seem that the compromise adopted an even less satisfactory position than the proposal.

The SPC is a *sui generis* form of intellectual property right which supplements the marketing authorisation of a product issued in accordance with drug regulatory requirements[78] and was designed to assist in

---

SPC to agrochemicals which also have problems of patent life erosion due to testing and authorisation requirements: Regulation 1610/96 concerning the creation of a supplementary protection certificate for plant protection products [1996] OJ L198/30.

[72] Regulation 1768/92, Article 2.

[73] Regulation 1768/92, Article 13.

[74] *Ibid.*

[75] See Proposal for Council Regulation (EEC) concerning creation of a supplementary protection certificate for medicinal products COM(90) 101 final – SYN 255 Brussels (11 April 1990) Article 8.1, and pp. 8, 37; R. Whaite and N. Jones, 'Pharmaceutical Patent Term Restoration' [1990] *EIPR* 179.

[76] See R. Whaite and N. Jones, 'Pharmaceutical Patent Term Restoration: The European Commission's Regulation' [1992] *EIPR* 324 at 325 and W. R. Cornish, *Intellectual Property: Patents, Copyright, Trade Marks and Allied Rights* (4th edn, London: Sweet & Maxwell, 1999) p. 159.

[77] Common Law Institute of Intellectual Property (CLIP) Report, *Supplementary Protection Certificates* (London: CLIP, 1991) pp. 21–3.

[78] H. P. Kunz-Hallstein, 'The Compatibility of a Community "Certificate for the Restoration of Protection"' [1990] *EIPR* 209, pp. 213–14. It has also been suggested that SPCs create a new intellectual property right different from patents since the link

the process of patent restoration for pharmaceuticals, viz. to help 'underpin [industry] resolve' to take the considerable risk of producing new drugs which would cope with serious gaps in therapy, particularly those arising from chronic diseases in the ageing population.[79] This principle is much less applicable to countries significantly reliant on the generic drug industry.[80] Ironically, it seems that the upper limit for the duration of the SPC of five years has penalised medicinal products with a development time greater than ten years by awarding them a shorter effective patent life, thus prejudicing products for the treatment of chronic diseases, where chronic toxicity tests, carcinogenicity tests and long-term efficacy tests necessarily result in longer testing-periods and development times.[81] SPCs are now recognised as 'essential to the

between investment and innovation is *indirect*, whereas SPCs *directly* protect the successful investment, since SPCs are only applied for in respect of successful products: CLIP Report, p. 18. Cf. Holyoak and Torremans, who disagree with the view that SPCs protect only successful inventions. They consider that patented inventions are successful by fulfilment of the patentability requirements and that the pharmaceutical industry often finds lucrative opportunities even for patented products which are not granted marketing authorisations as medicinal products. They say that the real tests for success are the drugs' sales figures. J. Holyoak and P. Torremans, *Intellectual Property* (2nd edn, London: Butterworths, 1998) p. 155. It is submitted that a marketing authorisation is a *sine qua non* for a medicinal product's success and that without such authorisation, a pharmaceutical product cannot properly be exploited. It would appear, therefore, that CLIP's observations are correct.

[79] Redwood, *Pharmaceutical Patent Term Restoration*, p. 1.

[80] In 1995, in Case C-350/92 *Kingdom of Spain* v. *Council of the European Union* [1995] ECR I-1985; [1996] FSR 73, Spain brought proceedings before the ECJ seeking the annulment of the Regulation creating the SPC. Spain claimed first that the Community had no competence to legislate in the area of patent law, relying on Articles 36 (now 30) EC and 222 (now 295) EC (the so-called '*ultra vires* argument'), and secondly that, in any event, Article 100a (now 95) EC was not the correct legal basis for the Regulation (the so-called 'legal basis argument'): *ibid.* §§75, 77, 82, 84. The ECJ held, in respect of the *ultra vires* argument, that neither Article 222 (now 295) EC nor Article 36 (now 30) EC reserved a power to delegate substantive patent law to the national legislature, to the exclusion of any Community action in the matter. The *ultra vires* argument was thus dismissed: *ibid.* §90. In respect of Spain's second claim, the legal basis argument, the ECJ held that the Regulation aimed to achieve the completion of the internal market and therefore was validly adopted on the basis of Article 95 EC (which empowered the Community to adopt measures for the approximation of the provisions laid down by law, regulation or administrative action in Member States): *ibid.*, §§91–2. Thus Spain's legal basis argument was also dismissed. Spain's motives in its proceedings before the ECJ were arguably coloured by its vested interest in relying heavily on the Spanish generic drug industry. It would also seem clear now that the enhancement of intellectual property on a Community-wide basis will only be held by the Court to be unjustified in the most exceptional of cases: Cornish, *Intellectual Property*, p. 25.

[81] H. von Morzé and P. Hanna, 'Critical and Practical Observations Regarding Pharmaceutical Patent Term Restoration in the European Communities' (1995) 77 *JPTOS* 479 at 518.

survival of a European R & D-based pharmaceutical industry'.[82] However, the majority of decisions have been on formal administrative requirements and technical issues affecting the operation of the SPC.[83]

[82] J. Adams, 'Supplementary Protection Certificates: The Challenge to EC Regulation 1768/92' [1994] *EIPR* 323 at 326.

[83] See, e.g., *Research Corporation's Supplementary Protection Certificate* [1994] RPC 387, 399; [1994] RPC 667, 674 (Patents Court) (both the SPC and the patent are subject to the same rights and limitations of a medicinal product (in terms of Article 5 of the Regulation) including the limitations of the licence of right provisions of the Patents Act 1977); *Research Corporation's Supplementary Protection Certificate* (No. 2) [1996] RPC 320, 327 (both the use of the active ingredient to formulate an authorised medicinal product and the medicinal product itself are protected by the SPC); *Farmitalia Carlo Erba Srl's SPC Application* [1996] RPC 111, 117 (applying the plain meaning of Article 13(1), the date of the first authorisation to place the product 'cabergoline' on the market in the Community was the date of an Italian authorisation for sale of a veterinary medicine (7 January 1987) as opposed to the date of a later Netherlands' authorisation for human use (21 October 1992)); *Centocar Inc.'s SPC Application* [1996] RPC 118, 121, 123 (claims of a basic patent, directed to a *combined* preparation of an anti-microbial agent and an antibody could not be regarded as protecting the *separate* administration of two separate products (one containing the antibody, the other containing the anti-microbial agent): such claims therefore did not protect an application of the antibody *per se*).
The scope of protection of the SPC was addressed in *Draco A.B.'s SPC Application* [1996] RPC 417, per Jacob J at 438–9, which held that the scope of protection was strictly confined to the product which obtained the authorisation, which had to be read using the definitions in Article 1(a) and (b) of the Regulation, and thus meant 'strictly confined to the active ingredient' of the medicinal product authorised to be placed on the market. New formulations of known drugs are thus not within the SPC's scope. A letter, permitting a company to supply a product for use in a particular clinical trial only, and which did not contain a summary of product characteristics in accordance with Article 8(1)(b), was held not to be a valid authorisation to place the product on the market as a medicinal product, in accordance with Article 3(b): *British Technology Group Ltd's SPC Application* [1997] RPC 118, 121. However, where a product in the form referred to in the marketing authorisation is protected by a basic patent in force, the SPC can cover that product as a medicinal product in *any* of the forms enjoying the protection of the basic patent: *Farmitalia Carlo Erba Srl* v. *Patentamt* ECJ (5th Chamber), 10 September 1999, §§21–2, 30.
In Case C-181/95 *Biogen Inc.* v. *SmithKline Beecham Biologicals SA* [1997] ECR I-357, the ECJ addressed two principal problems in respect of the granting of the SPC, viz. what transpires when a medicinal product is covered by several patents held by different companies, and what occurs when the holder of a basic patent and the holder of a marketing authorisation are different companies (a situation unforeseen at the time of drafting of Council Regulation 1768/92/EEC): see the Opinion of A.-G. Fennelly [1997] ECR I-357 at 360. The ECJ held that where a medicinal product is protected by a number of basic patents in force, which may belong to a number of patent holders, each holder of a basic patent may be granted an SPC, provided that only one certificate is granted for each basic patent: [1997] ECR I-357 at 395–6 and 401. The ECJ also held that where the basic patent and the marketing authorisation are held by different persons, and the patent holder is unable to provide a copy of the marketing authorisation in accordance with Article 8(1)(b) of the Regulation, the application for an SPC could not be refused on that ground alone since the national authority granting the SPC could obtain a copy of the marketing authorisation from the national authority which issued it, by virtue of simple co-operation between the authorities: [1997] ECR I-357 at 400, 402.

It has thus been observed that the rationale behind patent restoration and the emergence of the SPC has been the erosion of patent life, due to the time taken for a drug to receive its marketing authorisation. On closer examination, it could be argued that the real link is not solely between drug regulation and patent law but also between drug disasters, product liability and patent law. The emergence of an increase in the time for testing medicinal products could be linked to the occurrence of potential adverse drug reactions (ADRs) associated with such products. The ADRs associated with drugs used in pregnancy, e.g. thalidomide and Diethylstilbestrol, revealed the dangers of teratogenesis and second generation neoplasia respectively; the ADRs associated with certain non-steroidal anti-inflammatory drugs (NSAIDs), such as gastrointestinal haemorrhage, renal and hepatic reactions and dangers of their use in the elderly, gave important information. This provided the basis for requesting additional tests in clinical and preclinical trials for new related drugs. It is conceivable that increased testing has emerged, partly as a result of increased pharmacovigilance, but also as a result of product liability litigation associated with ADRs to certain drugs.

It is possible that increasing patent restoration or marketing exclusivity (the period of effective monopoly of a patented medicinal product) could be justified by several factors, other than the erosion of patent life, which might affect the costs sustained by pharmaceutical companies. Such factors could include the type and age of patient, the type of disease being treated and the nature of the drug,[84] where product liability litigation has been associated with similar drug structures.

Such developments remain possible,[85] but will be contingent upon future evidence as to whether product liability litigation will result in an increase in costs to pharmaceutical companies.

It has also been held by the ECJ that the grant of an SPC pursuant to the transitional provisions of Article 19 of Regulation 1768/92 is, in accordance with Article 3(b), conditional on a valid marketing authorisation having been granted in the Member State in which the application is submitted and at the date of that application: Case C-110/95, *Yamanouchi Pharmaceutical Co. Ltd* v. *Comptroller of Patents, Designs and Trade Marks* [1997] ECR I-3251 at 3277, §§28, 29.

[84] See the erosion of patent life in respect of anti-infective drugs, CVS drugs and CNS drugs in Y. Lis and S. Walker, *Pharmaceutical Patents: The Stimulus to Medicines Research* (Carshalton, Surrey: Centre for Medicines Research, 1988) p. 21 figure 8.

[85] Any further proposals to increase patent restoration or marketing exclusivity would need to consider the possibility of an overreaction to the strengthening of such intellectual property rights. Indeed, Professor Cornish has cautioned about extensions of a patent generally without 'most careful consideration': Cornish, *Intellectual Property*, p. 134.

Conclusion

In respect of the development risk defence, the ECJ decision, although generating some certainty over the issue as to whether Section 4(1)(e) properly implemented Article 7(e) of the EC Product Liability Directive, has arguably raised more questions than answers.

First, whatever the views of the European Court, it would seem that since the Section 4(1)(e) version of the defence has been constructed in a way which places emphasis upon the conduct of producers, it has been formulated in a manner which reflects the requirements of negligence. Secondly, it would appear that national courts will consider the issue of discoverability of a defect with, at the very least, a subjective element in their overall approach. Thirdly, the discoverability and accessibility of scientific and technical knowledge are more restrictive than the European Court's decision would at first suggest.

It is also arguable that the UK has benefited from the ambiguous way in which Section 4(1)(e) has been drafted. The apparent aborted outcome of the deliberations concerning the proposals of the European Parliament's Committee on the Environment, Public Health and Consumer Protection would appear to be a disappointment to consumer and patient interest groups, particularly in respect of their proposed abolition of the development risk defence. However, the European Commission's Green Paper seems to have re-opened the possibility of the defence's abolition. This will surely be a critical element of their second report on the Directive's operation, which is planned for the end of 2000.[86] It would seem that the development risk defence is one of the main obstacles to the achievement of strict liability under the Consumer Protection Act 1987, since discoverability by the manufacturer of unknowable defects of medicinal products will be decided in a manner likely to be identical to the requirements of negligence. Nevertheless, it could be argued that the defence is of possible assistance to therapeutic innovation and development within the pharmaceutical industry.[87]

Yet there would seem to be a reasoned argument for saying that the

---

[86] It has been predicted that the second report 'will be of outstanding importance in the design of the new millennium's system of product liability': J. J. I. Peris, 'Liability for Defective Products in the European Union: Developments since 1995 – the European Commission's Green Paper' [1999] *Consum. LJ* 331 at 346.

[87] There is considerable support both for excluding and for including liability for development risks under strict liability: see J. Fleming, 'Drug Injury Compensation Plans' (1982) 30 *Am. J Comp. L* 297 at 308–9. Compensation for development risks may be desirable for reason of compensating the injured from a 'deeper pocket'. However, it is unjustifiable on the grounds of inefficient resource allocation since development risks 'are unavoidable and preventable only by incurring socially undesirable costs' (e.g. longer testing): *ibid.* 312–13.

defence fails to take account of the very victims of innovation when therapeutic medicines may cause severe adverse effects. Indeed, the Pearson Commission recommended that, in introducing a system of strict liability for defective products, the 'producer should not be allowed a defence of development risk'[88] despite arguments that the cost of insurance might affect new product development. The dismissal of the defence was based on the premise that to include it 'would be to leave a gap in the compensation cover, through which, for example, the victims of another thalidomide disaster might easily slip'.[89] Similar concerns were raised before the defence's introduction into UK law.[90] At the time of the European Commission's first report on the application of the Product Liability Directive, the Commission had 'not considere[d] it necessary, at [that] stage, to submit any proposals for' the Directive's amendment,[91] and the future of the defence, given the absence of cases under the Directive, seemed fairly secure.[92] It is possible that this position may change in the Commission's second report, but the odds would seem to be against it. Professor Stapleton remains sceptical that the defence will eventually be abolished, because of its importance for technologically innovative sectors, such as the pharmaceutical industry, and also, more widely, because of its symbolic significance.[93]

---

[88] Royal Commission on Civil Liability and Compensation for Personal Injury, Cmnd 7054–1/1978, §1259. The Law Commission had similarly rejected the defence: Liability for Defective Products, Law Com. No. 82, Cmnd 6831/1977, §105.

[89] Royal Commission on Civil Liability and Compensation for Personal Injury, §1259. Professor Stapleton has recently reaffirmed the long-felt view of scholars in this area that the thalidomide children 'would fail under the Directive as they would have failed at common law': Stapleton, 'Products Liability', 61.

[90] A. Forte, 'Medical Products Liability' in S. McLean (ed.), *Legal Issues in Medicine* (Aldershot: Gower, 1981) p. 76; P. Cane, *Atiyah's Accidents Compensation and the Law* (4th edn, London: Weidenfeld & Nicolson, 1987) p. 145. See also the view of Miller that those who support the existence of the defence 'are saying in effect that liability for design or composition defects continues to be based on negligence or fault' and that although '[t]his is a perfectly tenable point of view', it is inconsistent with purporting to introduce strict liability along the lines of the Pearson Commission's or the Law Commission's proposals: Miller, *Product Liability and Safety Encyclopaedia*, Division III, §131.

[91] Commission of the European Communities, First Report on the Application of Council Directive on the Approximation of Laws, Regulations and Administrative Provisions of the Member States Concerning Liability for Defective Products (85/3741/EEC) p. 2.

[92] See C. J. S. Hodges, *Report for the Commission of the European Communities on the Application of Directive 85/374/EEC on the Liability for Defective Products* (London: McKenna & Co., 1994) p. 26, §77.

[93] Stapleton, 'Products Liability', 69. Professor Stapleton considers that the European perception of the US experience and the 'retrenchment of liability' of the Restatement Third, Torts: Products Liability will increase the justification for the defence's retention: *ibid.* Indeed, the *Restatement* has adopted a standard at least as negligence-

The chapter has finally addressed the scenario where the hurdles of causation, defectiveness and the development risk defence have been overcome in favour of the claimant. In this part of the chapter, an attempt has been made to develop the role of intellectual property rights as a means of addressing the problem of increased injury costs in medicinal product liability litigation. Thus, in addition to the use of insurance, the possibility has been mooted of increasing patent protection or marketing exclusivity through an adapted Supplementary Protection Certificate in circumstances where certain factors may affect the costs of pharmaceutical companies, e.g. where product liability litigation has affected innovation of similar drug structures for diseases of exceptional community need, such as AIDS, or pioneering approaches to therapeutics, including gene therapy. These advanced techniques have the potential of resulting in product liability litigation in the twenty-first century, yet in gene therapy we have a probable way of dealing with congenital disease, cancer and infections of worldwide significance. Such intellectual property developments will be dependent upon whether product liability litigation will produce a significant increase in costs to pharmaceutical companies in the future. Indeed, other unforeseeable factors may affect such costs. It may then be prudent to reconsider the possible option of increasing patent protection or marketing exclusivity with a reconceptualised Supplementary Protection Certificate.

---

orientated as our development risk defence in that §6(c) imposes liability only where the design of a prescription drug or prescription product poses sufficiently large foreseeable risks compared to its foreseeable therapeutic benefits that 'reasonable health care providers, knowing of such foreseeable risks and therapeutic benefits, would not prescribe the drug or medicinal device for any class of patients': American Law Institute, *Restatement of the Law Third, Torts: Products Liability* (St Paul, Minn.: American Law Institute Publishers, 1998). In essence, the plaintiff must prove that the drug or device should not have been on the market at all – arguably a kind of 'super' negligence standard, and one that could well be higher than that under Section 4(1)(e) of the Act: see T. M. Schwartz, 'The Impact of the New Products Liability Restatement on Prescription Products' (1995) 50 *Food and Drug Law Journal* 399 at 407. For the view that the EC Directive is a more protective regime for consumers than the Third Restatement, see Howells and Mildred, 'Is European Products Liability More Protective?' 1029. However, they also consider that accepting the principle of strict liability inevitably involves a rejection of the inclusion of the development risk defence: *ibid.* 1030. For products other than prescription drugs, Restatement Third, Torts: Products Liability §2(b) and (c) address, respectively, design defects and failure-to-warn defects, by requiring that 'foreseeable risks of harm' posed by design defects be avoided by the adoption of a 'reasonable alternative design' (§2(b)) and by requiring that 'foreseeable risks of harm' posed by failure-to-warn defects be avoided by the provision of 'reasonable instructions or warnings' (§2(c)). It would seem that such development risk considerations would exculpate defendants under the Third Restatement: *ibid.* 1025.

9   Transnational health care litigation and the
     Private International Law (Miscellaneous
     Provisions) Act 1995, Part III

Jonathan Harris

Introduction

The impact of the Conflict of Laws on health care litigation is considerable. The cross-border nature of manufacture, distribution and consumption of products makes the prospect of transnational disputes a
very real one. Since it might not be easy to determine where the
consequences of such action might be felt, the forum in which a
defective products case might be litigated cannot easily be predicted.
Furthermore, in the absence of harmonised choice of law rules, the law
applicable on the merits of a dispute cannot readily be foreseen. This is
a potentially serious problem for manufacturers of health care products.
Imagine a case where a manufacturer in State A produced pharmaceuticals sold in State B and consumed in England, where they are found to
be defective. All would be potentially available fora in which a consumer
might sue. If English courts would apply the law of the place of
consumption on the merits, the courts of State A the law of the place of
production, and the courts of State B the law of the place where the
goods were marketed, a manufacturer might need to comply with the
laws of three different States in order to satisfy himself that he would not
be exposed to tortious liability.[1] This could be said to be a major
impediment to the free movement of health care products throughout
Europe.

   Another major area of transnational litigation which is likely to arise
in the health care sphere concerns the violation of patents and trade

---

[1] Assuming that a particular court would characterise the claim as tortious and apply
choice of law in tort rules. The possibility that it would instead characterise the claim by
a consumer against a manufacturer as contractual cannot be ignored. See the discussion
of the scope of the Private International Law (Miscellaneous Provisions) Act 1995, Part
III, below.

marks in health care products.[2] Once again, the place where a violation occurs can be problematic. Furthermore, the territorial nature of these rights means that attempting to litigate the alleged infringement of a patent or trade mark in a foreign court can be unexpectedly complex.

Both product liability and infringement of intellectual property right disputes are areas which are heavily affected by the continuing tide of new legislation and case law on jurisdiction, enforcement of foreign judgments[3] and choice of law.[4] The focus of this chapter is ostensibly on the last of these three. The Private International Law (Miscellaneous Provisions) Act 1995, Part III, introduced major changes to the choice of law rules in tort in England. It is proposed to examine how these changes impact on transnational health care litigation in the two areas mentioned above.[5] An attempt will not be made to review the law

---

[2] See generally J. Fawcett and P. Torremans, *Intellectual Property and Private International Law* (Oxford: OUP, 1998).

[3] The present version of the Brussels Convention on Jurisdiction and Judgments (which was incorporated into English law by the Civil Jurisdiction and Judgments Act 1982) can be found in [1990] OJ C189/2. However, the Brussels Convention is to be replaced by a Regulation: see COM(99) 348 final. This has been made possible by the Treaty of Amsterdam, which entered into force on 1 May 1999, and which has brought judicial co-operation in civil matters having cross-border implications within the sphere of the EC Treaty (Article 65 (ex 73m) EC), in so far as necessary for the proper functioning of the internal market. The United Kingdom has an opt-out from Article 65 EC (Article 69 (ex 73q) EC preserves the Protocol on the position of the United Kingdom and Ireland, which can be found in [1997] OJ C340/99). The United Kingdom may choose to opt back in to individual initiatives. However, doing so would appear to grant the Community institutions an exclusive competence to act for the United Kingdom in matters within the Regulation's scope and remove the United Kingdom's right to enter into treaties in the area with non-Member States: see P. Beaumont, 'Current Developments in EC Law: ECJ and Jurisdiction and Enforcement of Judgments in Civil and Commercial Matters' (1999) 48 *ICLQ* 225, 228–9. There are also proposals for a Hague Worldwide Convention on Jurisdiction and Judgments in Civil and Commercial Matters ('the Worldwide Judgments Convention'), on which it is hoped to reach agreement at the Nineteenth Session of the Conference, which will conclude in late 2001 or early 2002. A preliminary draft of this Convention was adopted by the Special Commission on 30 October 1999. The drafting of the exclusive jurisdiction provisions relating to intellectual property in this Convention is likely to cause particular problems (see the draft versions of Article 12(4)–(6), Worldwide Judgments Convention).

[4] An Action Plan of the Council and Commission indicates that within two years of entry into force of the Treaty of Amsterdam, necessary revisions of the Rome Convention on the Law Applicable to Contractual Obligations (enacted into English law by the Contracts (Applicable Law) Act 1990) should have been completed and a legal instrument on the law applicable to non-contractual obligations drawn up ('Rome II'): see Action Plan of the Council and Commission on how best to implement the provisions of the Treaty of Amsterdam establishing an area of freedom, security and justice, adopted on 7 December 1998: [1999] OJ C19/1.

[5] I.e. product liability and infringement of intellectual property right claims. Discussion on the latter will focus henceforth primarily on the infringement of patents. However, the Conflict of Laws issues raised by both patents and trade marks overlap to a considerable extent.

comprehensively, but rather we will look at certain particularly dispu-
table issues. It will be demonstrated that the new legislation has
rendered the law in these areas unexpectedly complex. Moreover, the
impact of the reformed choice of law rules extends beyond the confines
of the scope of the legislation itself, since it also has a more subtle
impact upon the jurisdictional rules applied in an English court. It will
be shown that this interrelationship between the choice of law rules in
tort and those of jurisdiction is by no means a happy one.

Choice of law problems

The common law choice of law in tort rules

It is not proposed exhaustively to examine the common law rules, which
are discussed extensively elsewhere.[6] In essence, however, the claimant
was required to show both that the alleged wrong would have constituted a tort according to English domestic law and that it would also
have given rise to some form of civil liability by the law of the place
where the tort occurred (*lex loci delicti*).[7] This rule of 'double actionability', which had been developed in the nineteenth century[8] and recast
in the twentieth,[9] was a rather claimant-unfriendly one,[10] since it
required the availability of a particular cause of action under two
different laws.

Nonetheless, its effect on the law relating to defective products and to
intellectual property right violation claims was tolerably clear. A manufacturer domiciled in England could rest assured that, if he were to
export his health care product and it were to inflict harm overseas, he
could not be sued successfully in an English court if he had complied
with the requirements imposed by the English law of tort. In that sense,
trading activity might be said to have been promoted by the rule. As
regards infringement of patents, the position was even more stark. A
patent is territorial in its operation. It follows that, as a matter of English
law, a foreign patent cannot be infringed by an act committed in
England.[11] This meant that claims for infringement of a foreign patent

---

[6] See, e.g. L. Collins (ed.), *Dicey and Morris, The Conflict of Laws* (13th edn, London:
Sweet and Maxwell, 2000) ch. 35, pp. 1508–14, 1560–72; P. North and J. Fawcett
(eds.), *Cheshire and North's Private International Law* (13th edn, London: Butterworths,
1999) ch. 19, pp. 609–14.

[7] *Phillips* v. *Eyre* (1870) LR 6 QB 1.

[8] *Ibid.*

[9] *Boys* v. *Chaplin* [1971] AC 356.

[10] See *M'Elroy* v. *M'Allister* 1949 SC 110 for an example of the harshness of the rule.

[11] *Potter* v. *Broken Hill Pty Co. Ltd* (1906) 3 CLR 479; *Norbert, Steinhardt and Sons Ltd* v.

would quite simply not be entertained in an English court, since they were not actionable as a tort by English law and could be struck out as bound to fail on the merits.[12]

In any event, the perceived strictness of the double actionability rule had been significantly relaxed in recent years. In *Boys* v. *Chaplin*,[13] the House of Lords ruled that in a suitable case, the *lex loci delicti* could be disapplied in whole or in part, so that some or all issues could be resolved exclusively by English law. The precise operation of the exception was not wholly clear. Lord Wilberforce appeared to suggest that it could be applied where the *lex loci delicti* had no interest in being applied to a particular issue,[14] although it also seemed that if the centre of gravity was England, that could suffice to invoke the exception.[15] In *Red Sea Insurance Co. Ltd* v. *Bouygues SA*,[16] the Privy Council allowed 'single actionability' to work the other way, by holding that in an appropriate case English law could be disapplied in whole or in part and the *lex loci delicti* alone applied.

The introduction of these exceptions led to a choice of law rule well suited to the needs of transnational tort litigation. The importance of the *lex loci delicti* to most disputes (as the law of closest connection) is self-evident; but the exception in *Boys* dealt with cases where the locus of the tort might be arbitrary and where the connection with England was especially strong. The importance of English law stems from the intimate connection of tortious liability with the law of civil liberties. The fact that a claim had ordinarily to succeed by English domestic law as well meant that a claimant could not successfully sue a defendant in England for conduct which the latter was free to engage in by English domestic law. However, for torts where infringement of English civil liberties was less of a concern, the *lex loci delicti* alone could be applied if the matter had little real connection with England.[17]

The Private International Law (Miscellaneous Provisions) Act 1995,

---

Meth (1960) 105 CLR 440. See the discussion of justiciability and foreign intellectual property rights below.

[12] *Dicey and Morris, The Conflict of Laws*, p. 1521.

[13] [1971] AC 356.

[14] *Ibid.* 391.

[15] *Boys* itself was a case concerning a road accident in Malta involving two members of the armed forces resident in England. The exception was applied. See also *Johnson* v. *Coventry Churchill International Ltd* [1992] 3 All ER 14.

[16] [1995] 1 AC 190.

[17] The fact that a case has little connection with England does not necessarily mean that the English court would not take jurisdiction over it. If the common law jurisdiction rules are applicable, the English court would only stay proceedings if the defendant sought a stay; given the defendant-friendly choice of law rules in tort, he would be unlikely to do so. If the Brussels Convention applies, a court with jurisdiction may not ordinarily stay its proceedings on the grounds that the natural forum lies elsewhere.

Part III (hereafter 'the Act') has purported to replace the flexible double actionability rule with a simple choice of law rule in favour of the law of the place of the tort. It is no longer necessary that the alleged conduct be tortious by English domestic law, if it constitutes a tort by the *lex loci delicti*.

The Act has prompted a wave of criticism.[18] Briggs has commented that '[i]t is the view of this writer that legislation was unnecessary . . . and that the actual form taken by the legislation is user-hostile and intellectually weak'.[19] It is difficult to dissent from such a view. However, it is not intended to reiterate those criticisms here. Rather, it is proposed to show how some of these concerns weigh especially heavily when applied to potential tortious actions in the field of transnational health care litigation.

The scope of the Act

The Act is stated to apply to 'issues relating to tort'.[20] Section 9(2) provides that: 'The characterisation for the purposes of private international law of issues arising in a claim as issues relating to tort or delict is a matter for the courts of the forum.'

This is highly problematic. As the rule in *Boys* v. *Chaplin*[21] had generally required the claim to constitute a tort according to English domestic law, it followed that claims which would not be recognised as constituting tortious conduct by English domestic law were not brought in English courts.[22] Accordingly, no private international law definition of 'tort' had emerged and the Act offers no guidance on the matter.

Furthermore, even if a matter is to be characterised for private international law purposes as tortious, it does not follow that it will be

---

18 A. Briggs, 'Choice of Law in Tort and Delict' [1995] *LMCLQ* 519; P. Carter, 'The Private International Law (Miscellaneous Provisions) Act 1995' (1996) 112 *LQR* 190; J. Harris, 'Choice of Law in Tort – Blending in with the Landscape of the Conflict of Laws?' (1998) 61 *Modern Law Review* 33; C. Morse, 'Torts in Private International Law: A New Statutory Framework' (1996) 45 *ICLQ* 888; A. Reed, 'The Private International Law (Miscellaneous Provisions) Act 1995 and the Need for Escape Devices' (1996) 15 *CJQ* 305.

19 Briggs, 'Choice of Law', 520.

20 Section 9(1). See also Briggs, 'Choice of Law', 523.

21 [1971] AC 356, as interpreted in *Church of Scientology of California* v. *Commissioner of the Metropolitan Police* (1976) 120 *Sol. Jo.* 690 and *Coupland* v. *Arabian Gulf Oil Co.* [1983] 1 WLR 1136.

22 Although the exception introduced in *Red Sea Insurance* v. *Bouygues* [1995] 1 AC 190 would potentially have required an English court to deal with causes of action not known in England (or not regarded as matters relating to tort in English domestic law) where the matter was entirely connected with the place of the tort and the court was minded by exception to disapply English domestic law and apply solely the *lex loci delicti*.

governed by the Act, due to an unfortunate piece of legislative drafting. Section 14(2) states that 'nothing in this Part affects any rule of law (including rules of private international law) except those abolished by Section 10 above'. Section 10 is a statement of the double actionability rule and an abolition thereof.[23] It follows that some issues, although characterised for the purposes of private international law as tortious, will continue to be governed by the common law, since they were nonetheless not formerly part of the double actionability rule.[24]

This might be especially significant in the health care arena where an action is brought for breach of confidence. Though a claim which would be characterised for domestic law purposes as an equitable wrong, it might come within a private international law definition of 'tort'. However, whilst the precise choice of law rules applicable to equitable wrongs are unclear,[25] it does not appear that this type of claim was formerly governed by the common law double actionability rule. On one view, this means that it continues to be outside the Act.[26]

A more striking problem is with torts which occur in England. Section 9(6) states that, 'for the avoidance of doubt', the Act applies to events occurring in England as it applies to events occurring overseas, *subject to the provisions of Section 14*. However, torts occurring in England were *not* subject to the double actionability rule, but rather to a separate rule in *Szalatnay-Stacho* v. *Fink*[27] that English domestic law alone would always apply. If by Section 14(2) the Act only replaces the rule as stated in Section 10 and this rule was not part thereof, then arguably it was not abolished by Section 10 and replaced by the Act's provisions, despite the wording of Section 9(6).[28]

The result of this uncertainty is that it may be of critical importance in a defective product case in which, for example, a health care product is manufactured in State A, purchased in State B and consumed in England, to ascertain whether the locus of the tort is England, in order to determine whether to look to the statute at all. Patent infringements

---

[23] Save in the case of defamation and related claims, where the common law rule is preserved by Section 13.

[24] On this see Briggs, 'Choice of Law', 521.

[25] L. Barnard, 'Choice of Law in Equitable Wrongs: A Comparative Analysis' (1992) 51 CLJ 474.

[26] See Briggs, 'Choice of Law', 522.

[27] [1947] KB 1.

[28] Morse, 'Torts in Private International Law', 890 argues that the *Szalatnay* rule could be said to have become subsumed within the double actionability rule post-*Red Sea*, as the double actionability rule had become sufficiently flexible to deal with torts occurring in England. Whilst this reasoning attracts some support in *Dicey and Morris, The Conflict of Laws*, pp. 1516–17, it is somewhat speculative, given that there is no authority to this effect and that the *Szalatnay* rule is clearly distinct in origin. See also *Cheshire and North's Private International Law*, pp. 625–6.

are equally problematic. A UK patent cannot be infringed by an Act committed outside the jurisdiction;[29] hence it will be critical to determine the place of the infringement in the first instance. If infringement occurs in England and constitutes tortious conduct by English domestic law, a successful action could potentially be brought; but the Act may be inapplicable to the matter.

The implications of Section 9 stretch further still. As a matter of English domestic law, one would expect a claim brought by a consumer of a defective health care product against its manufacturer to sound in tort. However, the United Kingdom has enacted the Rome Convention on Choice of Law in Contract.[30] Where applicable, it is stated that its provisions 'shall apply'.[31] The Convention applies to 'contractual obligations involving a choice between the laws of different countries'.[32] The phrase 'contractual obligations' has a European autonomous meaning, but not one that has been defined.[33] In the Brussels Convention context, however, the term 'matters relating to contract' has been defined[34] in *Handte GmbH* v. *Traitements Mecano-Chimiques Des Surfaces*[35] as 'an undertaking freely entered into by one party in relation to another'. It is reasonable to assume that this European autonomous meaning will be closely followed for Rome Convention purposes. It might be argued that a manufacturer of a health care product voluntarily undertakes an obligation not just to the retailer, but also to anyone who purchases his product and thus falls within this definition. The impact of such a finding might be that the contractual choice of law rules of the Rome Convention would be applied to a defective product claim.

Handte itself concerned a manufacturer of a suction system which was sold to a buyer, who in turn sold the product on to a sub-buyer. The sub-buyer had wished to attach the system to metal-polishing machines which it had purchased elsewhere, but found the system unsuitable for this purpose. The sub-buyer sued in France. By French law, the claim was thought contractual, since the contractual rights of the buyer were assigned by law to the sub-buyer. The Court of Justice of the European Communities (ECJ) held that this did not suffice to render the matter one 'relating to contract'. But the decision is not free from doubt for two

---

[29] See the discussion of justiciability and foreign intellectual property rights below.
[30] Enacted by the Contracts (Applicable Law) Act 1990.
[31] Article 1(1) of the Rome Convention.
[32] *Ibid.*
[33] M. Plender, *European Contracts Convention* (London: Sweet and Maxwell, 1991) pp. 49–50.
[34] For the purposes of Article 5(1) of the Convention.
[35] Case C-26/91 *Jacob Handte GmbH* v. *Traitements Mecano-Chimiques Des Surfaces* [1992] ECR I-3967, §15.

reasons. First, Briggs and Rees[36] note that 'there was an obligation freely entered into; the right to enforce it passed to the claimant in *Handte*. It is not clear why the action did not fall within Article 5(1).' Secondly, it is true that a manufacturer of a health care product may have no idea where it might ultimately be consumed and by whom. But where a manufacturer sells his products to a retailer, he knows that the goods will be passed on for consumption by the ultimate user. In that sense, he can be said freely to enter into an obligation with any person who consumes his goods. It might follow that wherever a product is manufactured and distributed in circumstances where it is known[37] that the goods will be sold on, the case for treating such a claim as contractual for European autonomous purposes is a reasonable one, under both the Brussels and the Rome Conventions.

If a defective product claim may be characterised as contractual, the following question arises, namely, are the definitions of 'contract' in the Rome Convention and of 'tort' in the Act mutually exclusive? Given that the definition of 'contract' is a European autonomous one, and the definition of 'tort' is the product of a UK statute, this might seem unlikely. If there is no mutual exclusivity, it would appear to follow that the claimant in a defective products case might sometimes be free to choose whether to bring his claim in contract or in tort. His decision may depend largely on which law the choice of law rules in each area would lead to being applied in both cases. In other words, it would lead to 'choice of law shopping'.[38] The result would be to put the defendant firmly on the rack. Its effect on free trade throughout Europe would also be potentially great. A manufacturer who distributes health care products in England would need to have regard to the standards of care of the law designated by the Rome Convention and by the Act. In contrast, the purely domestic distributor in England would need to comply solely with English domestic law. The discriminatory effect of the choice of law rules would, in this scenario, be all too apparent.

However, it is possible to reason that the definitions of 'tort' and 'contract' in the Act and the Rome Convention are mutually exclusive. It could be said that when the Rome Convention was enacted, matters falling within its scope ceased to be governed by the rule of double actionability. If so, they were not touched by the Act, which does not

---

[36] A. Briggs and P. Rees, *Civil Jurisdiction and Judgments*, (2nd edn, Lloyd's of London Press, 1997) p. 93, n. 482.

[37] As opposed to being a mere possibility.

[38] The Giuliano and Lagarde Report (the official commentary on the Rome Convention) argues that uniform choice of law rules in Contracting States help prevent forum shopping and provide commercial certainty: [1980] OJ C282/5. Those aims are hardly promoted by this sort of confusion.

purport to affect anything other than the double actionability rule. In effect, such claims would be treated as exclusively contractual.

Nonetheless, it would be extraordinary if a UK statute characterised all defective product claims for the purposes of private international law as contractual. It is suggested that such actions should be treated as falling within the scope of the Act. It is likely, on the basis of the *Handte* decision, that such claims would fall outside the Rome Convention, save arguably in the case where there is an express assignment by the retailer of his contractual rights to the buyer. But the danger of overlap, and hence the need to comply with the law designated by both choice of law in contract and tort rules to avoid liability in an English court, will be ignored by a manufacturer at his peril.

It might appear that such characterisation problems can be avoided where infringement of a foreign intellectual property right is in issue. Such a claim seems unquestionably to be characterised as tortious. However, it is necessary to look beyond the form of the cause of action to the underlying issue. What if the only real issue in C's claim for infringement of a patent against D is D's defence that the patent was not valid? It is clear that in separate proceedings concerning the validity of a patent, the claim would ordinarily be characterised as a proprietary one. Dicey and Morris argue that a distinction should be drawn between questions concerning the title of the claimant to the right and whether that right has been violated. 'The first question is . . . governed by the *lex situs* . . . Nor, it is submitted, would it help the plaintiff that he could prove facts which would have been sufficient as a foundation of title according to the applicable law [of the tort] if they do not satisfy the requirements of the *lex situs*.'[39] In other words, violation of patent claims falls within the Act, but may not be exclusively determined by it.

It might be thought that, in the patent context, this discussion is of little importance. The place of the tort and the *lex situs* are highly likely to be the same. However, two points can be made. First, it may be that by law of a certain country, a patent can be violated by an act committed outside the State of registration. If so, the *lex loci delicti* and *lex situs* could differ. Secondly, even where the locus of the tort and its place of registration coincide, it should be recalled that in relation to proprietary disputes, but not to tortious disputes, the doctrine of *renvoi* may operate.[40] It is thus possible that a law other than the domestic law of the *lex situs* would determine the proprietary aspects of the claim.

---

[39] *Dicey and Morris, The Conflict of Laws*, pp. 1519–20.

[40] *Renvoi* involves the application not merely of the rules of the domestic legal system identified by English choice of law rules, but rather the application of the foreign legal system, including *its* choice of law rules. For example, suppose that English choice of

In any event, it will be necessary that the right acquired by the claimant (on application of property choice of law rules) is protected by the *lex loci delicti* in the sense that the latter law would not hold there to be a tortious violation of a right which it did not recognise as existing.

> *How will the* lex loci delicti *be identified? Are the common law authorities still a useful guide in this respect?*

Section 11(1) of the Act lays down the new general choice of law rule, namely that 'the applicable law is the law of the country in which the events constituting the tort or delict occur'. The word 'constituting' is not a helpful one as it is not one formerly used at common law and is not elucidated in the Act. However, the more problematic situation is where elements of these events occur in different countries. In that case, Section 11(2) states that the applicable rule shall be:

(a) for a cause of action in respect of personal injury caused to an individual or death resulting from personal injury,[41] the law of the country where the individual was when he sustained the injury;

(b) for a cause of action in respect of damage to property, the law of the country where the property was when it was damaged; and

(c) in any other case, the law of the country in which the most significant element or elements of those events occurred.

At common law, it was held in *Metall und Rohstoff AG* v. *Donaldson Lufkin & Jenrette Inc.*[42] that for the purpose of assessing where the natural forum is for jurisdictional purposes, one should ask where in substance the cause of action accrued. It was also established in *Armagas Ltd* v. *Mundogas SA*[43] that the place of the tort would be identical for jurisdictional and choice of law purposes. Given the lack of indication in the Act as to the presumed locus of a tort, one might assume that guidance should accordingly be drawn from the common

---

law rules tell us that French law should be applied to a dispute, but that a French court, had this matter arisen there, would actually have applied German law. Application of *renvoi* might lead to the application of German, not French, law in an English court. If *renvoi* were excluded, an English court in this situation would simply apply the domestic law of France. In transnational tort litigation, Section 9(5) of the Act excludes *renvoi*. However, in a proprietary claim, it appears that *renvoi* may be applied whether patents are characterised as movable or as immovable property: see *Re Ross* [1930] 1 Ch 377; *Re Duke of Wellington* [1947] Ch 506; *Winkworth* v. *Christie, Manson and Woods Ltd* [1980] Ch 496. For further discussion of the doctrine, see *Dicey and Morris, The Conflict of Laws*, ch. 4; *Cheshire and North's Private International Law*, ch. 5.

[41] Section 11(3) states that this definition includes 'disease or any impairment of physical or mental condition'.

[42] [1990] 1 QB 391.

[43] [1986] AC 71.

law jurisdiction cases.[44] In the defective products area, this would point to the place where goods were placed on the market without warning, not where they were manufactured. In *Distillers Co. (Biochemicals) Ltd* v. *Thompson*,[45] a drug containing thalidomide was manufactured in England and sold in New South Wales. The Privy Council held that the tort occurred in New South Wales, since the relevant part of the tort was the negligent failure to give an adequate warning of the dangers of the drug. Likewise, in *Castree* v. *E. R. Squibb Ltd*,[46] a centrifuge was manufactured in Germany but used in England, where it caused injury. The locus of the tort was held to be England.

Unfortunately, reference to the common law authorities is not facilitated by the drafting of the Act. Indeed, the statute is particularly unhelpful in identifying a choice of law rule in the sphere of health care litigation. Section 11(2), although phrased in terms of a particular cause of action, effectively determines the choice of law rule by reference to the head of damages sought. In the case of a toxic chemical substance, however, it is reasonable to suppose that a claim for damages might be brought both in respect of any consequential damage to property *and* for consequential physical harm from consumption thereof. Where such a good is manufactured and purchased in England and ultimately consumed in Germany, Section 11(2)(a) would appear to point to Germany as the place of the tort. But in relation to the claim for consequential damage to property, Section 11(2)(b) refers to the place where the property was when damaged. This could point to any place in which property was damaged, prior to its ultimate consumption in Germany. In particular, it could lead to the application of English law. Could it then be that different heads of damages resulting from harm caused by the same acts of manufacture, distribution and consumption, which would routinely be brought together, are in the ordinary case to be governed by different laws? If so, this puts the manufacturer of such products in an exceptionally awkward and uncertain position.

There might be two ways out of this unattractive situation. First, it could be said that Section 11(2) invites the court to assess the *principal* nature of the remedy sought. However, this would again make the outcome of litigation very difficult to predict in advance. Alternatively, it must be remembered that Section 11 is only the general rule. It may be displaced under Section 12(1) if, by comparing the factors which connect the tort to the *lex loci delicti* with those which connect it to another country, it is substantially more appropriate to apply the latter

---

[44] Briggs, 'Choice of Law', 524.
[45] [1971] AC 458.
[46] [1980] 1 WLR 1248.

law in whole or in part. Such factors include 'any of the events which constitute the tort . . . in question or . . . any of the circumstances or consequences of those events'.[47] This provision could be used to ensure that the same law is applied to both parts of the claim. Again, however, its fundamental uncertainty is a great weakness and makes defective product litigation unexpectedly hazardous.

Nor is the matter free from difficulty in relation to infringements of patents. Are these to be characterised as causes of action 'in respect of damage to property'? If so, the presumption would be that the applicable law would be that of the place where a patent was registered. But can it be said that a patent is 'damaged' by its violation? It is true that the property right has not been respected by the defendant. However, it is not obviously in itself damaged. In a similar way, one who vandalised another person's house has damaged the property; but a mere trespasser, whilst infringing the owner's right to exclusive occupation of the land, does not damage the land itself. For this reason, it may be that such claims fall outside Section 11(2)(b) and are instead governed by the law of the place where the most significant elements of the events occurred.[48] It might follow under that latter rule that where a patent in State A has been infringed by manufacture of a health care product in State A, but which is only distributed for commercial purposes in State B, the law of State B should determine whether a patent in State A has been infringed. Yet it would be surprising if the validity of a patent registered in State A were determined other than by the law of State A, given that English courts have always stressed the territorial nature of patents.[49]

In any event, a UK patent or trade mark cannot be infringed by an act committed outside the UK.[50] But what if a foreign law was held to apply by virtue of the Act on the merits and that foreign law *did* hold that a UK patent could be violated by an act committed overseas? It is fair to assume that where there are transnational elements to an alleged violation of a UK patent, an English court will strive to apply the *lex fori* wherever possible, even if the most significant elements of the alleged tort occur overseas. It might reach that result either by treating the application of English law[51] as a mandatory rule where violation of a UK intellectual property right is concerned,[52] or by holding that

---

[47] Section 12(2).
[48] Pursuant to Section 11(2)(c).
[49] See the discussion of justiciability and foreign intellectual property rights below.
[50] *Def Lepp Music* v. *Stuart-Brown* [1986] RPC 273; *James Burrough Distillers plc* v. *Speymalt Whisky Distributors Ltd* 1989 SLT 561.
[51] Such as the Patents Act 1977.
[52] The application of mandatory rules of English law designed to apply whatever the

application of a foreign law to violation of a UK patent is contrary to English public policy.[53] The latter route might be said to be almost calculated to cause offence, since it routinely emphasises the unacceptable nature of a foreign law. If the former route is to be taken as a matter of course in all cases of alleged violation of a UK patent, it would have been far better to have set down a special choice of law rule in the Act for violation of UK intellectual property rights, to the effect that the applicable law for all questions of violation would be the law of the forum. More generally, it might be questioned in relation to violations of foreign patents whether it is desirable to hold that the place of the tort is a country other than that where the patent is held, except in the most clear-cut of cases. It would be preferable to adopt a rebuttable presumption that the place of the alleged violation of a foreign patent is the country in which it is held for the purpose of identifying the applicable law.

It can be seen then that the reformed choice of law rules have created grave uncertainty in the law. Nor does the policy of the Act appear internally consistent. Reference exclusively to the *lex loci delicti* as a general rule suggests both that that is the law which has the closest connection with the dispute and that it has the greatest interest in application. However, Section 9(5) states that the applicable law 'shall exclude any choice of law rules forming part of the law of the country or countries concerned'. In other words, the doctrine of *renvoi* is excluded. At first sight, it might be thought that this simplifies the law and conforms to the expectation of the parties that the domestic law of the place of the tort will apply. However, if English choice of law rules point to the application of the law of State A, it is surprising that State A's domestic law will be applied, even if a court in State A would apply the law of State B. To an extent, application of the *lex loci delicti* by an English court is a substitute for the case actually being heard in the courts of the place where the tort occurred. If an English court is not prepared to apply the law that a court in State A would actually apply, that might be said to undermine the purpose of referring to the *lex loci delicti* in the first place, since the conditions in the foreign court will in no sense be reproduced. Moreover, if an English court would apply the law of State A on the merits, but the courts of State A would apply the law of State B on the merits, the possibility of forum shopping by the claimant to ensure litigation in the country which will apply the law most favourable to his case is a very real one. The result is that the

applicable law may be is preserved by Section 14(4). See Fawcett and Torremans, *Intellectual Property*, pp. 598–606.
[53] Invoking Section 14(3)(a)(i).

producer of a health care product marketed across Europe will find himself potentially exposed to tortious liability unless he satisfies the standard of care required under the law of more than one country, and hence he faces a real disincentive to trade in comparison to the purely domestic producer and retailer.

Conclusion

It has been seen that the Act has created choice of law rules which are opaque and whose policy is difficult to defend cogently. Those rules can be especially perplexing in areas of particular concern to health care litigation and have rendered the spectre of litigation before the English courts for health care product manufacturers unappealing, especially given the difficulty in foreseeing where the harmful effects of a defective product might be felt.

Jurisdictional problems

The reform of choice of law rules necessarily impacts on other areas of international litigation. In particular, there is little point in creating a *lex loci delicti* choice of law rule if its effects will be nullified by rules denying jurisdiction to the English courts in relation to torts committed abroad. Unfortunately, there is no evidence that this interaction was closely considered when the Act was drafted.[54]

Brussels Convention

The general rule of the Brussels Convention is that a defendant domiciled in a Contracting State may be sued where he is domiciled.[55] It follows that the English court will be jurisdictionally competent to hear cases brought under the Convention against an English defendant, even where a tort clearly occurs overseas and hence where a foreign law will be applicable on the merits.

However, Article 5 also lays down additional fora in which a defendant domiciled in a Contracting State may be sued.[56] Article 5(3) allocates jurisdiction in matters relating to tort to 'the place where the harmful event occurred'. The 'harmful event' refers either to the place

---

[54] See further Harris, 'Choice of Law in Tort'.
[55] Article 2.
[56] The fact that several States' courts have jurisdiction does not mean that they all may exercise it. Only the State whose courts are first seised of the matter may hear the case: Article 21.

of the act giving rise to damage, or to any place where immediate damage is suffered by the claimant.[57] It has been held by the ECJ in *Kalfelis* v. *Schroder, Munchmayer, Hengst and Co.*[58] that Article 5(3) applies to 'all actions which seek to establish the liability of a defendant and which are not related to contract within the meaning of Article 5(1)'.[59] Hence the definitions of 'contract' and 'tort' for Convention purposes are mutually exclusive.

Article 5(1) allocates jurisdiction in matters relating to contract to 'the courts for the place of performance of the obligation in question'. 'Matters relating to contract', it will be recalled, covers obligations freely entered into by one party towards another.[60] In order to work out where the obligation[61] was to be performed, an English court should refer to the applicable law of the contract.[62]

The definitions of 'tort' for the purposes of the Brussels Convention and the Act are almost certainly different.[63] It follows that for jurisdictional purposes, it is at least arguable that defective health care product litigation between a consumer and a manufacturer might be treated as contractual, whereas on the merits the claim may sound in tort.[64] Advocate-General Jacobs expressly envisaged in *Handte*[65] that a claim might be characterised differently for jurisdictional and choice of law purposes and saw no principled objection thereto.

---

[57] Case 21/76 *Bier* v. *Mines de Potasse d'Alsace* [1976] ECR 1735; Case C-220/88 *Dumez France* v. *Hessische Landesbank* [1990] ECR I-49; Case 364/93 *Marinari* v. *Lloyd's Bank* [1995] ECR I-2719; Case C-51/97 *Réunion Européenne SA* v. *Spliethoff's Bevrachtingskantoor NV* [1998] ECR I-6511.

[58] Case 189/87 [1988] ECR 5565.

[59] *Ibid.* 5585. The word 'liability' may be a limiting expression that excludes claims not seeking compensation: see Briggs and Rees, *Civil Jurisdiction and Judgments*, pp. 112–14.

[60] Case C-26/91 *Jacob Handte GmbH* v. *Traitements Mecano-Chimiques Des Surfaces* [1992] ECR I-3967, §15. See the discussion of the scope of the Act above.

[61] I.e. the obligation in respect of which the claimant sues: Case 14/76 *De Bloos* v. *Bouyer* [1976] ECR 1497.

[62] Case 12/76 *Industrie Tessili Italiana Como* v. *Dunlop AG* [1976] ECR 1473; Case C-288/92 *Custom Made Commercial Ltd* v. *Stawa Metallbau GmbH* [1994] ECR I-2913; Case C-440/97 *GIE Groupe Concorde* v. *Suhadiwarno Panjan* [1999] CLC 1976. The draft Brussels Regulation (on which see above, n. 3) alters matters somewhat, by providing an autonomous meaning to 'place of performance' for certain contracts. Article 5(1) states that, unless otherwise agreed, the place of performance in sale of goods contracts is the Member State where the goods were delivered or should have been delivered; in contracts of service, the relevant place is the State where under the contract the services were provided or should have been provided. But for all other contractual matters, the position remains unchanged.

[63] This is an inevitable consequence of the Act covering only such claims as were previously governed by the double actionability rule.

[64] Not least because the definitions of 'contract' and 'tort' for choice of law purposes may not be mutually exclusive. See the discussion of the scope of the Act above.

[65] Case C-26/91, [1992] ECR I-3967, §24 of the Opinion.

If a defective product claim could fall within Article 5(1),[66] the English court would have to identify where the *contractual* obligation of the manufacturer of a defective product to a consumer was to be performed (which might be where the manufacturer was based, where his product was distributed, or anywhere where his product was consumed), even though the claimant's claim on the merits could be characterised as tortious for choice of law purposes. This curious result is one which cannot at present be ruled out.

Claims for infringement of a patent or trade mark might seem to fall within the scope of Article 5(3) as matters relating to tort. However, matters are complicated where the validity of the patent or trade mark is pleaded as a defence to the infringement action. In such circumstances, the claim may be caught by the exclusive jurisdiction provisions of Article 16. Where a provision of Article 16 applies, the courts of the State specified therein will alone have jurisdiction, by way of exception to the defendant domicile rule. Article 16(4) allocates such jurisdiction

in proceedings concerned with the registration or validity of patents, trademarks, designs, or other similar rights required to be deposited or registered, [to] the courts of the Contracting State in which the deposit or registration has been applied for, has taken place or is under the terms of an international convention deemed to have taken place.

In *Coin Controls v. Suzo International (UK) Ltd*,[67] Laddie J held that where validity is a *substantial* issue in infringement proceedings, the entire infringement action should be heard exclusively in the place of registration. This is so even if the *principal* issue is one of infringement. However, Fawcett and Torremans point out[68] that this result is not required by Article 19, which states that

Where a court of a Contracting State is seised of a claim which is principally concerned with a matter over which the courts of another Contracting State have exclusive jurisdiction by virtue of Article 16, it shall declare of its own motion that it has no jurisdiction.

A literal interpretation would suggest that where the claim is principally concerned with infringement (i.e. the validity of the patent is not the major issue in determining whether it has been infringed), the fact that validity is a substantial issue in the case should not deprive the court of jurisdiction. 'It is hard to believe that the drafters of the Brussels Convention used the word "principally" in Article 19 when what they

---

[66] See the discussion of the scope of the Act above.
[67] [1999] Ch 33; followed on this point in *Fort Dodge Animal Health Ltd and Others* v. *Akzo Nobel NV and Another* [1998] FSR 222. The point was conceded without argument by the parties in *Sepracor Inv.* v. *Hoechst Marion Roussel Ltd* [1999] FSR 746. See also Case 288/82 *Duijnstee* v. *Goderbauer* [1983] ECR 3663.
[68] Fawcett and Torremans, *Intellectual Property*, p. 203.

actually meant was the very different, and much wider concept, of "not arising incidentally".[69] The result also allows a defendant to an infringement action to frustrate proceedings by contesting validity and thereby bringing the matter within Article 16(4).

However, the most pertinent point for present purposes is that many claims to which the new choice of law rules in tort might have been applied, at least in part, will not in any event be heard in an English court. Imagine an action for infringement of a German patent brought against an English domiciliary, which for choice of law purposes would have been characterised as tortious and to which German law would have been applied on the merits. If the defendant raises a serious arguable case as to the validity of the patent, the English court will decline jurisdiction in favour of the German court. It follows that the opportunities to apply the Act to foreign intellectual property rights might be rather limited in practice.[70]

Common law

The principal application of common law jurisdiction rules in the health care sphere will be where the defendant is not domiciled in a Contracting State to the Brussels Convention.[71] It is suggested that the practical application of the Private International Law (Miscellaneous Provisions) Act's provisions on the merits may be somewhat limited in defective product cases where common law jurisdiction rules apply, since an English court will be reluctant to hear a case where the tort occurred overseas.

An English court will have jurisdiction as of right if the defendant is present in England to be served with a claim form[72] or submits to the court's jurisdiction.[73] However, the defendant may apply for a stay of

---

[69] *Ibid.* p. 204.
[70] Although an English court will have jurisdiction in relation to a UK patent infringement where its validity is contested, it is arguable that the Act does not apply to torts committed in England: see the discussion of the scope of the Act above.
[71] A matter which is civil or commercial will fall within the Convention. However, if the exclusive jurisdiction, consumer or insurance provisions do not apply and there is no submission to another Contracting State's courts or a choice of court clause for another Contracting State, Article 4 of the Convention instructs a national court to apply its own idiosyncratic national jurisdictional rules, if the defendant is not domiciled in a Contracting State. In England, this will be the common law rules. However, since the matter is *ex hypothesi* within the Convention, the English court's jurisdiction will be subject to the *lis alibi pendens* provisions of Articles 21 and 22, and an English judgement will still be entitled to recognition under the liberal Convention rules in other Contracting States.
[72] *Maharanee of Baroda* v. *Wildenstein* [1972] QB 283.
[73] *Williams and Glyn's Bank plc* v. *Astro Dinamico Cia Naviera SA* [1984] 1 WLR 438.

proceedings, on the grounds that England is a *forum non conveniens*. Lord Goff in *Spiliada Maritime Corp.* v. *Cansulex*[74] laid down a two-stage test to determine whether the stay will be granted, which can be summarised briefly as follows. First, the defendant must prove that there is another available forum which is clearly or distinctly more appropriate for resolution of the dispute. If he succeeds, the burden of proof passes to the claimant, who may resist a stay if he shows that it would be unjust to require him to sue overseas. However, in the context of tortious litigation, it was said in *The Albaforth*[75] that the natural forum is presumed to be the place where the tort occurred. In other words, in situations where foreign law might have been applicable on the merits, an English court is likely to stay its proceedings upon application by the defendant.

Where the court has no jurisdiction as of right, the claimant must apply for permission to serve a claim form outside the jurisdiction pursuant to CPR 6.20.[76] He must show a good arguable case that his claim falls within a provision thereof[77] and also that the court should exercise its discretion to serve out thereunder. In particular, for present purposes, sub-rule 6.20 (8) provides that service may be made where 'a claim is made in tort where – (a) the damage was sustained within the jurisdiction; or (b) the damage sustained resulted from an act committed within the jurisdiction'. This broad formulation avoids the need to identify a single locus of the tort. Imagine a case where a defective health care product is manufactured in England and distributed abroad, where it causes harm. It would seem to suffice under this sub-rule that the defendant manufactured the product in England, even if he sold it exclusively abroad. However, the claimant has also to show that England is the natural forum,[78] if he is to persuade the court to exercise its discretion. In order to demonstrate this, he must, on *The Albaforth* reasoning, show that the tort occurred in England. In other words, although CPR 6.20 (8) does not require the court to identify a single locus for the tort, the court's discretion whether to allow service out under that sub-rule *will* be determined by where the tort occurred. The locus of the tort in a defective product case is the place where the product was placed on the market without warning.[79] In our example, it

---

[74] [1987] AC 460.

[75] *Cordoba Shipping Co.* v. *National State Bank, Elizabeth, New Jersey: The Albaforth* [1984] 2 Lloyd's Rep. 91, 94.

[76] This replaced the rules contained in RSC Ord. 11 with effect from 2 May 2000.

[77] *Seaconsar Far East Ltd* v. *Bank Markazi Jomhouri Islami Iran* [1994] 1 AC 438.

[78] *Spiliada* v. *Cansulex* [1987] AC 460.

[79] *Distillers Co. (Biochemicals) Ltd* v. *Thompson* [1971] AC 458; *Castree* v. *E. R. Squibb Ltd* [1980] 1 WLR 1248.

would follow that service out would not after all be permitted. It would also then follow that service out will usually only be possible in cases where English law is applicable on the merits.[80] In short, the practical effect of the Act on defective product claims may be rather less than one might expect, given the limited opportunities of the court to take jurisdiction at common law where the *locus delicti* lies overseas.

Justiciability and foreign intellectual property rights

Perhaps the most significant potential impact of the Act on health care litigation is on the bringing of actions for infringement of foreign intellectual property rights in English courts. Prior to the Act, the position was clear: claims for infringement of foreign intellectual property rights could not be brought in England at common law. One reason for this lay in the choice of law rules applicable prior to the Act. The double actionability rule required the act complained of to constitute a tort by English domestic law. However, as a matter of English domestic law an intellectual property right is strictly territorial in its operation. It follows that by English domestic law an alleged infringement of a foreign right cannot constitute a tort and hence that such claims would inevitably fail on the merits.

It is less clear whether the refusal of English courts to hear such cases was based solely on their lack of substance or also on a separate rule that foreign intellectual property right claims 'belonged' exclusively in the courts of the State in which they were registered and should not, as a matter of policy, be entertained under any circumstances in an English court. Put differently, it might be said that such claims *were not justiciable* in an English court.[81] Dicey and Morris observed on the non-justiciability argument that, 'It seems highly unlikely that this adds anything constructive to the analysis of the problem, though it can readily be admitted that the analysis produces no difference in result.'[82] However, this is no longer the case. The choice of law objection to an English court entertaining an alleged foreign intellectual property right violation has disappeared, since the Act requires only that the claim succeed by the *lex loci delicti* and not that it must also succeed by English domestic law. It follows that the only possible residual objection to the bringing of

[80] And where hence, on one view, the Act will not be applicable at all.
[81] On patents, see *Potter* v. *Broken Hill Pty Co. Ltd* (1906) 3 CLR 478, *Norbert Steinhardt & Son Ltd* v. *Meth* (1961) 105 CLR 440; on trade marks, see *L. A. Gear Inc.* v. *Gerald Whelan and Sons Ltd* [1991] FSR 670; on copyright, see *Def Lepp Music* v. *Stuart-Brown* [1986] RPC 273, *Tyburn Productions Ltd* v. *Conan Doyle* [1991] Ch 75.
[82] *Dicey and Morris, The Conflict of Laws*, (4th supplement to 12th edn, London: Sweet and Maxwell, 1997) p. 232. This sentence has been removed from the 13th edition.

such actions could be their non-justiciability in English courts. Hence it is necessary to examine this second objection.

In *British South Africa Co. v. Cia de Moçambique*,[83] the House of Lords ruled that it had no jurisdiction to entertain an action for trespass to land situated abroad. Lord Herschell explained that 'our Courts did not exercise jurisdiction in matters arising abroad "which were in their nature local"'.[84] In other words, the fact that such actions would inevitably be most closely connected with the State where the land was situated led to a blanket rule that these claims would not be heard in England.

A similar rule apparently evolved in relation to infringement of foreign intellectual property rights. On one view, this could have been because such property, like land, was classified as immovable. This is not especially convincing. Whilst it might not be possible to register a State A patent elsewhere than in State A, it does not follow that it is not possible to move the registration from one State to another. Laddie J in *Coin Controls v. Suzo International (UK) Ltd*,[85] when addressing the description of a patent by Griffiths CJ in *Potter v. Broken Hill Pty Co. Ltd*[86] as 'analogous to an immovable', remarked: 'I accept that the *Moçambique* rule has been applied to intellectual property by analogy. But that fact emphasises that, whatever the similarities may be, patents and other intellectual property rights are not accurately described as immovables.'[87]

Another justification was put forward by Aldous LJ in *Plastus Kreativ AB v. Minnesota Mining and Manufacturing Co.*[88] namely that,

although patent actions appear on their face to be disputes between two parties, in reality they also concern the public. A finding of infringement is a finding that a monopoly granted by the State is to be enforced. The result is that the public have to pay higher prices than if the monopoly did not exist . . . That result should . . . come about from a decision of a court situated in the State where the public have to pay the higher prices.

This is unpersuasive, in that it is difficult to see the limits of the argument. In particular, it could argue for all claims which involve upholding State restrictions on the free market mechanism to be localised; yet there has never been a suggestion that this should represent the law. The implications for State policy of an intellectual property

[83] [1893] AC 602.
[84] *Ibid.* 621, discussing the judgment of Buller J in *Doulson v. Matthews* (1792) 4 Term Rep. 503, 504.
[85] [1999] Ch 33.
[86] (1906) 3 CLR 479, 494.
[87] [1999] Ch 33, 44.
[88] [1995] RPC 438, 447.

right infringement claim are too indirect to justify an absolute rule of non-justiciability in what is clearly a private law dispute.

Yet Laddie J in *Coin Controls* was emphatic that the non-justiciability rule had in the past been good law and that the double actionability rule alone had not been the reason why foreign intellectual property rights infringements could not be heard in England. 'The *Moçambique* rule has nothing to do with double actionability. It is a principle of public policy based on the undesirability of our courts adjudicating on issues which are essentially foreign and local.'[89] If so, it would follow that the removal of double actionability by the Act would not have removed the justiciability bar.

It is somewhat surprising in the light of the authorities that Roch LJ in *Pearce* v. *Ove Arup Partnership Ltd*[90] should have taken the view that the *Moçambique* rule did not extend to infringements of foreign copyrights. In that case (which involved a pre-Act claim to which common law rules would be applicable on the merits) it was held that the English court had jurisdiction[91] in an action for alleged breach of Dutch copyrights brought against Dutch co-defendants to a claim against the first defendant on the basis of his UK domicile. Lloyd J had held at first instance that the matter would previously have been treated as non-justiciable in an English court.[92] Roch LJ reviewed the authorities in some depth. He distinguished *Tyburn Production Ltd* v. *Doyle*,[93] a case involving alleged infringement of copyright and trade mark in the works of Sir Arthur Conan Doyle in the United States, where Vinelott J had held that he could not entertain a claim for infringement of these rights. In that case, validity of the foreign intellectual property rights was an important issue in the infringement proceedings and Roch LJ acknowledged the correctness of the decision, noting that any English judgment might not have been enforced in the United States. However, he did not consider the case a binding precedent where validity of the foreign right was not an issue in infringement proceedings.[94] *Def Lepp Music* v. *Stuart-Brown*,[95] a

---

[89] [1999] Ch 33, 43.
[90] [1999] 1 All ER 769; see J. Harris, 'Justiciability, Choice of Law and the Brussels Convention' [1999] *LMCLQ* 360.
[91] By Article 6(1).
[92] [1997] Ch 293; noted by M. Tugendhat, 'Media Law and the Brussels Convention' (1997) 113 *LQR* 360, A. Briggs, 'Two Undesirable Side-Effects of the Brussels Convention?' (1997) 113 *LQR* 364.
[93] [1991] Ch 75.
[94] [1999] 1 All ER 769, 799. For a similar reason, the Australian decision in *Potter* v. *Broken Hill Pty Co. Ltd* (1906) 3 CLR 479 was regarded as an authority for the principle that claims concerning validity of foreign patents should be brought in the State where the patent was allegedly granted, but not as conclusive where validity was not in dispute.
[95] [1986] RPC 273.

case where the English court refused jurisdiction in a claim for alleged infringement of a United Kingdom copyright by acts committed overseas, was also regarded as of no help where the issue in question was infringement of a *foreign* right in that *foreign* country.[96] Whilst the judgment is a masterly example of distinction of authorities, one might wonder why the granting of a foreign intellectual property right should be treated as an intrinsically local matter, yet the conditions under which that right is infringed should not be so regarded.[97] In the event, however, Roch LJ did not regard it as crucial to determine conclusively whether the justiciability bar operated where jurisdiction was taken at common law in infringement cases involving no question of validity. Even if the rule existed in that context, it could not survive where the Brussels Convention was applicable.[98]

Roch LJ also held that the double actionability rule could not be invoked to prevent the English court hearing the case on the ground that it was bound to fail on the merits.[99] Unfortunately, he offered no real exposition as to why this objection was invalid. The matter was considered at first instance by Lloyd J, who held that the non-justiciability rule and the double actionability rule could not be invoked to prevent the English court hearing the case. Lloyd J pointed to the ECJ's view in *Kongress Agentur Hagen GmbH* v. *Zeehaghe BV* that national procedural rules may nonetheless not impair the effectiveness of the Convention and must not lay down conditions of admissibility which restrict the application of jurisdictional rules in the Convention.[100] Moreover the Schlosser Report states that 'where the courts of several Contracting States have jurisdiction, the plaintiff has deliberately been given a right of choice, which should not be weakened by application of the doctrine of *forum conveniens*'.[101] Lloyd J regarded both the non-justiciability and the double actionability rules as 'measures having equivalent effect' to rules of jurisdiction.[102] 'If the terri-

---

[96] [1999] 1 All ER 769, 798.
[97] One possible answer where the Brussels Convention is applicable is that a judgment of a Contracting State in infringement proceedings must be recognised in other Contracting States. In contrast, a judgment in relation to the validity of a foreign patent or trade mark which was given in a Contracting State other than that where the right in question was granted or deposited would breach the exclusive jurisdiction provisions of Article 16(4). In such a case, Article 28 states that recognition of the judgment throughout Europe should be refused.
[98] [1999] 1 All ER 769, 797. In this respect, the judgement accords with the views of Laddie J in *Coin Controls*, [1999] Ch 33 and of Lloyd J at first instance in *Pearce* itself: [1997] Ch 293.
[99] [1999] 1 All ER 769, 802–4.
[100] Case 365/88, [1990] ECR I-1845, §20.
[101] [1979] OJ C59/71, 97.
[102] [1997] Ch 293, 308.

torial approach of English law were applied so as to exclude an action being brought against a defendant domiciled in the United Kingdom . . . for breach of a Dutch copyright, the quixotic position would be reached that the court is required to accept jurisdiction under Article 2 but would immediately strike out that action as non justiciable.'[103] He was unmoved by statements in *Hagen*[104] and in *Sanicentral GmbH* v. *Collin*[105] that the Brussels Convention did not affect national procedural or choice of law rules. However, Lloyd J's view is not obviously correct. Choice of law rules are designed to select the most appropriate law to apply on the merits. They may be more or less favourable to the claimant, but they do not purport to remove jurisdictional competence from the English court. Nor are the limits to Lloyd J's statement of principle clear. Could it be said as a result that any choice of law rule will be struck down if it does not give the claimant at least a serious opportunity of success on the merits?[106]

Yet Roch LJ was prepared to go further still. Although he accepted that choice of law rules are not designed to address jurisdictional questions, he reasoned that, in cases of alleged infringement of foreign intellectual property rights, one would expect an English court, when applying its common law choice of law rules, to apply solely the *lex loci delicti*. He reasoned that double actionability would not be applied in such a case and that an English court would invoke the *Red Sea* exception[107] so as to disapply English law, since 'this is not a case in which the claim is in respect of some wrong which is conceptually unknown in English law'.[108] With respect, this approach is open to question. The *Red Sea* exception was precisely that: it was not intended to become a rule to the effect that English law would be routinely disapplied for certain typical claims, such as foreign intellectual property right violations. Such an approach makes the traditional understanding of English law as the *lex causae* under the common law double actionability principle unsustainable. Nor is there any indication in the *Red Sea* case that application of the exception should be affected by the jurisdiction rules of the Brussels Convention.

In any event, the new choice of law rules in the Act appear to be compatible with the Brussels Convention, as they do not condemn the claimant to failure on the merits in a foreign intellectual property right

---

[103] *Ibid.* 303.
[104] Case 365/88, [1990] ECR I-1845.
[105] Case 25/79, [1979] ECR 3423.
[106] See further Briggs, 'Two Undesirable Side-Effects'; Harris, 'Choice of Law in Tort'.
[107] See the discussion of the common law choice of law in tort rules above.
[108] [1999] 1 All ER 769, 803.

violation claim.[109] More pertinent for future purposes is whether the non-justiciability rule still has a role to play. It is suggested that it does not. However, this is not necessarily because the Brussels Convention so dictates, but rather is due to the nature of the new choice of law rules contained in the Act. With the removal of double actionability, English courts ought in principle to be prepared to hear cases relating to foreign intellectual property right infringements both under the Brussels Convention *and* at common law. It would be surprising if the prospect of a successful claim on the merits which the Act offers the claimant was at once removed because the English court was held in all cases not to be an available forum. Otherwise, to adopt the terminology of Lloyd J in *Pearce*, the non-justiciability rule could be said to be a 'measure having equivalent effect' to a choice of law rule.

The argument that such claims are in their nature local and cannot be adjudicated upon elsewhere carries little conviction. 'Why, for example, is a breach abroad of a foreign copyright to be seen as being in its nature local, but the commission of a tort or other civil wrong is not usually designated local in nature?'[110] Carter argues that no principled objection can be maintained and that pragmatism must determine which so-called 'localised' actions may be brought in an English court. Hence whilst disputes relating to land were initially considered to be localised, extensive erosion of this rule has been made by statute[111] and case law[112] in cases where it was not necessary that the courts of the *situs* of the property had exclusive jurisdiction. Likewise, there is no obvious reason why a blanket exclusion needs to apply to foreign intellectual property right infringements. If, for example, it is alleged that an English domiciliary has simultaneously infringed patents in England, France and Brazil, it is not obviously undesirable that all three actions be brought together in an English court. This point was well made in *Sepracor Inv.* v. *Hoechst Marion Roussel Ltd*[113] by Laddie J, who noted that where infringement of patents in a number of European jurisdictions is in issue, resolution of the whole claim in the courts of one State would be 'quicker, cheaper . . . more convenient . . . [and] reduce the possibility of conflicting decisions on the same . . . issues'. Moreover, the Schlosser Report[114] makes plain that the fact that a foreign law will

---

[109] Although Section 13 excludes defamation, which will continue to be governed by the double actionability rule.

[110] Carter, 'Decisions of British Courts during 1990 involving Questions of Public or Private International Law – B. Private International Law' (1990) 61 *BYIL* 401.

[111] Section 30, Civil Jurisdiction and Judgments Act 1982.

[112] See, e.g. *Re Duke of Wellington* [1948] Ch 118.

[113] [1999] FSR 746, 754.

[114] [1979] OJ C59/71, 97.

be applied on the merits is not a reason to decline jurisdiction. Indeed, it is in the nature of the choice of law reforms of the Act that claims which could succeed by the *lex loci delicti* but not by English domestic law can successfully be brought in an English court.

In summary, it is suggested that the view that the Brussels Convention dictates that foreign intellectual property right violations may be entertained in an English court is questionable. However, the effect of the Act is to render the non-justiciability bar particularly inappropriate, whichever scheme of jurisdictional rules applies, and it should be regarded as having removed it. Nevertheless, it is regrettable that the Act at no point addresses the issue and that such a shadow of uncertainty should have been cast on this question.

Conclusion

Litigation in England under the double actionability rule may not have been especially attractive to a claimant, but the effect of the law on product liability and intellectual property right violations was reasonably clear. The Act's choice of law rules may ostensibly be more claimant-friendly, but they have spawned grave uncertainties in these areas. It will henceforth be uncertain whether a health care product manufacturer might be exposed to liability in contract and/or in tort; and where the Act is found to apply, the applicable law cannot be stated with any confidence. The holder of a foreign intellectual property right in such a product faces similar uncertainties as to the scope and application of the Act, and additional opaqueness as to when he will be able to bring a claim for infringement before an English court. The result is that those involved in transnational health care development and production who have dealings in England must tread with extreme caution. Legally and commercially this is a most undesirable situation and potentially a major obstacle to free trade. It is far from clear that the common law model was broken; it is abundantly clear that the Act has not fixed it.

Index

parallel trade, 29, 31, 32–4, 79–83
passing off, 28
price differentials, 15–16, 81
registration, 27–9
repackaging/relabelling, 33–4, 35–6, 79–82
transnational litigation, 205–6
United Kingdom, 27–9
Trade-Related Aspects of Intellectual Property Rights (TRIPs)
international exhaustion, 12–13, 23, 42
morality clauses, 159
United States, 12

United Kingdom
alternative medicine, 47
choice of law, 207–18
development risk defence, 186–97
essential similarity, 119
import licensing, 83, 85
Licensing Authority, 102
marketing authorisations, 101–3, 114
MCA *see* Medicines Control Agency
medical profession, 65–6
National Health Service (NHS), 178
patents, 21, 23
private international law, 205–29
product liability, 185–97
Research Ethics Committees (RECs), 178

term of protection, 113, 123
trade marks, 27–9
United States
Food and Drug Administration (FDA), 143, 148, 153
medical profession, 64–5
morality clauses, 161
TRIPs, 12
welfare benefits, 54, 73
Uruguay Round, 42

Variation
minor/major changes, 125
mutual recognition, 145
new indications, 85
new research, 122–3
non-indication changes, 127
term of protection, 85, 116–17, 128
Veterinary medicine
centralised assessment, 145
CVMP *see* Committee for Veterinary Medicinal Products
free movement of persons, 55
Veterinary International Conference on Harmonisation (VICH), 151

World Health Organisation (WHO), 125, 136, 138, 153
World Trade Organisation (WTO), fair trade, 12